T0319722

EXTERNAL CONTACTS AND THE ECONOMY OF LATE ROMAN AND POST-ROMAN BRITAIN

This book brings together new archaeological, historical and palaeo-ecological approaches to the transition from the Romano-British to medieval Celtic economy between the fourth and ninth centuries AD, re-examining well-known sources of evidence and introducing new material. While the emphasis is on the Celtic-speaking areas of Britain after AD 400, the geographical and chronological scope of the contributions is wide-ranging.

The articles include a reassessment of the end of the Romano-British economy, suggesting that the conventional interpretation – a sudden collapse in production in the early fifth century – is incorrect; pollen analysis is a key approach in understanding the end of the agricultural economy, and here, for the first time, all relevant pollen sequences are catalogued and discussed. A fresh investigation into imported pottery and glass and inscribed stone monuments clarifies an understanding of these problematical sources, while the nature of the contacts which brought imports into Britain and Ireland is re-evaluated from new evidence which, together with archaeological material from shipwrecks of AD 400–600 (of which a catalogue is presented here) and historical data, indicate that Byzantine contacts with Britain are unlikely to have been on entirely commercial grounds.

Dr K.R. Dark teaches at the University of Reading.

EXTERNAL CONTACTS AND THE ECONOMY OF LATE ROMAN AND POST-ROMAN BRITAIN

Edited by

K. R. DARK

THE BOYDELL PRESS

First published 1996
The Boydell Press, Woodbridge

Transferred to digital printing

ISBN 978-0-85115-655-2

The Boydell Press is an imprint of Boydell & Brewer Ltd
PO Box 9, Woodbridge, Suffolk IP12 3DF, UK
and of Boydell & Brewer Inc.
668 Mt Hope Avenue, Rochester, NY 14620, USA
website: www.boydellandbrewer.com

A catalogue record for this book is available
from the British Library

This publication is printed on acid-free paper

CONTENTS

FIGURES

PREFACE

The transformation from the ancient to the medieval economy is an enduring problem of both archaeological and historical studies. Recent years have also seen a renewed interest in the end of the Roman Empire and specifically the end of Roman Britain.

This book differs from many studies of these questions in two principal ways. First, it concentrates on the parts of Roman Britain to remain in British political control after the fifth century: until the seventh century these areas comprised the majority of what had been Roman Britain. Second, it links processes of transformation beginning in the fourth century with developments in the 'Celtic' areas of Britain in the post-Roman period.

The focus of the book is, therefore, on mainland Britain south of Hadrian's Wall and especially on the western part of that geographical area, although the geographical spread of the evidence discussed ranges from Ireland to the Byzantine Empire. The papers use archaeological, palaeoecological, historical and epigraphic sources to examine continuity and discontinuity in both agriculture and manufacturing and to elucidate changing patterns of production and overseas contacts through the period from the fourth to the ninth centuries.

The first three chapters reinterpret the end of the Romano-British economy. Chapters 4 to 6 examine the evidence provided by imported pottery and glass and by historical evidence for overseas trade. Epigraphic evidence for long-range contacts is discussed in Chapter 7, and the evidence of a specific excavated site – Poundbury – is reinterpreted by its excavator (in relation to themes of long-range contact and its local economy) in the final chapter.

These contributions do not aim to produce an integrated synthesis or to set a common interpretation, but to present the latest analyses and evidence, and to introduce new debates on key questions. Together, the papers present new directions of research of interest to all those working on the social, environmental, political or economic history of Britain and the transformation of the Roman Imperial economy into that of medieval Europe.

It must be stressed, in conclusion, that the interpretations put forward in this book represent those of the individual authors of chapters, not of all the scholars whose work is included here. Finally, I would like to thank all those involved in the production of this work, especially Richard Barber, Claire Orchard (the sub-editor), David Dumville and, of course, the contributors.

K. R. Dark
July 1995

vii

CONVENTIONS

'Britain and Ireland' are used geographically to refer to the islands rather than political units. Likewise, 'England', 'Scotland' and 'Wales' are used as geographical terms to refer to parts of Britain rather than in a cultural or national sense. The Irish spelling 'ogom' is preferred here to 'ogam' or 'ogham'.

I

PROTO-INDUSTRUALISATION
AND THE END OF THE ROMAN ECONOMY

K. R. Dark

Modern scholars have been unanimous in their opinion that the Roman economy was not industrialised.[1] They have been sure that the Roman economic system was predominantly agricultural.[2] Some have taken an extreme view of this agricultural economy and seen long-range trade and crafts-production as serving only to supply the needs of the ruling élite.[3] Others have minimalised the economic importance of urban life, especially in Britain, and viewed towns as no more than élite settlements, comprising only the mansions of the rich and service elements for them.[4]

Scholars such as Fulford and Greene, with more sophisticated concepts of the Roman economic system, have emphasised long-range trade, the efficiency of communications, maritime aspects, and the commercial character of urban life.[5] They have tended to see towns as crafts and exchange centres with substantial populations.

Another approach has been to emphasise the role of the economy in supporting the army, the bureaucracy, or the frontier zones. The most convincing argument of this kind has been proposed by Fulford, who suggests that the Mediterranean economy 'fed' wealth and surplus into the poorer peripheral areas rather than *vice versa*.[6]

In a recent alternative view, Woolf[7] has emphasised the role of territorial expansion in the economy, implying that this afforded opportunities for economic growth in the economy, although it is hard to consider frontier maintenance on the Roman model other than a drain on resources. Despite these contrasts of interpretation, and contrary to the minimalist view,

---

1 Greene, *The Archaeology*, pp. 14–16.
2 *Ibid.*, p. 67.
3 Whittaker, 'Late Roman Trade'.
4 Dixon, 'Life after Wroxeter' Reece, 'Town and Country'.
5 Greene, *The Archaeology*; Fulford, 'Demonstrating Britannia's Economic Dependence'; Fulford, 'Pottery and Britain's Foreign Trade'; Fulford, 'The Economy of Roman Britain'.
6 Fulford, 'Territorial Expansion'.
7 Woolf, 'Imperialism, Empire'.

K. R. Dark

Greene has proposed an archaeological interpretation of the whole Roman economic system stressing trade, transport, and monetary exchange.[8] His view is that, although there was no industrialisation, the Roman economy was both efficient and based on a market system; he has noted that technology was applied, to a limited extent, in the solution of economic problems.[9]

There are, therefore, many alternative views of the scale and character of the Roman economy, and there is plentiful evidence from which to work. It is a huge topic, and it will be possible, here, only to set out a new interpretation, test it against evidence from Roman Britain and elsewhere, and to consider its implications. As I hope to show, its implications elucidate the end of the Roman economy both in Britain and elsewhere, and, in particular, enable us to explain the extremely rapid decline of large-scale production by some of Roman Britain's most notable 'industries', such as pottery production.

Obviously, there is much scope for future elaboration and examination of this new model, but this analysis will, hopefully, demonstrate its applicability and potential. First, however, it is necessary to consider the definition of some economic types.

The agriculturally-based economy has been characterised as a 'subsistence' or 'peasant' economy.[10] In her fascinating study of the quantitative evidence for the Late Roman agricultural economy, Tamara Lewit has proposed that the agricultural economy of the third to fifth century was flourishing, not in decline.[11] The one period of brief recession seems to have been in the mid-third century, an observation which historians will find unsurprising.

In the peasant, or subsistence, agricultural economy the majority of wealth is produced on the land, and this underlies such élite use of surplus as exists. An agricultural economy need not employ monetary exchange, nor necessarily are towns required for it to function. In such an economy, trade, (especially long-distance trade) has a minor, subsidiary, role and artefacts are produced by specialist craftsmen, not factory, or 'manufactory', workers.

This, of course, is in contrast to the industrial economy.[12] An industrial economy is one in which we see mass-production facilitated by the

8 Greene, *The Archaeology*.
9 Greene, 'Perspectives'.
10 Lewit, *Agricultural Production*. On 'peasant' economies see: Hodges, *Primitive and Peasant Markets*.
11 Lewit, *Agricultural Production*.
12 See Deane, *The First Industrial Revolution* for a definition of the industrial economy.
13 Mendels, 'Proto-Industrialisation: the First Phase of the Industrialisation Process'.
14 For example, Berg, Hudson and Sonenscher, 'Manufacture in Town and Country'; Berg, *The Age of Manufactures*.

2

application of technology, efficient communications, widespread intensive capital investment in production and distribution, the supply of regional or international markets, and a monetary market-based exchange network. Often, as we all know, there will be factories employing large numbers of production workers, an administrative bureaucracy, and a new élite whose wealth is based on capital gained from industrial production. There will also be, essentially, a concentration of systematic production in urban communities whose livelihood derives from employment in that production, rather than from agriculture. The need for a mass-market will usually, although not necessarily, require the existence of substantial population concentrations.

Although models and definitions of what we mean by an 'industrialised economy' might cause controversy, this definition could, I hope, be acceptable to most economists, historians and geographers. Yet there is, however, an intermediary stage between an agriculturally-based economy, and one based on industry. This is the 'proto-industrial', or industrialising economy.[13] Such an economy is one undergoing the process of industrialisation but not fully industrialised.

The characteristics of the proto-industrial economy are subject to debate[14] but a widely accepted definition would be that such an economy has a monetary market-based exchange system, efficient communications, regional or national markets, and large-scale, rural, production. This type of economy existed in its classic form in the fifteenth to the eighteenth century in England and is claimed to have first developed into the full industrial economy in the late eighteenth century.[15] This event, the famous Industrial Revolution, is usually considered unique, but proto-industrial economies have been found to be extremely widespread in the early modern world – for example, in pre-colonial Asia.[16]

These types of economy are, of course, only themselves broad categories within which there may be much variation. They can certainly be read as a sequence: from an agricultural ('peasant') to proto-industrial to industrial economy. But the use of these categories need not be evolutionary, nor need one type of economy always develop into the next: the uniqueness of the Industrial Revolution would seem at once to refute the suggestion that it need do so. Importantly, here, we must not be so narrow-minded as to view the process of industrialisation in terms of the closeness of the physical resemblance of production centres to those of the modern industrial period. It would be possible to meet all the criteria of industrialisation in very different physical settings, and with different technology.

I shall not try to show that the Roman economy was a fully industrial

---

15 Blair and Ramsey, *English Medieval Industries* Crossley, *Medieval Industry*; Ashton, *The Industrial Revolution*, pp. 39–44.
16 Perlin, 'Proto-Industrialisation and Pre-Colonial South Asia'.

system. The proto-industrial, or industrialising, economy would, however, seem to be a far better fit for the Late Roman economy than the 'subsistance', or 'peasant', agricultural economy, although it has never been applied to the Ancient world. Those interested in Late Saxon England and Viking-Age Scandinavia might also note the proto-industrial model. It is doubtful, however, whether mass-production was ever as fully developed in the period *ca* 400 to 1100, as it was during the period *ca* 200 to 400, at least in Britain.[17]

In order to show the relevance of the proto-industrial model to Late Roman Britain, I shall first consider the prerequisites of a proto-industrial economy (money, efficient transport, a market economy, and towns) and then examine, albeit briefly, two of the 'industries' of Roman Britain, in order to test the model. Finally, this test will be placed in a broader Imperial context by considering the *fabricae* of the third to sixth centuries in other parts of the Empire, including the East, and conclude by discussing the implications of the model for the end of the Roman, and especially Romano-British, economy and the uniqueness of the Industrial Revolution.

To conduct a broad discussion of this type one must lean heavily on the work of other scholars presented in secondary sources. I have, therefore, taken especial care to select only those which are widely accepted as authoritative by specialists, rather than the more interpretative, or controversial, sources. As already mentioned, there is an especially large amount of data for this period, which relates to economic activity, and this has received extremely rigorous study by archaeologists working both on national and regional scales.

Prerequisites of proto-industrialisation

The Proto-industrial economy cannot function without coinage, transport, markets and population nucleation. This section will attempt to show that each of these features existed in Late Roman Britain in such a way as to facilitate the development of an industrialising economy.

The transport network of Roman Britain is very well studied.[18] There was an extensive network of roads, which, if not as straight as popularly supposed, were unsurpassed until the modern period. There were also many ports, the number of which is probably even now underestimated.[19] Maritime technology was sufficiently developed so as to produce both shallow-draught vessels capable of carrying heavy loads, and efficient sea-going

[17] Hodges, *The Anglo-Saxon Achievement*; Hodges, *Dark-Age Economics*.
[18] For example, Chevalier, *Roman Roads*, pp. 158–9; Jones and Mattingly, *An Atlas*, pp. 175–78.
[19] Jones and Mattingly, *An Atlas*, pp. 198–200.

sailing ships capable of loading large cargoes.[20] Kevin Greene has noted that the cargo capacity of Roman ships was not exceeded until the fifteenth century, and that of the largest Roman ships not until the nineteenth century.[21]

The later medieval communications network in England and Wales covers the same geographical area as Roman Britain, and the late medieval road network was closely modelled on that of the fourth century.[22] If so, then it seems logical to suppose that the Romano-British communication system was as efficient as that of the Middle Ages.[23] The later medieval British communications network was the basis of that employed by the proto-industrial economy until the Industrial Revolution. This similarity between Roman and later proto-industrial communications networks is reinforced by the comparison, made by Jones, of Roman and eighteenth-century transport costs. He noted cost-ratios for the Roman period of:[24]

	Roman period	*Early eighteenth century*
Sea transport	1.0	1.0
Inland waterways	4.7	4.9
Road transport	22.6	28.0

This degree of transport efficiency is presumably why, in the early fourth century, the Roman garrison of northern Britain could use pottery provided by suppliers located in the south of England.[25]

The market economy is not simply a matter of competitive, price-based exchange, and of fairs or trading places. Not only are specialised physical settings for exchange usually required, but mechanisms of exchange enabling the tender and storage of capital and investment. These are all well attested in Late Roman Britain.

The later Roman period was the British heyday of low-value copper-alloy coinage.[26] This was in very wide circulation and coins were often used so intensely as to be worn illegible. Large amounts of coinage, therefore, existed, and were used in Roman Britain for low-value transactions for the storage of wealth. Many specialised settings, such as *fora*, *macella*, and simple shops or fairs, existed for trade based on coinage use.[27] The

---

[20] Greene, *The Archaeology*, p. 25.
[21] *Ibid.*
[22] See Chevalier, *Roman Roads*.
[23] For the rate of communication in the Roman world, see Meijer and van Nijf, *Trade, Transport and Society*, esp. pp. 136–58 and 178–9.
[24] Duncan-Jones, *The Economy of the Roman Empire*, pp. 366–69.
[25] Jones and Mattingly, *An Atlas*, pp. 210 and 212 fig. 6:30 and 6:31.
[26] Fulford, 'Coin-circulation and Mint-activity', p. 90.
[27] Mackreth, 'Roman Public Buildings' pp. 134–36.

coinage-based market is well attested, therefore, and to judge from the commodities found on Romano-British settlement sites, this mainly involved the products of mass-production.

Investment is a more difficult area to demonstrate. Textual evidence, except for one of the early Roman Vindolanda tablets, does not greatly inform us of such matters in Britain.[28] Despite this, Romans certainly had banks, and the concept of capital investment is attested,[29] but neither feature in something which we can either confidently confirm or discount when considering Britain in the third to fourth centuries.

Population concentrations are important to proto-industrialisation as they provide a market for the products manufactured. Debate over the character of the Late Romano-British town is not yet resolved, but it is now realised that the well-known plans of Caerwent and Silchester are principally plans of the towns as they were in the fourth century.[30] Increasingly, scholars have looked at the widespread evidence of 'dark earth' deposits, associated with domestic occupation and with production, as evidence of modified remnants of low-status, poorly-built houses, not as evidence for desertion.[31] This view has been reinforced by Macphail's important work on soil micromorphology, suggesting that the 'dark earth' represents debris from such buildings. If so, then fourth-century towns were larger population concentrations of consumers of mass-produced goods (as represented among the finds in the 'dark earth'[32]) than were first- to third-century towns in Britain. In Biddle's phrase, they were 'more urban than they had ever been'.[33] As he points out, this view is confirmed by the extensive fourth-century cemeteries found outside towns, such as Winchester and Dorchester (Dorset).[34] It would appear that Late Roman British towns were sufficient population concentrations to provide a market, and work-force for mass-producing industries.[35] The presence of large quantities of pottery and coinage in the 'dark earth' deposits of fourth-century British towns supports this view.[36]

In Late Roman Britain we can recognise, therefore, the prerequisites of a proto-industrial economic system. The single unattested characteristic cannot be shown to have been either present or absent, and is certainly found elsewhere in the Roman Empire.

[28] Bowman, *Life and Letters*, pp. 46–7, 70 and 136–8.
[29] Greene, *The Archaeology*, pp. 63–65.
[30] Esmonde Cleary, *The Ending of Roman Britain*, pp. 75–77.
[31] Biddle, 'The Study of Winchester', Dark, *Civitas*, pp. 15–18.
[32] Courty, Goldberg and Macphail, *Soils and micromorphology*, pp. 261–68.
[33] Biddle, 'The Study of Winchester', p. 319.
[34] *Ibid.*, pp. 318–19; see also Sparey Green, this volume.
[35] Biddle, 'The Study of Winchester', p. 317; Evans, 'Towns and the End of Roman Britain', p. 146; Dark *Civitas*, pp. 16 and 18–19.
[36] For example, Biddle, 'The Study of Winchester', p. 318; Dark, *Civitas*, p. 15.

Consequently, there is no obvious reason why Late Roman Britain need not have had a proto-industrial economy. This does not show that it had such a system, only that it could have supported one. In order to examine the data for positive evidence we may consider two specific 'industries': pottery and iron-smelting. These are probably the most fully understood Romano-British 'industries',[37] and each can show proto-industrial characteristics. It is interesting that these were among the first 'industries' to be fully industrialised in the late eighteenth century, perhaps suggesting that they are especially amenable to industrialisation.

Ceramics

Pottery and tile were widely used in Roman Britain.[38] The population was dependent, after the mid-third century, on a few British production centres. Regrettably, little is known about the workshops of these potteries, although a few workshop buildings have been excavated.[39] It is difficult, therefore, to estimate output from the workshop sites, although Fulford has suggested an output of between two- and fifteen thousand pots per kiln.[40] As pottery use was widespread and intensive – Greene notes that fine-wares only became as widely used again in the eighteenth century[41] – the output of these centres must have been considerable. This can be demonstrated by the following calculation.

Allowing for a population of four million in Late Roman Britain,[42] each of the eight contemporary major producers[43] would have to make half a million pots per annum, or about ten thousand per week, to provide each individual with a pot of any of the major types each year. The quantities of pottery found at settlement sites in Roman Britain suggest that these are, if anything, low averages, although it is, of course, unlikely that everyone acquired a new pot each year.[44]

These pots were wheel-turned, and often slipped and decorated, so it is

---

[37] Cleere, 'Industry in the Romano-British Countryside'.
[38] Fulford and Huddleston, *The current state of Romano-British pottery studies*; McWhirr, *Roman Brick*.
[39] Young, *Oxfordshire Roman Pottery*, pp. 44–50; Fulford, *New Forest Roman Pottery*, pp. 18–20; Swan, *The Pottery Kilns*, p. 36.
[40] Fulford, *New Forest Roman Pottery*, p. 22.
[41] Greene, *The Archaeology*, p. 167.
[42] Millett, *The Romanisation of Britain*, p. 185.
[43] Swan, *The Pottery Kilns*, p. 13 map 7.
[44] Reliable figures for pottery usage at Romano-British settlement sites are hard to obtain because of problems of sampling, curation, and regional variation. While pottery use was probably far more intense than indicated here on villa and town sites, far lower figures might be expected at 'native' rural settlements in relatively un-Romanised highland areas.

incredible, as Fulford has independently argued on the evidence of the production sites, that ten potters working for each producer could have each made one thousand such pots per week.[45] This would require each potter throwing about one hundred and forty vessels per day. If each potter produced a hundred pots per week[46] – one every hour, non-stop, during a fifteen-hour, seven-day week throughout the year – this would require a hundred potters working for each producer.[47] Although production rates may have been higher than this, one must also take account of the time needed to maintain and load kilns, or to acquire raw materials. This estimate also takes no account of the necessary staff to transport, store, and market the wares, and any administrative staff. The figure of a hundred 'employees' to each Late Roman pottery producer could, then, be only a minimum estimate.

It might be supposed that as these 'employees' were dispersed through several contemporary production sites, they constituted only a regional concentration of independent producers. If so, each producer could have been producing pottery on the small scale envisaged by conventional studies. But a consideration of the pottery itself seems to discount this, because the most notable characteristic of the late fourth-century ceramics 'industry' is its standardisation.[48] From the mid-fourth century until their collapse all the major 'industries' produced only standardised products. This has been seen as decline and 'stagnation', but I know of no demonstration by anthropological or historical analogy that this must be the case[49] and Carver has drawn attention to evidence that refutes this proposition.[50] This

---

45 Fulford, *New Forest Roman Pottery*, pp. 12 and 22. Young (*Oxfordshire Roman Pottery*, pp. 43–44 and 50) estimates that a workforce of one or two potters could have produced 40,000 pots per annum, but we might doubt if it is possible for his hypothetical potter to have produced 700–800 pots per week. For comparison, each six-man team of potters of modern Thrapsanos, Crete, produces 400–500 storage jars in a season, from late May to mid-September, or under 100 per month. The figures for Thrapsanos are from Peacock, *Pottery in the Roman World*, p. 27.

46 Ethnographic data for the rate of production of handmade pottery are available in van der Leeuw, 'Dust to Dust'. Van der Leeuw gives the following figures: a 'household industry' produced 200–300 vessels per month, and a workshop over 400 vessels per month: that is, an estimate of 100 vessels produced each week by a potter is approximately equivalent to a workshop scale of production.

47 For comparison, Josiah Wedgwood employed 270 workers in 1790 (Peacock, *Pottery in the Roman World*, p. 44) and a hundred workers would be more than were used by the proto-industrial manufacturers of late eighteenth-century Staffordshire (Peacock, *Pottery in the Roman World*, p. 45).

48 Fulford, 'Pottery Production and Trade at the End of Roman Britain', p. 121.

49 Rice, 'Change and Conservatism in Pottery-producing Systems', p. 240; Benco, 'Morphological Standardisation'. Both argue that standardisation is linked to increasing the efficiency of production. A similar point is made by Going, 'Economic "Long Waves" ', pp. 101–102.

50 Carver, *Underneath English Towns*, p. 43.

8

may be similar to the standardisation identified elsewhere in the Late Roman economy by Simon James,[51] as denoting mass-production. No moulds or machines are known to have been used to form the vessels, so this standardisation may have been prompted by a need similar to that noted in James's study of the production of fourth-century helmets, where design was simplified to speed up production. Importantly, standardisation also shows co-operation or unity among the kilns of each of the producers. For example, Oxfordshire pottery, as we define it today, was seen by its contemporaries, including its producer(s), as a single unitary product. The eight major contemporary pottery producers of fourth-century Britain represent, therefore, eight manufacturers, not eight geographical groups of independent potters. It is irrelevant to the question of proto-industrialisation whether these manufacturers were organised as collectives, or owned by a single 'industrialist'.

The discussion suggests that the conventional view of the Late Roman pottery 'industry' – that it entirely consisted of 'cash-cropping' by farmers at low points in the agricultural year – is misguided.[52] This is not to say that no Roman pottery was produced by such 'cash-cropping', only that these 'industries' represent major manufacturers with substantial workforces operating all year round. This is the most credible way to account for the quantity and standardisation observed by other scholars. Even if the exact numbers given above are nowhere near the actual figures, they are more likely to be too low in their estimation of both the amount of pottery used and the labour-time involved in its production, than too high.

So, it seems implausible that the Late Roman pottery 'industry' was no more than an adjunct to agriculture, and it seems likely that standardisation was a product of mass-production, with each producer employing a hundred or more workers. These workers may have been distributed over a number of contemporary production sites, as the available evidence suggests that each consisted of clusters of kiln and production foci in contemporary use. The absence of single, large, pottery-making 'factories' where workers toil under a single roof, should not dissuade us from considering them proto-industrial.

'Industries' such as the Oxfordshire-ware and Alice Holt potteries were located on rivers or so as to take advantage of the road network, and at the boundaries of two or more (up to four) *civitates*.[53] Their products were widely marketed within these *civitates* and their location suggests that they were intended, from their establishment, to furnish a market beyond their immediate locality. Given the monetarisation of fourth-century Britain, this was probably achieved by utilising the money-based economy.

---

[51] James, 'The *fabricae*', pp. 271–72.
[52] Cleary, *The Ending of Roman Britain*, p. 88.
[53] Millett, *The Romanisation*, p. 166 fig. 68.

Tile production also involved large-scale, standardised, manufacture.[54] Fourth-century Britain was the heyday of the pre-modern tile-roofed house; tile was also used in buildings and for non-structural purposes. Tile production is not as extensively studied as pottery-making, but it provides one important piece of evidence. Tile manufacture in Roman Britain included production-line manufacture under a single roof.[55] If so, this 'factory' (or, to use Peacock's term, 'manufactory') is a classic industrial feature in a very early context.[56]

Almost certainly, if tile production centres were static, tile in bulk had to be widely distributed to keep them in business. Like pottery-producing centres, tile kilns could be located at *civitas* boundaries, presumably to take advantage of a wider market.[57] So, again, a regional market and bulk transport is evidenced by tile distribution.

Both tile and pottery production, therefore, exhibit every indication of proto-industrialisation. Monetarisation and the market economy were used to distribute mass-produced standardised products in regional (and wider) markets. There is even evidence of the concentration of workers into a single 'manufactory', and of the application of systematic solutions to production problems. But, such clearcut evidence of proto-industrialisation notwithstanding, pottery and tile were not the only, or even clearest, cases of proto-industrial manufacturing in Late Roman Britain. Another 'proto-industry' was iron-smelting and this presents an even stronger case.

Ironsmelting[58]

By the fourth century ironsmelting was carried out at three major locations: Dean, Weald, and the 'Jurassic ridge' and each had a market area approximately equivalent to a fourth-century province[59] so far as can now be discerned by archaeometallurgy. They were located so as to take advantage of road and river networks, and, of course, sited on ore deposits.

Ironsmelting had, therefore, a regional market for which production was orientated, and was connected to the communication network so as to reach that custom. It also shows evidence of capital investment and return.

These characteristics would in themselves imply proto-industrial production, but when the scale of the industry is considered, the importance of iron-working to the Roman economy is clarified. In the Weald the third-

[54] McWhirr, *Roman Brick*.
[55] Green, 'A Tilemaker's Workshop'.
[56] Peacock, *Pottery in the Roman World*, pp. 9–10 and 43–46.
[57] Millett, *The Romanisation*, p. 128.
[58] For a recent general account see, Cleere, 'Ironmaking'.
[59] *Ibid.*, p. 5 fig. 4.

and fourth-century slag-tips are very large – at Beauport Park three acres were covered by high slag heaps representing fifty to sixty thousand tons of iron over 160 or 170 years.[60] The Forest of Dean tips were so large, in fact, that mining them became a commercial undertaking in the sixteenth and seventeenth centuries.[61]

Beauport Park was only one of at least sixteen contemporary ironsmelting complexes in the Weald.[62] Together, the known Wealden sites produced up to 7,500 tonnes of iron per annum in the fourth century, and there were many more Roman-period ironsmelting sites in this area than there were in the middle ages.[63] A recent survey located forty ironsmelting sites in the Weald, of which all but seven were Romano-British, in contrast to five medieval sites.[64]

Nor was the Weald the principal fourth-century iron producer; of the four contemporary major smelting sites (each a cluster of iron-working centres) it was not the largest. At Ariconium, in the Dean fields, there were also slag-tips of ironsmelting waste. These covered not seven acres (as in the largest Wealden example), but two hundred acres.[65] This suggests very large-scale production even by early modern standards. It may be no coincidence that these tips were so close to a small town – perhaps the wealth of the community and its reasons for existence was the iron-industry.

A large producer-site has recently been excavated among the ironsmelting complexes of the Jurassic ridge in Northamptonshire.[66] At the site, Laxton, iron-working debris spread over at least 400 square metres, and up to 100 metres from the excavated site. Beyond this, slag-heaps were found 450 metres from the site and, most remarkably, a 100 metre-wide valley running parallel with the site was filled with slag and debris.

The iron produced by these sites was widely distributed throughout their regions. Their spacing could also indicate that each 'industry' provided all the iron required by one or more Late Roman provinces.

There can be no denying, therefore, that the iron-industry in Late Roman Britain was proto-industrial. In scale, in concentrated numbers of smelting centres, and in the amount of iron annually produced, it exceeds the proto-industrial late medieval iron-industry.

[60] Cleere, 'The Roman Iron Industry', p. 184.
[61] Cleere, 'Ironmaking', p. 3.
[62] Cleere, 'The Roman Iron Industry'.
[63] Crossley, 'Medieval Ironsmelting', p. 33.
[64] Hodgkinson and Tebbutt, 'A Fieldwork Study of the Romano-British Iron Industry', p. 162.
[65] Healy, *Mining and Metallurgy*, p. 65.
[66] Jackson and Tylecote, 'Two New Romano-British Iron-working Sites'.

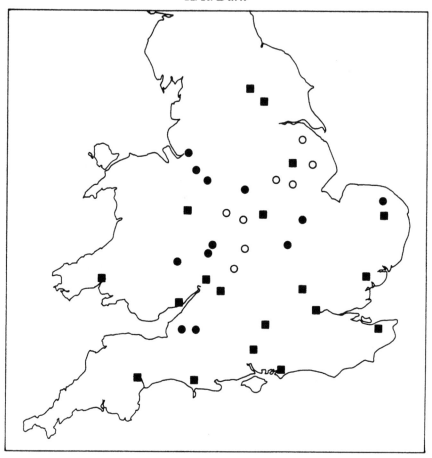

Figure 1. Proto-industrialisation and urbanism in Late Roman Britain 'Small towns' with economies apparently dependent on mass-production (filled circles) in relation to 'major towns' (filled squares) and 'minor defended settlements' (open circles). Based on data in Burnham and Wacher, 1990, with three sites excluded from the latter category. These are: Neatham, on chronological grounds, and both Margidunum and Cambridge on the grounds that they are more readily seen as 'walled small towns' rather than analogous to sites such as Dorn.

Industrial towns in Roman Britain

Proto-industrialisation is mainly concerned with the industrialisation of rural production, but in Roman Britain there were urban communities closely connected with proto-industrial production. The small town of Ariconium has already been mentioned, and it is conventional to argue that the small town of Charterhouse was located for, and probably dependent upon, the lead mines adjacent to it.[67] The two towns named *Salinae* were so called because of their salt-production.[68] That is, the 'industry' characterised these places, yet they were certainly not the only salting sites in Roman Britain.[69] The most obvious explanation is that it was the scale of production, not the production itself, that was the characteristic, hence its name. There are several other sites, such as Water Newton which might be seen as specialised 'industrial' settlements, with a major part of their population employed in production.[70] While such communities are not a requirement of proto-industrialisation, clearly their existence shows that production could provide a large part of the support and employment required to maintain substantial communities.

An especially interesting aspect of the distribution of such sites in Roman Britain is shown when they are mapped. A group of 'industrial' small-towns including Middlewich, Little Chester, Droitwich, Kenchester and possibly Worcester, form a zone of settlements across what is today the West Midlands.[71] There are very few other urban settlements in this area, apart from Wroxeter itself, and it seems that the landscape of the West Midlands was characterised by a series of 'industrial towns' on the fringe of the 'military zone' (where there were few villas, no major towns and forts) and the 'civil zone' (where villas were widespread and there were major towns, but only rarely forts), with this zone roughly delineated of the east by a series of 'minor defended settlements', such as Dorn, Wall, Chesterton-on-Foss, Manceter and, perhaps, Thorpe-by-Newark. Although 'industrial towns', notably Water Newton, did occur to the east of this line, it separates the concentration of such sites across the West Midlands from the area (distinguished by containing more villas and larger towns) to the east.

---

[67] Burnham and Wacher, *The Small Towns*, pp. 208–11.
[68] *Ibid.*, p. 211.
[69] Jones and Mattingly, *An Atlas*, pp. 224, 226 map 6:43, 227 map 6:44, and 228.
[70] *Ibid.*, pp. 195 map 6:14, 209 map 6:27, and 210; Burnham and Wacher, *The Small Towns*, pp. 203–34, provide a general account.
[71] Burnham and Wacher, *The Small Towns*, pp. 2 and 203–34. For the 'minor defended settlements', pp. 234–78.

Whether or not this is coincidence, or due to an abundance of natural resources, it is intriguing that this is an area closely associated with the origins of the eighteenth-century Industrial Revolution.

Conclusion

The criteria of proto-industrialisation are all present in fourth-century Britain. Industries produced for regional, and wider, markets and supported whole communities by the marketing of these products in the monetary economy. Standardisation, the application of systematic solutions to production difficulties, the use of efficient networks of communication, are all evidenced.

There are hints, in the Weald, and in the much more widespread use of some manufactured items, such as pottery, that the Late Roman economy was industrialised more intensely than that of the late Middle Ages – the classic period of proto-industrialisation. Recognising the proto-industrial character of the late Romano-British economy does not mean that artisan production did not exist. Clearly, it continued alongside larger-scale manufacture. This is what we find in the eighteenth-nineteenth century – local blacksmiths do not disprove the existence of an iron-industry.

It must be stressed, however, that evidence of proto-industrialisation is not evidence that an industrial revolution had taken place, or would inevitably have taken place in Roman Britain given time. It merely indicates an *industrialising* economy.

The British data cannot be seen in isolation, however, and again, in order to place Britain in a clearer perspective, we may consider some evidence from other parts of the Roman Empire. This will show that Britain was by no means the most industrialised part of the Late Roman world. This must, of course, be a highly selective account of a large subject, and so I shall concentrate on the most straightforward piece of evidence, the so-called 'factories', of the Late Empire, which are directly relevant to Roman Britain as there was a 'factory' at a British town called *Uenta*: presumably either Caerwent or Winchester.[72] Their study in more amply documented provinces may elucidate the character of these sites, and help place British proto-industrial production in its wider perspective.

---

[72] James, 'The *fabricae*'; Jones, *The Later Roman Empire*, 2, pp. 834–37; Wild, 'The Gynaeceum at *Venta*'. For the cloth industry in general see, Wild, *Textile Manufacture*.

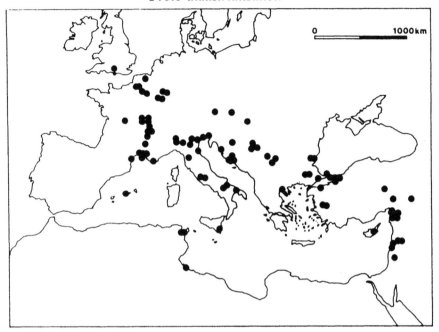

Figure 2. Textually attested 'factories' in the Late Roman empire. The one site in Britain is identified here as Winchester, after Randsborg (1991), on whose maps this drawing is based.

Industrialisation in other parts of the Roman Empire

The most striking archaeological example of a proto-industrial complex in fourth-century Europe is at Barbégal, in Gaul.[73] A series of large, vertical wheel, water-mills were arranged in sequence down the hillside. These, it has been estimated, could have produced enough grain for twelve thousand people. The intended market was probably only the nearby town, but the use of technology in this way, and scale of production, must demand, at least, the description 'proto-industrial' for this site.

Gaul had also, of course, a notable proto-industrial complex prior to the fourth century. The samian ware 'industry', with its international mass-markets, mould-made, standardised, products, and its massive scale of production is the most striking.[74] There are other examples, of course, but

[73] Benoit, 'L'usine de Meunerie Hydralique de Barbégal (Arles)'; Sagui, 'Le Meunerie de Barbégal'; Peacock, *Pottery in the Roman World*, p. 10.

[74] Peacock, *Pottery in the Roman World*, pp. 122–28.

this will suffice to form a background to the discussion of the proto-industrialised factories of the Late Roman world.

The number and nature of Late Roman 'factories'

In an excellent study, Simon James has clarified the character and number of *fabricae*.[75] These Late Roman 'factories' were widespread, they were urban production centres, and are usually assumed, on no strong evidence, to have been small artisan workshops of under fifty employees, although they were equated with army regiments by the bureaucracy.[76] Yet, as James points out, there are no certainly identified excavated examples of *fabricae*.[77] There are possible instances from Sardis, where the building is unexcavated, and at Amiens, where extensive manufacturing took place in a disused public building: a characteristic of Late Roman urban archaeology evidenced in Britain at York and Silchester.[78] This latter group of sites seems to indicate the 'industrial' use of large buildings, whether or not the structure at Sardis has been correctly identified, and the textual indications of size suggested to McMullen that there were two hundred, and to A. H. M. Jones four to five hundred employees in each official 'factory'.[79] No official record exists of the metalworking attested at York and Silchester and this may suggest that many undocumented (although not, necessarily, unofficial) 'factories' existed.

The figure for the number of employees given by Jones, although based on speculation, is probably the more accurate estimate: the clearest available evidence of the size of *fabricae* is in descriptions of the population of Tarsus, Caesarea, and Cyzicus.[80] A large part of the population of each of these towns comprised 'industrial' employees in these 'factories'. For example, the majority of the inhabitants of Cyzicus were employed in the two 'factories': the mints and the armoury.[81]

These towns may have been exceptional, of course, but there is no reason to suppose that they were unlike other eastern cities, such as Antioch or Sardis. Towns with more than one *fabrica* were widespread.

[75] James, 'The *fabricae*'.
[76] Jones, *The Later Roman Empire*, vol. 2, p. 835.
[77] James, 'The *fabricae*'.
[78] Vann, *The Unexcavated Buildings*, pp. 11–22; Bayard and Massy, *Amiens Romain*; Wacher, *The Towns of Roman Britain*, p.289; Cleary, *The Ending of Roman Britain*, pp. 70–71; Phillips and Heywood, *Excavations at York Minster*; Carver, *Arguments in Stone*, p. 59.
[79] James, 'The *fabricae*', p. 276.
[80] *Ibid.*, p. 281; Jones, *The Later Roman Empire*, vol. 2, p. 836; Jones, 'The Economic Life of the Roman Towns', p. 51.
[81] Jones, *The Later Roman Empire*, vol. 2, pp. 836–37.

It is, therefore, reasonable to take the evidence of Tarsus, Caesarea, and Cyzicus as a guide to the size of *fabricae*, at least in the eastern Empire. It may be noted that although texts inform us especially about government factories, the *Novels* of Justinian make it clear that by the sixth century, at latest, private arms production existed on a substantial scale.[82] We must, therefore, recognise that government-owned *fabricae* were not the only mass-producers in the Mediterranean.

Consequently, even a brief consideration of fabricae shows that large, unitary[83] organised, urban, production centres were widespread in Europe and the Mediterranean from the fourth century onward. If we adopt such an interpretation, then, factories, no less, were widespread in Late Antique Europe and the Mediterranean.[84] There is also evidence that, in the fourth century, technology, especially water-power, was applied to solving mass-production problems.[85] Even in the West, as David Peacock has noted, Barbégal seems to show this tendency.[86] These are characteristics of a fully industrial system, not merely of proto-industrialisation, suggesting that the process of industrialisation was sufficiently advanced in the Late Roman Mediterranean to show the first indications of a transition from a proto-industrial to industrial system. Certainly, there were production centres in the fourth-century Mediterranean which may well have been larger than those of eighteenth-century England.

In conclusion, then, the proto-industrial model fits Britain well, but in the most technologically advanced and urbanised areas of the Empire the economy was not only proto-industrialised but showing the first tendencies towards full industrialisation.[87] The lack of evidence for further development of industrialisation in the eastern Roman Empire might be explained

82 James, 'The *fabricae*', p. 282.
83 *Ibid.*, p. 281; Jones, *The Later Roman Empire*, vol. 2, p. 836; Jones, 'The Economic Life of the Roman Towns', p. 51.
84 These urban production centres might be taken to show greater evidence of industriali-sation than is encompassed within conventional definitions of proto-industrial production, as, for example, by Kemp: Kemp, *Historical Patterns*. Kemp defines proto-industrialisation as 'a growth market-orientated industry, mainly rural, and still organised on traditional lines', p. 43.
85 White, *Greek and Roman Technology*; Greene, 'Perspectives'. For Britain see, Spain, 'Romano-British Watermills'. Spain notes that at Ickham the mill may have run a trip-hammer, rather than been used for grinding corn alone.
86 Peacock, *Pottery in the Roman World*, p. 10.
87 In a statistical study, Clark has noted that levels of production in Italy were, in A.D. 300, equivalent to those of Britain in A.D. 1800. Clark also estimates that the value of income per man-year for the Roman economy for the third to the sixth century, was higher, according to a standard measure (the I.U. or International Unit) than that of Greece in the 1950s. This study seems to have been overlooked by archaeologists and historians, perhaps because it was by an economist and published in a work principally concerned with modern economics. Clark, *The Conditions of Economic Progress*, pp. 676–77.

in many ways: a crisis of confidence leading to reluctance on the part of investors and potential industrialists, or a slow rate of technological development provide equally plausible explanations of this.

Such conclusions throw doubt upon not only the conventional interpretation of the Roman economy, but the uniqueness of the eighteenth-century Industrial Revolution. Unlike the proto-industrial economy of the early modern period, the Roman economy collapsed, and mass-production ceased.

This raises the question of the relationship between proto-industrialisation and the end of the Roman economy. There is, I think, a very close relationship between the two. It is to this relationship which we must now turn.

Proto-industrialisation and the end of the Roman economy

Proto-industrial and industrial economic systems are, to use Kent Flannery's term, highly 'coherent'.[88] That is, they depend upon a constant inter-relationship of elements of production and exchange. They require the maintenance of a cost-efficient means of production and distribution, and the will both to invest in production and, on the part of the consumer, to obtain the product.

'Coherence' is an interesting phenomenon, because it has been shown that very coherent systems exhibit a general proneness to collapse extremely suddenly. This tendency can be described, and to an extent explained, by the application of catastrophe-theory.

Catastrophe-theory[89] is a mathematical means of explaining and modelling very sudden negative change, hence its name. In basis, it works on the assumption that a gradual build-up of factors limiting choice causes the restriction of options in decision-making to those which promote collapse. Because this only occurs when options narrow to the critical point of leaving no option other than one causing decline, this decline occurs suddenly and dramatically.[90]

When an economic system becomes so 'coherent' that it cannot adapt to changed circumstances it can, therefore, be 'catastrophic' in the mathematical sense. The options are narrowed because the only way for it to operate is to maintain a constant relationship between its constituent parts. Flannery has called such systems 'hypercoherent'[91] and it is, I suggest, an adequate description of Late Roman proto-industrial economics. Unlike agricultural

---

88 Flannery, 'The Cultural Evolution of Civilizations'.
89 Renfrew, *Approaches to Social Archaeology*, pp. 359–60.
90 *Ibid.*, pp. 372–74.
91 Flannery, 'The Cultural Evolution'.

or other production, they required the maintenance of low-value coinage employed in market-based exchange, efficient networks of road and water communication, a substantial concentrated (urban) market, and the maintenance of a minium of technology. They also required confidence on the part of the workforce, and investor, in the future of the market-based system and of demand for the products. In the late fourth to early fifth centuries, communications were probably disrupted by barbarian raiding and migration, confidence in the future maintenance of the Roman world order probably declined, and the money-based urban economy was also disrupted.

Conversely, if we consider that the Late Roman economy was proto-industrial, it was a 'hypercoherent' system which, at the start of the fifth century, was faced with an abrupt discontinuity in the necessities of its continued operation. Catastrophic change, therefore, occurred.

Returning to Roman Britain, this is what we see in many industries. For example, pottery ceased to be mass-produced in the early fifth century,[92] and the villa-system was almost certainly no longer functioning by the mid-fifth century.[93] Whatever the exact fate of the money-using economy and towns, there seems little doubt that large population concentrations like Roman Wroxeter did not exist by *ca* 500 at the latest and the building industry had collapsed by the middle of the preceding century.[94] Even in colloquial terms, the end of Romano-British mass-production industries was 'catastrophic', and it probably occurred in a short time-span from the late fourth century to the early fifth century.

After *ca* 450, it is impossible to find anything approaching industrialised production in Britain for the remainder of the period of British political independence. In Gaul and Italy there is also evidence of rapid industrial decline, with only a few production centres surviving into the fifth to sixth centuries.[95] The survival of even these might be linked to the different survival of towns and coinage-use, providing both markets and work-forces, and to the maintenance of confidence by the Late Roman élite during the fifth century. In Britain large parts of the industrial base had been in the areas which passed under Germanic control in the fifth century.[96]

Only in the East did large-scale production survive longer, but then so did all its prerequisites. There collapse was not in the fifth century, but in

---

[92] Fulford, 'Pottery Production', especially pp. 123–25.

[93] Dark, *Discovery*, pp. 95–98; *Civitas*, p.59; and 'St Patrick's *uillula*'.

[94] For sub-Roman Wroxeter and an example of a fifth-century mortared stone building see, White, 'Excavations on the Site of the Baths Basilica'. For my dating of the final phase of occupation at Wroxeter see, Dark, *Discovery*, p. 94.

[95] Fulford, 'Pottery Production', pp. 122–23.

[96] For the area under Anglo-Saxon control in the fifth century see, Hines, 'Philology, Archaeology', p. 34 fig. 1; Dark, *Civitas* p. 219.

the seventh century, and it was notably similar in spread and totality.[97] Late medieval Sardis was an agricultural village, not an 'industrial' town.[98]

Consequently, the catastrophe-theory model of rapid collapse closely fits the observable evidence for the end of Late Roman mass-production. It is interesting to see the close relationship between areas where towns survived and those where mass-production continued, suggesting a relationship between producer and market. This may suggest that these towns were greater population centres in the fifth to sixth centuries, than some have supposed.

It is also relevant to return to the assertion that the eighteenth-century Industrial Revolution was a unique historical event, for this discussion sheds light both on the Late Roman and early modern situations. The 'hypercoherent' nature of the Roman economy raises the possibility that 'hypercoherence' and catastrophic collapse are general characteristics of industrialising economic systems. If so, then the pattern which we might expect of those states which could be considered as proto-industrial would be of logistic curves of economic growth, followed by catastrophic collapse. But clearly the post-eighteenth-century industrial economy has not been 'hypercoherent' – it survives today, so we might assume that it would not show such a pattern of growth and sudden decline. Interestingly, this is exactly the pattern of medieval and modern economic change favoured by economic historians and geographers. They see the 'pre-industrial' (that is, pre-eighteenth century) economy, as exhibiting logistic patterns of slow growth and then sudden decline on quantitative data derived from late medieval and early modern textual sources.[99] In contrast, the industrial economy is frequently viewed as showing 'long-waves' of economic growth and decline, as first suggested by N. D. Kondratieff.[100] Again, quantitative data from modern textual sources enable this interpretation to be corroborated.

This digression into modern economic history is, therefore, not without relevance for the study of the end of the Roman economy, nor is the study of the Roman economy irrelevant to that of the modern world. It has been shown that the mass-production component of the Late Roman economy seems to prescribe a logistic wave and sudden collapse. This is consistent with the more strongly attested pattern of the fifteenth- to eighteenth-century economy, with which we have been comparing that of the Late Roman Empire. The relationship is reflexive, in that the significance of the Roman economy as a proto-industrial system enables us to take these

---

[97] Mango, *Byzantium*, pp. 60–87.
[98] Foss, *Byzantine and Turkish Sardis*.
[99] E.g. Taylor, *Political Geography*, pp. 14–15.
[100] *Ibid.*, pp. 13–14. Recently, Going has attempted to demonstrate 'long-waves' in the Romano-British economy: Going, 'Economic "long waves" '.

patterns of logistic growth and decline back still further in time, and to suggest that their cause is the 'coherence' of the economies of industrialising urban states. This would seem to be true of all 'pre-industrial' states; all seem to show proto-industrial characteristics. If this is so, it enables us to note that the Industrial Revolution of the eighteenth century was not unique because of the process of industrialisation, but because it overcame the apparently inherent 'hypercoherence' of the proto-industrial system, enabling a full Industrial Revolution to occur. The reasons for this are not, however, appropriate material for further discussion here.

Nevertheless, I suggest that by seeing the Roman economy in this comparative perspective, and by using models employed elsewhere in economics, we may clarify the character of the Roman mass-productive economy. This model may also explain why it failed to survive in Britain after the first quarter of the fifth century.

II

PALAEOECOLOGICAL EVIDENCE FOR LANDSCAPE CONTINUITY AND CHANGE IN BRITAIN *ca* A.D. 400–800

*S. P. Dark**

Palaeoecological evidence is being used increasingly in conjunction with archaeological and historical sources in studying past society and economy. This application results from the potential of such evidence to provide reconstructions of the environmental setting of human activities, and the timing, nature and scale of human impacts (both direct and via grazing animals) on the landscape. Effort has largely been concentrated on prehistoric periods, however, partly because sequences of organic deposits from later periods have often been disturbed by human activity, such as peat digging, and perhaps also because it has been thought less necessary to apply such techniques when written evidence is available.

Palaeoecology has much to offer in the study of historical periods, since, for example, it provides evidence unbiased by past human perceptions and enables continuous long-term 'monitoring' of changes in land-use patterns, such as would be impossible using archaeological or historical data alone. Of special importance to the study of the period A.D. 400–800 is the question of whether there was continuity of landscape use after the end of the Roman period, or general collapse of agricultural systems and widespread abandonment of land. Did similar crops to those used in the Roman period continue to be grown, or was there a shift to other types of production? Such questions can be addressed by pollen analysis of sequences of waterlogged organic deposits which have accumulated during the relevant time interval. These sequences provide a record of vegetational change through time which, if independently dated, can be correlated with archaeological and historical sources. This chapter brings together the evidence from radiocarbon-dated pollen sequences from Britain spanning the period A.D. 400–800 to provide a picture of regional differentiation in landscape use and continuity after the end of the Roman period.

* Formerly Day.

23

The Palaeoecological Approach

On- and off-site evidence

Biological remains with the potential to shed light on past human activity may be retrieved from two main sources – archaeological contexts ('on-site' samples), and sequences of organic deposits not directly associated with archaeological sites ('off-site' samples).

On-site environmental evidence generally consists of assemblages deposited at one time, or over a period of a few years or decades, such as wood charcoal and charred cereal remains from a hearth. These assemblages are important in providing evidence for the types of plant utilised by the occupants of the site, but, since they result from non-random selection of plants growing an unknown distance away, they are of little practical use in providing an idea of its general environmental setting. In contrast, off-site sequences of organic deposits which have accumulated in lakes, peat bogs etc., may provide a continuous record of environmental change over thousands of years, unbiased by past human sampling. Because these sequences are not directly associated with archaeological material, they enable reconstructions of human impacts on the landscape in general, rather than relating only to the immediate vicinity of a particular settlement site. It is this type of evidence which will be considered here.[1]

Pollen analysis

At its simplest level, pollen analysis involves taking small samples at regular intervals from a sediment sequence, concentrating the pollen by chemical preparation techniques, and identifying and counting the different pollen types under a microscope. Pollen diagrams are then produced showing the way in which the relative frequencies of different pollen types have changed through time. Interpretation of pollen diagrams requires consideration of a range of factors affecting the relationship between the pollen assemblages obtained and the original vegetation.[2]

Some plants are well represented in the palynological record due to high pollen production and/or widespread dispersal of their pollen grains. This group includes wind-pollinated plants, such as birch, oak, and grasses. Other plants produce small numbers of pollen grains that are dispersed only short distances. This group includes most insect-pollinated plants, which tend to be poorly represented, even if they are abundant in the local

---

[1] For a discussion of the merits of the 'off-site' pollen record see Edwards, 'Using space'. 'On-site' assemblages of macroscopic plant remains from Dark Age contexts are, in fact, few, as emphasised in a review by Greig, 'The British Isles'.

[2] For details of the production and interpretation of pollen sequences see Moore, Webb and Collinson, *Pollen Analysis*, and Faegri and Iversen, *Textbook*.

vegetation. Furthermore, the area of vegetation represented in a pollen sequence depends on the type of deposit analysed. In general, large lakes and bogs give a regional picture, while peat which accumulates in small hollows registers only local events.[3]

Changes in pollen sequences may be the result of natural processes, or human activity, or both. The separation of local from regional-scale effects and natural from human impacts relies on detailed knowledge of the ecology of the plant types represented, dispersal characteristics of their pollen grains, and sampling properties of the deposit studied. For example, an increase in frequency of tree and shrub pollen in a sequence might reflect local encroachment of trees onto drying peat deposits, or woodland regeneration on abandoned agricultural land some distance from the site. In this example, if the increase in tree pollen consists only of willow and/or alder, plants which occur predominantly on damp soils, and with pollen grains that travel relatively short distances, then it is likely to be only of local significance.

The extent to which pollen analysis can be used to detect changes in crop exploitation is limited by the fact that the pollen of many groups of plants, such as legumes, cannot be separated into cultivated and 'wild' types. Some cereals, or groups of cereals, can be distinguished from their pollen,[4] although this is not consistently attempted by all workers. Pollen of hemp (*Cannabis sativa*) – an important fibre plant – often first appears in the Roman or Dark Age/Anglo-Saxon part of a sequence, but it is not always possible to separate its pollen from that of the hop (*Humulus lupulus*), which is in the same family (Cannabaceae).[5] In this case the pollen may be referred to the family or designated '*Cannabis* type' although it is generally considered that fossil grains of this type are usually hemp.

Because of the time and expense involved in palynological studies, a single sequence is usually analysed from the deepest part of a lake or bog. Comparison of adjacent pollen profiles from the same site has indicated that lateral variation in pollen sequences is not great, although significant differences in the representation of local wetland plants may occur.[6]

Correlation of changes in a pollen sequence with events recognised from archaeological or historical sources requires the acquisition of a series of 'absolute' dates, usually produced by radiocarbon-dating. The process of obtaining a radiocarbon date involves a series of factors which affect the

3 Jacobson and Bradshaw, 'The selection of sites'.
4 See, for example, Andersen, 'Identification'.
5 See Godwin, 'Pollen-analytical evidence' and Whittington and Gordon, 'The differentiation', for separation of pollen of hop and hemp.
6 Turner, Innes and Simmons, 'Two pollen diagrams'; Whittington *et al.*, 'Late- and post-glacial'; Stewart *et al.*, 'Pollen diagrams from Dubh Lochan'; Chambers, 'Three radiocarbon-dated pollen diagrams'; and Smith and Green, 'Topogenous peat development'.

age-range covered by the result. Firstly, samples for radiocarbon-dating from sediment or peat cores generally consist of slices of the deposit spanning a depth of several centimetres, which will have accumulated over a period of decades or even centuries. The possibility of contamination by younger roots, or older inwashed material has long been recognised as a potential problem, but the recent practice of dating separate components of sediment samples has revealed the possibility of further problems with the usual 'bulk' dates. For example, significant discrepancies were found between 'bulk' and 'humin' dates obtained for a pollen sequence from Extwistle Moor, Lancashire, making the chronology of vegetation change around the site in the first millennium A.D. uncertain.[7]

The error term for the date (which allows for laboratory error) is usually quoted at one standard deviation, meaning that there is a 68% chance that the true age falls within the quoted range of the experimental result. At two standard deviations of the result (obtained by doubling the error term) there is a 95% chance that the age falls within the given range. Radiocarbon dates are generally quoted in uncalibrated years 'Before Present' (B.P.), where 'Present' is taken as A.D. 1950.

Calibration of radiocarbon dates is required because past fluctuations in the level of carbon-14 in the atmosphere mean that radiocarbon years are not strictly equivalent to calendar years. Calibration curves have been produced by radiocarbon-dating of wood samples of known age (dated by dendrochronology), of which the most recent covering the period under consideration here is that of Stuiver and Pearson.[8] For example, a radiocarbon date centred on 1660 B.P. is equivalent to A.D. 300 in radiocarbon years (i.e. 1950 – 1660 = 290), but calibration shows that the true date in calendar years is A.D. 410. The radiocarbon date therefore provided an over-estimate of the age of the sample in this case. Calibrated radiocarbon dates are conventionally cited as 'cal. A.D.' to distinguish them from true historical dates.

In some instances, calibration may substantially increase the time-span represented by a radiocarbon date, due to plateaux and 'wiggles' in the calibration curve. In such cases a single radiocarbon date may be equivalent to more than one calendar age. For example, a radiocarbon date centred on 1580 B.P. intersects the calibration curve on plateau lasting from A.D. 450–530 in calendar years. Furthermore, the error term attached to the radiocarbon date should also be calibrated to provide a true idea of the possible range of the date.[9] Radiocarbon dating therefore provides an age range for a sample rather than a single date, a fact which is of critical

---

[7] Bartley and Chambers, 'A pollen diagram'.
[8] Stuiver and Pearson, 'High precision bidecadal calibration'.
[9] See Bowman, *Radiocarbon Dating*, for methods of calibrating date ranges.

importance when attempts are made to correlate different sources of information for a period.[10]

For pollen diagrams, levels chosen for dating tend to be those where major changes in pollen spectra occur, with dates for intervening events being estimated by interpolation on a plot of radiocarbon dates against sample depth, assuming constant accumulation rate. This is generally a safe assumption for lake deposits, but peat sequences may contain breaks due to cessation of accumulation in dry periods or removal by peat cutting. Such breaks can usually be detected by sharp changes in the pollen spectra. As mentioned previously, removal of the upper layers of bogs by peat cutting is often responsible for the absence of post-Roman deposits in peat sequences.

A further important consideration is sampling resolution of the pollen sequence. Where samples are separated by periods of centuries, temporal resolution will be inadequate to enable changes in vegetation between the Roman period and later centuries to be detected. For example, a pollen sequence from Wilden Marsh, in the West Midlands,[11] covers the period A.D. 400–800, but probably only one sample falls within this timespan. This means that a major phase of woodland regeneration or other vegetational change could have been missed.

These considerations require a critical approach in the use of palaeoecology in relation to historical periods, since the temporal resolution of most pollen diagrams, and errors associated with their radiocarbon dates, mean that investigation of local events on short time-scales is not feasible.[12] Pollen analysis is, however, well suited to addressing questions relating to environmental change on a landscape scale, and the study of a group of sites enables some of the shortcomings in the record from individual locations to be overcome.

Previous work

Early attempts at reconstructing vegetational change in relation to particular phases of human activity were hampered by a lack of radiocarbon dates,[13] and observed phases of clearance and regeneration tended to be assigned to particular periods in relation to the presence, or absence, of archaeological or historical evidence for activity nearby. It was often assumed that wood-

---

[10] A problem discussed by Baillie, 'Suck-in and smear', and Dumayne *et al.*, 'Problems associated with'.

[11] Brown, 'The palaeoecology'.

[12] See Edwards, 'Palynological and temporal', for discussion of problems in using palynological data in prehistoric contexts.

[13] See, for example, Turner, 'Post-neolithic disturbance'.

land regeneration phases identified in undated pollen sequences were immediately post-Roman.[14]

By the late 1970s sufficient radiocarbon-dated pollen diagrams had been produced from north-eastern England to enable Turner to attempt a reconstruction of the environment in the Roman period.[15] She argued that much of the area was cleared of woodland in the late Iron Age, and farmed throughout the Roman period until at least the sixth century, followed by woodland regeneration. Turner's suggestion of an initial period of post-Roman continuity was based on radiocarbon dates associated with regeneration phases, but at some of the sites, such as Fellend Moss and Steng Moss, Northumberland,[16] regeneration actually began *before* the radiocarbon-dated level. Most of the sites probably do not, in fact, show an initial period of continuity.

A later, and brief, account of vegetation of the immediately post-Roman period incorporated further dated sites, mainly from northern England and Scotland.[17] This led Turner to the conclusion that 'the majority of pollen diagrams indicate a regenerated forest and a lower proportion of arable and pasture land. . . . Some show no change and only a very small proportion indicate a higher level of activity than in the Iron Age'.[18] This evidence has subsequently been extrapolated to other areas, resulting in a general perception that abandonment of land and woodland regeneration were widespread after Roman withdrawal from Britain, a view recently challenged by Bell.[19]

Over the last decade many new radiocarbon-dated pollen sequences have been produced from most parts of Britain, but there has been no synthesis of this body of data to provide a reconstruction of the environment of fifth- to ninth-century Britain and its similarity, or otherwise, to that of the Roman period.

Background

Obviously, the wide geographical coverage of this chapter means that a considerable amount of vegetational variation between sites will result from different local conditions of topography, geology, soil, and climate, independently of land-use practices. Any vegetational response to changing pressure of land-use will also, therefore, vary accordingly. In most lowland

---

[14] For example, Moore, 'Human influence'.

[15] Turner, 'The environment of north-east England'.

[16] Davies and Turner, 'Pollen diagrams from Northumberland'.

[17] Turner, 'The vegetation'.

[18] *Ibid.*, p. 71.

[19] Bell, 'Environmental archaeology'.

areas, cessation of grazing or ploughing, and abandonment of land, will enable colonisation by scrub leading to the formation of woodland. Conversely, in some upland areas progressive soil deterioration and hydrological changes following initial woodland clearance may mitigate against tree growth, so that cessation, or reduction, of grazing pressure may result in the spread of heathland.[20]

Although most vegetational change observed in pollen sequences covering the last five thousand years is probably due to human activity, either directly or indirectly, natural environmental factors, particularly climatic change, should also be considered. Proxy climatic information for the first millennium A.D. has been obtained from a number of sources, of which studies of peat bog stratigraphy have been most widely used. This method uses variations in the degree of decomposition of plant remains making up the peat as an indication of bog surface wetness at the time of accumulation. The results are by no means unequivocal. Barber suggested climatic deterioration at *ca* 1170 B.P. (cal. A.D. 890) from studies of Bolton Fell Moss, Cumbria,[21] while data on peat humification[22] from five sites in northern England, Wales, and Ireland, suggest a shift to increased wetness of bog surfaces from *ca* 1400 B.P. (cal. A.D. 650).[23] Climatic cooling and/or increased climatic wetness could be responsible for these changes.

The onset of blanket peat-formation in this period at some Welsh sites might be argued to lend additional support to suggestions of climatic deterioration.[24] Not all sites provide evidence for climatic change at this time, however,[25] while some peat sequences have been interpreted to suggest lower rainfall or climatic warming. Examples are provided by the 'retardation layers'[26] at Helsington Moss, Morecambe Bay, radiocarbon dated to around 1500 B.P. (cal. A.D. 600),[27] and similar changes in peat deposition at Burnfoothill Moss, Dumfries and Galloway, dated to *ca* cal. A.D. 350–450.[28] A problem with such studies is that peat growth in different areas is likely to vary in its response to climatic change, and will also be affected by local hydrological factors which may, in turn, be connected with human activity.

---

[20] Moore, Merryfield and Price, 'The vegetation and development'; Miles, 'Vegetation and soil change'.

[21] Barber, *Peat stratigraphy*.

[22] A measure of the extent to which decomposition has occurred, and therefore dryness of the peat surface at the time of accumulation.

[23] Blackford and Chambers, 'Proxy records'.

[24] Chambers, 'Three radiocarbon-dated pollen diagrams'.

[25] For example, Quick Moss, Northumberland, where peat humification data show no change from the Roman period, Rowell and Turner, 'Litho-'.

[26] That is, points in the sequence where peat growth has ceased for a time, presumably due to drier conditions, followed by renewed growth.

[27] Smith, 'The mires'; Pennington, 'Vegetation history in the north-west'.

[28] Tipping, 'Holocene evolution of a lowland Scottish landscape: Kirkpatrick Fleming. Part I'.

Notwithstanding the problems associated with peat bog stratigraphy, other sources of evidence would seem to confirm the existence of widespread climatic deterioration in the immediate post-Roman period.[29] It is particularly notable that studies of European tree-rings suggest a series of unfavourable growing seasons at a period centred on the A.D. 540s, the decade of the Justinianic plague.[30] This coincides with historical references to a dust-veil from Britain, the Mediterranean and China at around A.D. 536, possibly the result of a major volcanic eruption. It was originally thought that this could be related to a phase of increased acidity in the Greenland ice sheet, probably the result of ash fallout from a major volcanic eruption dated to A.D. 540 ± 10.[31] The date of this event has subsequently been revised to A.D. 516 ± 4, however,[32] so there is currently no clear link between the ice-core and dendrochronological and historical evidence for a major eruption at A.D. 536. Analysis of other ice-cores may yet resolve this issue.

The results of any such volcanic eruption are unlikely to have affected the climate for more than a few years – tree-ring studies have been interpreted as suggesting reduced temperatures for about a decade,[33] but a mechanism has recently been suggested for more severe and prolonged environmental effects.[34] Volcanic emissions would have resulted in acid gas deposition which may have increased the acidity of nutrient-poor soils in upland areas, perhaps pushing them across a threshold beyond which they could no longer be farmed. The resulting soil changes might be irreversible, and thus lead to permanent abandonment of land. Similarly, any climatic change that did occur may only have been significant in areas which were already marginal for cultivation.

The present study of vegetational change in the period A.D. 400–800 provides the additional opportunity to examine the effect of any possible climatic deterioration or volcanically-induced soil changes, since, if sufficiently severe to affect vegetation and settlement, they would be expected to have led to abandonment of, at least, the more marginal upland sites.

[29] Lamb, 'Climate'; Randsborg, *The first millennium*, chapter 3.
[30] Baillie and Munro, 'Irish tree rings'; Baillie, 'Do Irish bog oaks'; Baillie, 'Dendrochronology raises questions'.
[31] Hammer, Clausen and Dansgaard, 'Greenland ice sheet'.
[32] Hammer, 'Traces of volcanic eruptions'.
[33] Baillie, 'Dendrochronology raises questions'.
[34] Grattan and Gilbertson, 'Acid-loading from Icelandic tephra'; Grattan and Charman, 'Non-climatic factors'.

Approach

The aim of this paper is to provide a catalogue of dated pollen sequences from fifth- to ninth-century Britain, and to illustrate patterns of change in landscape use between this and the preceding Roman period. The study area incorporates regions in which agricultural activity was probably strongly linked with the market economy of the later Roman empire, regions under Roman control but not fully integrated with the Roman economic structure, and regions beyond the fourth-century Roman frontier. If romanisation had affected landscape use significantly, these different areas might be expected to vary in the extent to which vegetational change occurred in the fifth- to ninth centuries.

Pollen sequences used in this study are those which I consider to be sufficiently well-dated, and with an adequate sampling (temporal) resolution, to illustrate any significant vegetational change around the site in the period *ca* A.D. 400–800. This has meant excluding some sequences which have previously been employed in discussions of the period, such as Thorpe Bulmer and Neasham Fen,[35] the latter due to poor temporal resolution (samples approximately three hundred years apart) and the former due both to poor resolution and a possible problem with the radiocarbon dates.

For each sequence a comparison has been made between the vegetation of the Roman period and succeeding centuries. The sites have been classified, with respect to levels of human activity, as falling within one of the following categories:

Continuity: the general character of the vegetation remained the same before and after A.D. 400. This category can be divided into two groups – sites where vegetation had suffered little human impact previously, and continued not to be exploited (*continuity of non-exploitation*), and those where the local landscape was exploited during the Roman period and continued to be used to a similar degree in the centuries immediately following it (*continuity of exploitation*). In a few instances the pollen sequences is sufficiently detailed, and the radiocarbon dates have sufficiently small error terms, to enable identification of an initial period of continuity after A.D. 400, followed by a later change in level of activity.

Reduced activity: changes in the pollen spectra, such as an increase in frequency of tree and shrub pollen, and/or decrease in frequency of pollen of cereal and weeds generally associated with agricultural activity, occurred.

---

[35] Bartley, Chambers and Hart-Jones, 'The vegetational history', discussed by Turner, 'The vegetation'.

31

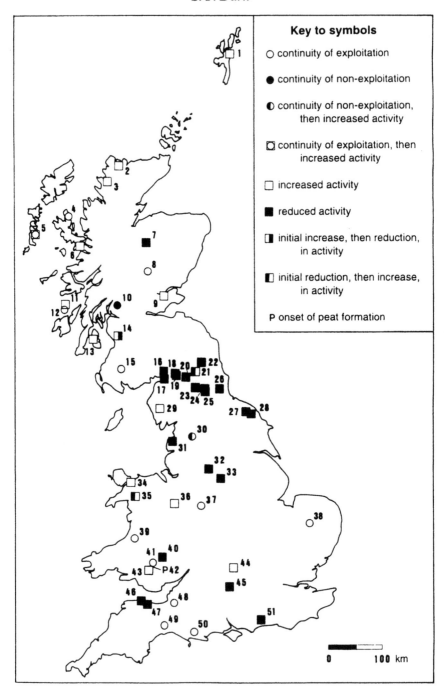

Figure 1. Locations of pollen sequences used in this study and evidence for environmental continuity and change in the period A.D. 400–800.

Increased activity: changes in the pollen spectra, such as a decrease in frequency of tree and shrub pollen, and/or increase in types associated with agricultural activity, occurred.

As well as changes in the intensity of land-use, the occurrence of particular crop types is assessed to detect any changes in the nature of agricultural exploitation. In many instances where long pollen sequences have been produced, the investigator has not specifically commented on the vegetation of the period A.D. 400–800, in which case the interpretation of events is my own.

The distribution of sites used and the category into which they have been placed is shown in figure 1. The appendix contains a list of the sites with a brief description of the general character of the vegetation in the period *ca* A.D. 400–800, and any change from that of the Roman period. Where radiocarbon dates are available for vegetation changes they are given in uncalibrated radiocarbon years B.P. with one standard deviation of the error term, and a calibration of the central date is given using the Stuiver and Pearson calibration curve. It must be remembered, however, that the actual possible spread of the date is often well in excess of one hundred years. Not all of the sites employed have radiocarbon dates falling within this period, in which case the relevant part of the sequence has been identified by interpolation between earlier and later radiocarbon dates, assuming a constant rate of sediment accumulation between the dated levels. The dating of the sequences is thus far from precise, and the overall picture shown by clusters of sites will obviously be more reliable than that from individual localities.

Key to Figure 1

1 Dallican Water	18 Bolton Fell Moss	36 Crose Mere
2 An Druim	19 Walton Moss	37 King's Pool
3 Loch Assynt	20 Fellend Moss	38 Hockham Mere
4 Loch Cleat	21 Fozy Moss	39 Tregaron Bog
5 Loch Lang	22 Steng Moss	40 Waun Fach South
6 Loch Meodal	23 Quick Moss	41 Brecon Beacons
7 Loch Pityoulish	24 Stewart Shield Meadow	42 Coed Taf
8 Carn Dubh	25 Bollihope Bog	43 Cefn Glas
9 Black Loch	26 Hallowell Moss	44 Sidlings Copse
10 Dubh Lochan	27 Wheeldale Gill	45 Snelsmore
11 Loch Cholla	28 Fen Bogs	46 The Chains
12 An t-Aoradh	29 Burnmoor Tarn	47 Hoar Moor
13 Machrie Moor	30 White Moss	48 Meare Heath
14 Bloak Moss	31 Fenton Cottage	49 Aller Farm
15 Round Loch of	32 Featherbed Moss	50 Rimsmoor
Glenhead	33 Leash Fen	51 Amberley Wild Brooks
16 Burnfoothill Moss	34 Llyn Cororion	
17 Glasson Moss	35 Bryn y Castell	

Table 1. *Altitudes of sites shown in Figure 1*

	0–150m	151–300m	301–450m	451–600m	601m+
Continuity					
Aller Farm	+				
An t-Aoradh	+				
Brecon Beacons					+
Carn Dubh			+		
Dubh Lochan	+				
Hockham Mere	+				
King's Pool	+				
Loch Cleat		+			
Loch Lang	+				
Meare Heath	+				
Rimsmoor	+				
Round Loch		+			
Tregaron Bog		+			
White Moss		+			
Increased activity					
An Druim	+				
Black Loch	+				
Bloak Moss	+				
Burnmoor Tarn		+			
Cefn Glas				+	
Crose Mere	+				
Dallican Water	+				
Llyn Cororion	+				
Loch Assynt	+				
Loch Cholla	+				
Loch Meodal	+				
Machrie Moor	+				
Sidlings Copse	+				

	0–150m	151–300m	301–450m	451–600m	601m+
Reduced activity					
Amberley	+				
Bollihope Bog			+		
Bolton Fell Moss	+				
Bryn y Castell			+		
Burnfoothill Moss	+				
Featherbed Moss				+	
Fellend Moss		+			
Fen Bogs		+			
Fenton Cottage	+				
Fozy Moss		+			
Glasson Moss	+				
Hallowell Moss	+				
Hoar Moor			+		
Leash Fen		+			
Loch Pityoulish		+			
Quick Moss				+	
Snelsmore	+				
Steng Moss			+		
Stewart Shield			+		
The Chains				+	
Walton Moss	+				
Waun Fach					+
Wheeldale Gill		+			

Results

The available radiocarbon dated pollen sequences are mainly thinly scattered, with a concentration of sites in northern England. Unfortunately, suitable sites are absent from the potentially interesting areas of the south-western peninsula of England, south-west Wales, and much of central England. Work on Bodmin Moor and Dartmoor[36] has produced detailed pollen sequences with acceptable radiocarbon dates only for the early

[36] Brown, 'Late Devensian'; Simmons *et al.*, 'A further pollen analytical study'.

prehistoric period. The site at Blacka Brook, south-west Dartmoor, investigated as part of the Shaugh Moor Project,[37] produced a pollen diagram which almost certainly spans this period, but in view of the inconsistencies of the dates and poor sample resolution, the diagram has not been included here. There are similar problems with a sequence from Dozmary Pool on Bodmin Moor.[38]

The available pollen sequences indicate that by A.D. 400 much of Britain had been cleared of its former woodland cover, leaving isolated woods in a landscape of open agricultural land, moorland and bog. Extensive tracts of woodland did remain in some areas, as around Dubh Lochan, Central Scotland, which remained wooded throughout the Dark Ages.[39]

Despite the uneven distribution of the sites, a clear pattern emerges. Of the fifty-one pollen sequences used, twenty-four show signs of reduced human activity in the period A.D. 400–800, and half of these are in the extreme north of England, in the area of the Hadrianic frontier. All but two of the seventeen Scottish sites show either continuity or increased activity, although in one case (Bloak Moss, Strathclyde) an initial increase of activity seems to have been followed by woodland regeneration. Similarly, of the seven Welsh sites, only two show evidence for reduced activity in this period, and at one of these (Bryn y Castell) this was probably followed by later clearance prior to A.D. 800. It is, therefore, clear that the fifth to ninth centuries were not a general period of agricultural stagnation in Britain, and in many areas there was an expansion of agricultural activity.

The consistent pattern of land abandonment in the extreme north of England is a striking exception to this pattern, however, and is in direct opposition to previous interpretations of the palynological record from the area (see later). The most obvious explanation for this relaxation of land-use is that it reflects a reliance on markets provided by the Roman army which could not be replaced by local demand once the troops were withdrawn.

With reference to the effects of any possible climatic change in this period, the overall picture of continuity or increased activity suggests that any such change was not significant enough to affect detrimentally environmental exploitation across the whole of Britain. It is notable, however, that most of the sites where there is evidence for reduced human activity are at altitudes greater than 150 metres, while sites where there was continuity or increased activity are mainly at lower altitudes (Table 1). This could be taken to suggest that climatic deterioration caused land abandonment in some areas which were already marginal for agriculture. Similarly, this could lend some support to the suggestion of upland soil deterioration due to acidification by volcanic emissions. Several high-altitude sites show

[37] Smith *et al.*, 'The Shaugh Moor Project'.
[38] Simmons, Rand and Crabtree, 'Dozmary Pool'.
[39] Stewart, Walker, and Dickson, 'Pollen diagrams from Dubh Lochan'.

continuity or increased activity, however, so it seems unlikely that deterioration of climate or soil were significant enough alone to cause abandonment of upland areas.

It is possible that there was an inter-play between 'cultural' and environmental factors, in which environmental change may have tipped the balance to land-abandonment in areas where, for example, changing market forces themselves encouraged relaxation of land-use. Abandonment of upland sites and concentration on lowland areas might, however, be expected to occur, irrespective of external environmental factors, if contraction of agricultural activity occurred, since one would expect a concentration on the, presumably more productive, lowland areas. The role of climatic and/or soil deterioration in leading to abandonment of upland sites in this period, therefore, remains unclear.

Turning to a consideration of some of the sites in greater detail, they will be discussed according to the category in which they have been placed.

Sites showing continuity of non-exploitation

As mentioned previously, few areas of Britain appear to have remained untouched by agriculture in this period, and the remaining woodland consisted of isolated patches in a substantially open landscape. The only pollen sequence suggesting continued major woodland cover throughout is from Dubh Lochan in Central Scotland. The area around White Moss, Lancashire, may also have remained wooded for much of the Dark Ages, although the large error term attached to the radiocarbon date for the onset of clearance (1470 ± 100 B.P.), and discrepancies between the date of this event from two different parts of the site, make this uncertain.[40]

Sites showing continuity of exploitation

In most areas agriculture had become well-established long before the fifth century. For example, at sites as far apart as Meare Heath, Somerset, and Round Loch of Glenhead, Galloway, cereal pollen occurs before, during, and after the Dark Age part of the sequences, suggesting the continued local importance of arable agriculture.[41]

In some instances the general character of the vegetation remained substantially the same, but with a change in agricultural emphasis. At Hockham Mere, Norfolk, there appears to have been a minor reduction in cereal cultivation in favour of pastoralism in this period,[42] while at King's Pool, Stafford, hemp apparently began to be grown, or used, locally at a

40 Bartley, Jones, and Smith, 'Studies in the Flandrian'.
41 Beckett and Hibbert, 'Vegetational change'; Jones, Stevenson and Battarbee, 'Acidification of lakes'.
42 Sims, 'The anthropogenic factor'.

level radiocarbon dated to 1370 ± 70 B.P. (WAT-275) (cal. A.D. 660)[43] The importance of hemp is also evident at Crose Mere, Shropshire, and Leash Fen, Derbyshire (discussed later).[44]

Sites with increased activity
Several of the sites show evidence for increased activity at around A.D. 400, the nature of which varies in different environments. At Sidlings Copse, Oxfordshire, most local woodland on well-drained soils had already been cleared in the Bronze Age. A minor phase of woodland regeneration in the Iron Age resulted in a small amount of woodland which persisted into the Roman period, but all local woodland appears to have been destroyed at the beginning of the Anglo-Saxon period.[45]

The spread of heathland at the expense of woodland occurs at several Scottish sites, such as Loch Assynt, Sutherland, and Loch Meodal, Isle of Skye,[46] suggesting an increase of grazing pressure. Sometimes this was accompanied by cereal cultivation, as at Black Loch, Fife. Here, '*Avena/Triticum* type' (oat or wheat) pollen was first recorded after *ca* 1430 B.P. (cal. A.D. 640), previous records for cereal being of barley (*Hordeum*).[47] At Loch Lang, South Uist,[48] and Burnmoor Tarn, in the Lake District,[49] the expansion of heathland is accompanied by the first records for cereal pollen from any part of the sequence.

At Bloak Moss, Strathclyde,[50] and Tregaron Bog, Dyfed,[51] a decrease in frequency of tree and shrub pollen was accompanied by an increase of grasses, ribwort plantain (*Plantago lanceolata*), and bracken (*Pteridium aquilinum*), suggesting creation of open land for pasture. At Crose Mere, Shropshire,[52] increased woodland clearance was apparently associated with high levels of Cannabaceae (probably hemp) pollen between levels radiocarbon dated to 1610 ± 75 B.P. (Q-1231) and 1055 ± 72 B.P. (Q-1230), that is between *ca* cal. A.D. 430 and cal. A.D. 1000. The frequency of cereal pollen remained constant in this period.

Sites with reduced activity
Abandonment of land is typically indicated by an increase in frequency of tree pollen (often birch (*Betula*) and oak (*Quercus*) and a decline in pollen

[43] Bartley and Morgan, 'The palynological'.
[44] Beales, 'The Late Devensian'; Hicks, 'Pollen-analytical evidence'.
[45] Day, 'Post-glacial vegetational history', 'Woodland origin'.
[46] Birks, 'Quaternary vegetational'; Birks and Williams, 'Late-Quaternary'.
[47] Whittington, Edwards and Cundill, 'Late- and post-glacial'.
[48] Bennett et al., 'Holocene vegetational'.
[49] Pennington, 'Vegetation history'.
[50] Turner, 'A contribution'.
[51] Turner, 'The anthropogenic factor'.
[52] Beales, 'The Late Devensian'.

frequency of grasses, bracken, ribwort plantain, and sorrel (*Rumex*). The behaviour of heather (*Calluna vulgaris*) varies – it declines along with the other herbs at Steng Moss, Northumberland,[53] while at The Chains, Exmoor,[54] it increases with birch and hazel (*Corylus avellana*). At Fen Bogs, North Yorkshire,[55] and Steng Moss and Stewart Shield Meadow, in Durham,[56] cereal pollen also disappears in the Dark Age phase, while at The Chains it declines in frequency.

In some areas there seems to have been a lower intensity of exploitation and shift in agricultural emphasis, rather than complete withdrawal. For example, at Leash Fen, Derbyshire, an increase in frequency of oak and decline of cereals suggests possible abandonment of agricultural land, but the presence of hemp pollen suggests that this plant may have been grown in some fields formerly used for cereals.[57]

At Fozy Moss, Northumberland, initial woodland regeneration at *ca* cal. A.D. 400 is followed by renewed clearance and cereal cultivation from *ca* cal. A.D. 600.[58] Unfortunately, however, many sites lack a sufficient sampling resolution and narrowness of radiocarbon error terms to enable such short initial periods of regeneration to be detected.

Conclusion

One of the most notable patterns to emerge from these data is the evidence for a major reduction of agricultural activity and widespread woodland regeneration in the north of England, in the vicinity of the Hadrianic frontier. All sites in this area show evidence for abandonment of agricultural land and woodland regeneration. As mentioned previously, this pattern may reflect collapse of agricultural systems which had previously supplied the Roman forces based on, and around, Hadrian's Wall. This contrasts strongly with previous arguments for an initial period of continuity in this area, which have been based on a fairly small number of pollen diagrams, often with poor sample resolution and dating control.[59] Obviously, this makes the often-stated view, recently reiterated by Casey[60] that fort-communities along the Wall and in the rest of northern England 'stayed put' after the end of Roman rule, unlikely.

In contrast, most sites in the rest of England and in Wales show continued

[53] Davies and Turner, 'Pollen diagrams'.
[54] Merryfield and Moore, 'Prehistoric human'.
[55] Atherden, 'Late Quaternary'.
[56] Roberts, Turner and Ward, 'Recent forest history'.
[57] Hicks, 'Pollen-analytical evidence'.
[58] Dumayne and Barber, 'The impact of the Romans'.
[59] For example, Higham, *The Northern Counties*.
[60] Casey, 'The end of garrisons'.

landscape use or even intensified activity in the immediate post-Roman period. In areas outside the distribution of Roman-period villas as, for example, in north-west Wales, this may reflect the lack of integration into the Roman agricultural economy, so that Imperial withdrawal had little negative impact. The general picture of increased activity, or continuity of exploitation, in Scotland again presumably reflects the lack of integration of the area into the Roman economy. Evidence for continuity in more 'romanised' regions, such as south-east Wales and Dorset, suggests that economic change, and the collapse of the villa-economy, following Roman withdrawal did not generally result in widespread landscape discontinuity in these areas either. Unfortunately, too few sequences are available from areas where the villa-economy was well-developed to enable more than tentative conclusions to be drawn, although the recently analysed pollen sequence from Sidlings Copse, Oxfordshire, indicates post-Roman agricultural expansion in such an area.[61]

In conclusion, then, it would seem that much of Britain experienced little change in landscape-use in the period A.D. 400–800, with similar, or increased, levels of exploitation to those of the Roman period. Major discontinuity in this period is only apparent in the extreme north of England, where the economy may have been highly dependent on the market provided by Roman forces on Hadrian's Wall.

Acknowledgements

I thank Drs K. R. Dark and K. D. Bennett for their comments on the manuscript.

Appendix

The appendix gives details of the sites shown in Figure 1 (p. 32). The layout of the appendix is as follows.

Site name and county
Author(s) and year of publication
Ordnance Survey grid reference, altitude in metres above sea level, site type
(a) General character of vegetation in the period A.D. 400–800.
(b) Changes, if any, in pollen spectra between the Roman period and the

---

[61] Day, 'Post-glacial vegetational history', 'Woodland origin'.

ninth century. Radiocarbon dates, where available, are given with one standard deviation of the error term, and the laboratory code number. A calibration of the central date is given using the Stuiver and Pearson calibration curve. Where radiocarbon dates are not available for events in this period, interpolated dates (interp.) are given.
Category as shown in Fig. 1

Aller Farm, Stockland, Devon
Hatton and Caseldine 1992
ST 245044, 120m, valley peat
(a) Mosaic of woodland, grassland and probably arable.
Continuity of exploitation

Amberley Wild Brooks, Sussex
Waton 1982
TQ 037145, 60m, bog
(a) Substantial woodland with areas of grassland, following major regeneration in the late Roman or early Anglo-Saxon period.
(b) Increase of hazel and decline of grasses.
Reduced activity

An Druim, Eriboll, Sutherland
Birks 1980
NC 434567, 25m, lake
(a) Extensive areas of woodland with some grassland and heath.
(b) Decrease of birch (*Betula*) and alder (*Alnus glutinosa*), increase of grasses and ribwort plantain (*Plantago lanceolata*).
Increased activity

An t-Aoradh, Oronsay
Andrews, Beck, Gilbertson and Switsur 1987
NR 358893, 20m, bog
(a) Open environment with very little woodland.
Continuity of exploitation

Black Loch, Fife
Whittington, Edwards and Cundill 1991
NO 261149, 90m, lake
(a) Open landscape with little woodland.
(b) Decline of hazel (*Corylus avellana*), increase of heather (*Calluna vulgaris*), grasses, cereals and ribwort plantain. 'Avena/Triticum type' (oat/wheat) appears after *ca* 1430 B.P. (interp.) = *ca* cal. A.D. 640 (previously only 'Hordeum type' – probably barley).
Increased activity

Bloak Moss, Strathclyde
Turner 1965
NS 361460,72m, bog
(a) Open landscape with some woodland.
(b) Decrease of tree and shrub pollen, increase of grasses, ribwort plantain and bracken (*Pteridium aquilinum*) at *ca* 1500 B.P. (interp.) = cal. A.D. 600. Then decline of herbs and increase of trees and shrubs at 1370 ± 105 B.P. (Q-724) = cal. A.D. 660.
Increased activity then woodland regeneration

Bollihope Bog, Durham
Roberts, Turner and Ward 1973
NY 980358, 360m, bog
(a) Fairly open landscape with some woodland, the extent of which exceeds that in the Roman phase.
(b) Decrease of heather and herbs, increase of hazel.
Reduced activity

Bolton Fell Moss, Cumbria
Barber 1981
NY 488692, l07m, bog
(a) Fairly open landscape with some woodland, the extent of which increases throughout the fourth-to-eighth centuries.
(b) Decrease of grasses, ribwort plantain, and bracken, increase of birch and ash (*Fraxinus excelsior*). Sporadic cereal pollen prior to levels dated to the ninth century A.D., then small cereal peak from 1185 ± 60 B.P. (Hv-3083) = cal. A.D. 880.
Reduced activity

Brecon Beacons, Powys
Chambers 1982
SO 043196, 715m, blanket bog
(a) Predominantly open moorland landscape, probably with some arable (cereal present).
Continuity of exploitation

Bryn y Castell, Gwynedd
Mighall and Chambers 1989, 1995
SH 730432, 360m, valley bog (two sequences with relevant dates)
(a) Open landscape with some woodland.
(b) Site BYC: Decrease of birch and alder, increase of ribwort plantain, cereal, heather and charcoal at 1610 ± 70 B.P. (HAR-6104) = cal. A.D. 430. Site 2 (greater sampling resolution): increase of oak, alder and heather at 1655 ± 50 B.P. (GrN-17582) = cal. A.D. 410; increase then decline of hazel,

decline then increase of grasses. Cereal type pollen disappears initially then returns.
Reduction then increase of activity

Burnfoothill Moss, Dumfries and Galloway
Tipping 1995
NY 263737, 100m, raised bog
(a) Mosaic of woodland, grassland and heath; woodland increasing throughout.
(b) Increase of alder, birch, oak and hazel. Decline of grasses and ribwort plantain.
Reduced activity

Burnmoor Tarn, Cumbria
Pennington 1970
NY 183044, 259m, lake
(a) Mosaic of woodland, grassland and raised bog, with spread of heathland in Dark Age phase.
(b) Increase of heather at 1560 ± 30 B.P. = cal. A.D. 460–530 (on plateau of calibration curve).
Increased activity

Carn Dubh, Perthshire
Tipping 1995
NN 985607, 350m, valley peat
a) Mosaic of woodland, grassland and heath.
Continuity of exploitation

Cefn Glas, Glamorganshire
Smith and Green, 1995
SN 923025, 490m, valley bog
(a) Predominantly open landscape with extensive areas of blanket bog.
(b) Decline of birch and hazel, increase of grasses at 1700 ± 70 B.P. (CAR-415) = cal. A.D. 380.
Increased activity

Coed Taf, Powys
Chambers 1983
SN 988108, 420m, blanket bog
Peat initiation in a non-forested environment dated to 1435 ± 55 B.P. (CAR-77) = cal. A.D. 640 at site A. Dates of 1310 ± 70 B.P. (CAR-48F) and 1630 ± 60 B.P. (CAR-48C) were produced from different fractions of the same sample to date peat initiation at site B.

Crose Mere, Shropshire
Beales 1980
SJ 430305, 90m, lake
(a) Open environment with some woodland. Cereal present before, during and after the Dark Age phase.
(b) Decrease of alder and hazel, increase of grasses at 1610 ± 75 B.P. (Q-1231) = cal. A.D. 420. High 'Cannabaceae', probably hemp, between this level and 1055 ± 72 B.P. (Q-1230) = cal. A.D. 1000.
Increased activity

Dallican Water, Shetland
Bennett, Boreham, Sharp and Switsur 1992
HU 498674, 56m, lake
(a) Generally treeless environment with heath and blanket bog.
(b) Increased heather at 1565 ± 65 B.P. = cal. A.D. 530 and slightly more frequent records for '*Hordeum* type' pollen (probably barley).
Increased activity

Dubh Lochan, near Loch Lomond, Central Scotland
Stewart, Walker and Dickson 1984
NS 377963, 30m, lake
(a) Wooded with some open areas.
Continuity of non-exploitation (no substantial disforestation until the last thousand years, but authors suggest slightly increased activity at *ca* 1600 B.P. (interp.) = cal. A.D. 430).

Featherbed Moss, Derbyshire
Tallis and Switsur 1973
SK 091928, 500m, blanket bog
(a) Mosaic of woodland, grassland and heath, extent of woodland exceeds that in the Roman period.
(b) Decrease of grasses and bracken, increase of birch and oak, disappearance of cereal, just below level dated to 1400 ± 50 B.P. (Q-852) = cal. A.D. 650.
Reduced activity

Fellend Moss, Northumberland
Davies and Turner 1979
NY 679658, 200m, bog (100m from vallum of Hadrian's Wall)
(a) Fairly open environment with substantial woodland, extent of which is increasing.
(b) Decrease of grasses, ribwort plantain, and bracken, increase of tree pollen at *ca* 1650 B.P. (interp.) = cal. A.D. 400.
Reduced activity (authors suggest continuity until level radiocarbon dated

to 1330 ± 40 B.P. (SRR-875) = cal. A.D. 670, but there is some woodland regeneration before this)

Fen Bogs, North Yorkshire
Atherden 1976
SE853977, 164m, valley bog
(a) Open environment with some woodland.
(b) Decrease of grasses, ribwort plantain and bracken, cessation of cereal, increase of birch, oak, alder, hazel and heather at 1530 ± 130 B.P. (T-1086) = cal. A.D. 550.
Reduced activity

Fenton Cottage, Over Wyre, Lancashire
Huckerby, Wells and Middleton 1992
SD 404449, 6m, raised bog
(a) Mosaic of woodland, grassland, heath and arable land.
(b) Decrease of grasses and ribwort plantain, increase of heather, birch, alder, oak and ash. Cereal continues to occur sporadically.
Reduced activity

Fozy Moss, Northumberland
Dumayne and Barber 1994
NY 830714, 230m, valley bog
(a) Predominantly open landscape of grassland and heath, extent of woodland first increases then declines.
(b) Decrease of grasses, increase of hazel, oak and heather at cal. A.D. 400 (interp.), but at cal. A.D. 600 trend is reversed and rye (*Secale cereale*) and '*Avena/Triticum* type' (oat/wheat) pollen appear.
Reduced then increased activity

Glasson Moss, Northumberland
Dumayne and Barber 1994
NY 238603, 10m, raised bog
(a) Mosaic of woodland, grassland and heath; woodland increasing gradually throughout.
(b) Increase of hazel and heather, decline of grasses. '*Avena-Triticum* type' (oat/wheat) and '*Cannabis* type', probably hemp, pollen from *ca* cal. A.D. 600 (interp.).
Reduced activity   but with later increase of arable

Hallowell Moss, Durham
Donaldson and Turner 1977
NZ 251439, 90m, raised bog
(a) Landscape almost totally cleared by the end of the Roman period, but

regeneration resulted in some woodland in a still predominantly open landscape. The precise date of the start of regeneration is uncertain due to the inversion of dates of 1522 ± 65 B.P. (SRR-412) and 1355 ± 50 B.P. (SRR-413), which are separated by just 2cm of peat.
(b) Decrease of grasses, ribwort plantain, and bracken, increase of tree and shrub pollen, and disappearance of cereal pollen.
Reduced activity

Hoar Moor, Exmoor, Somerset
Francis and Slater 1990
SS 862407, 410m, blanket bog
(a) Open landscape with heath and some woodland
(b) Decrease of grasses and cessation of cereal records, with increase of trees, shrubs, and heather.
Reduced activity

Hockham Mere, Norfolk
Sims 1978
TL 933937, 33m, former lake
(a) Mixed landscape of woodland, heath and agricultural land. Cereals, including rye, cultivated, as well as hemp.
(b) Possible minor shift from cereal cultivation to pastoralism.
Continuity of exploitation

King's Pool, Staffordshire
Bartley and Morgan 1990
SJ 926234, 76m, bog
(a) Open landscape with little woodland.
(b) Peak of cereal and small increase of hemp pollen at a level dated to 1370 ± 70 B.P. (WAT-275) = cal. A.D. 660.
Continuity of exploitation

Leash Fen, Derbyshire
Hicks 1971
SK 296741, 290m, bog
(a) Open landscape with a little woodland.
(b) Decrease of grasses, cereal and sorrel, and increase of oak, birch, heather and ribwort plantain. '*Cannabis/Humulus*', probably hemp, constant, after first being recorded in the late Roman or early Dark Age phase.
Reduced activity   with change in type of agriculture

Llyn Cororion, Gwynedd
Watkins 1990
SH597688, 83m, lake

(a) Substantial areas of local woodland. Sporadic cereal pollen before and during Dark Age phase.

(b) Decline in frequency of tree and shrub pollen and increase in frequency of grasses continues from Roman period.

Increased activity

By Loch Assynt, Sutherland

Birks 1980

NC 215253, 110m, peaty hollow on north side of Loch Assynt

(a) Predominantly open environment, but with substantial areas of woodland. Extent of heathland increasing.

(b) Birch, alder and willow (*Salix*) decline, hazel, heather and sedges increase.

Increased activity

Loch Cholla, Colonsay

Andrews, Beck, Gilbertson and Switsur 1987

NR 382917, 30m, lake

(a) Landscape virtually treeless, with grassland, pasture and heath. (Some woodland had been present in the Roman period.)

(b) Decrease of birch and willow and increase of grasses at level dated to 1650 ± 50 B.P. (Q-3160) = cal. A.D. 410.

Increased activity

Loch Cleat, Isle of Skye

Birks and Williams 1983

NG 447673, 160m, lake

(a) Landscape mainly treeless with patches of scrub.

(b) Decrease of grasses and heather, with increase of birch, alder ribwort plantain and bracken.

?Continuity of exploitation

Loch Lang, South Uist

Bennett, Fossitt, Sharp and Switsur 1990

NF 806295, 80m, lake

(a) Open landscape with some woodland, extent of heathland increasing.

(b) Decrease of birch and increase of heather, with first record for 'Cereal type' pollen at *ca* 1500 B.P. (interp.) = cal. A.D. 600.

Initial continuity of exploitation then increased activity

Loch Meodal, Isle of Skye

Birks and Williams 1983

NG 656112, 120m, lake

(a) Open landscape of grassland, heath, and bog with some woodland.

(b) Spread of heather.
Increased activity

Loch Pityoulish, Highland Scotland
O'Sullivan 1976
NH 920135, 210m, lake
(a) Landscape substantially wooded, extent of open areas decreasing.
(b) Decrease of grasses and spread of woodland.
Reduced activity

Machrie Moor, Arran
Robinson and Dickson 1988
NR 905315, 75m, bog
(a) Predominantly open environment with blanket bog, some 'cereal type' pollen recorded.
(b) Birch, alder and hazel declining, heather and grasses increasing between levels dated 1615 ± 55 B.P. (GU-1349) = cal. A.D. 430 and 1120 ± 60 B.P. (GU-1348) = cal. A.D. 900–960.
Increased activity

Meare Heath, Somerset
Beckett and Hibbert 1979
ST 444406, 15m, bog
(a) Fairly open but with substantial wooded areas. Cereal present before, during, and after the Dark Age phase.
Continuity of exploitation

Quick Moss, Northumberland
Rowell and Turner 1985
NY878467, 510m, blanket bog
(a) Blanket bog with some woodland, grassland and heath. Single record for cereal.
(b) Decrease of ribwort plantain, grasses and heather, increase of hazel.
Reduced activity

Rimsmoor, Dorset
Waton 1982
SY 814922, 45m, bog
(a) Open landscape with some woodland.
(b) Complex changes in tree pollen curves, increase of herbs.
Continuity of exploitation

Round Loch of Glenhead, Dumfries and Galloway
Jones, Stevenson and Battarbee 1989

NX 450804, 300m, lake
(a) Predominantly open landscape with heathland, blanket bog and some woodland.
Cereal pollen occurs before, during and after the Dark Age phase.
Continuity of exploitation

Sidlings Copse, Oxfordshire
Day 1991, 1993
SP 556096, 100m, valley mire
(a) Clearance of all woodland which had been present in the Roman period resulted in an open landscape with arable and pastoral agriculture.
(b) Decline of hazel and oak, increase of grasses and ribwort plantain.
Increased activity

Snelsmore, Berkshire
Waton 1982
SU 463704, 70m, valley mire
(a) Substantial areas of woodland with some grassland, and arable with rye cultivation.
(b) Increase of birch and alder, decrease of oak and grasses.
Reduced activity

Steng Moss, Northumberland
Davies and Turner 1979
NY 965913, 305m, bog
(a) Open environment with increasing amount of woodland.
(b) Decrease of grasses, ribwort plantain, heather and bracken, cessation of cereal cultivation, and increase of trees and shrubs, just below level dated to 1490 ± 60 B.P. (Q-519) = cal. A.D. 600.
Reduced activity   (authors suggest initial continuity)

Stewart Shield Meadow, Durham
Roberts, Turner and Ward 1973
NY 980428, 380m, bog
(a) Landscape open with scattered woodland.
(b) Decrease of ribwort plantain and heather, increase of willow and oak at *ca* 1650 B.P. (interp.) = cal. A.D. 410.
Reduced activity   (Turner 1979, 1981 suggests reversion to woodland at level dated to 840 ± 100 B.P. (GaK-3/032) = cal. A.D. 1220, but regeneration began before this)

The Chains, Exmoor, Somerset
Merryfield and Moore 1974; Moore, Merryfield and Price 1984
SS 735425, 472m, blanket bog

(a) Open environment with increasing woodland cover.
(b) Decrease of grasses, ribwort plantain, bracken and cereal, increase of birch, hazel and heather just below level dated to 1500 ± 60 B.P. (UB-816) = cal. A.D. 600.
Reduced activity

Tregaron Bog, Dyfed
Turner 1964
SN 685621, 168m, bog
(a) Open landscape with some woodland.
(b) Grasses and ribwort plantain increasing at level dated to 1477 ± 90 B.P. (Q-391) = cal. A.D. 600, continuing a trend initiated in the late Iron Age or Roman period.
Continuity of exploitation

Walton Moss, Cumbria
Dumayne and Barber 1994
NY 504667, 100m, raised bog
(a) Mosaic of woodland, grassland, heath and arable land with cereal ('*Avena/Triticum* type') and perhaps hemp ('*Cannabis* type') cultivation, the latter occurring for the first time.
(b) Increase of alder and hazel, decline of grasses.
Reduced activity

Waun Fach South, Black Mountains, Powys
Moore, Merryfield and Price 1984; Price and Moore 1984
SO 218300, 810m, blanket bog
(a) Uncertain as only partial pollen diagrams available.
(b) Decline of ribwort plantain at level dated to 1550 ± 75 B.P. = *ca* cal. A.D. 540.
Reduced activity

Wheeldale Gill, North Yorkshire
Simmons and Cundill 1974
SE 760997, 200m, blanket bog
(a) Major clearance in the Roman period had created an open environment in which the spread of heathland and some woodland regeneration occurred during the Dark Age phase.
(b) Decrease of ribwort plantain and sorrel, increase of heather and tree and shrub pollen at level dated to 1570 ± 90 B.P. (GaK-3879) = cal. A.D. 530.
Reduced activity

White Moss, North Yorkshire
Bartley, Jones and Smith 1990

SD 792546, 190m, bog
(a) Substantially wooded landscape, with decrease of trees and shrubs, and increase of ribwort plantain, grasses and sorrel, immediately after level dated to 1470 ± 100 B.P. (Birm-666) = cal. A.D. 610 (later date for this event from smaller western part of the site).
?Continuity of non-exploitation then increased activity

III

POTTERY AND LOCAL PRODUCTION AT THE END OF ROMAN BRITAIN

K. R. Dark

When mass-production ceased in the early fifth century, the population did not desert the fields in despair. There is no evidence that the collapse of the proto-industrial component of the Roman economy caused agricultural disruption, and in the majority of Britain there is no reason to suppose that barbarian incursions had driven the population abroad or into hiding by the middle of the century.[1] When migration to Brittany, and probably Spain, did occur – in the fifth century and later – this may have involved migrants from areas undergoing settlement by barbarian peoples, in eastern England, rather than sub-Romans in the west, or, even less plausibly, north.[2]

The settlement-evidence for the sub-Roman period is scarce, but does encompass settlements continuing from the Roman to sub-Roman centuries without abandonment. The close correlation between later medieval settlements and low-status Romano-British settlements on Anglesey, in Somerset and Dorset and in Cornwall, is suggestive of local continuity in the rural settlement in these regions.[3]

The evidence that there was a settlement-shift within this period is not, alone, enough to demonstrate agricultural discontinuity, as low-status farmsteads were constantly shifting location to adjacent sites throughout the first millennium.[4] This process is especially noticeable in the seventh century, and need not indicate population or economic change, merely a relocation of domestic occupation.

The circumstances under which sub-Roman lower-status farmers lived are little known. At Drim, Pant y Saer, and in Cornwall, they could, evidently, obtain some luxuries, whether penannular brooches or imported bowls.[5] There are indications of the occupation of rectilinear and curvilinear

1 Böhme, 'Das ende der Romerherrschaft'; Dark, *Civitas*, p. 219.
2 D. N. Dumville, 'The Insular Churches in the Age of the Saints', unpublished O'Donnell Lecture, 1983.
3 Leech, 'The Roman Interlude'; Preston-Jones and Rose, 'Medieval Cornwall'; Royal Commission on Ancient and Historical Monuments in Wales, *Inventories Anglesey*.
4 Randsborg, *The First Millennium*, pp. 40–81.
5 Dark, *Discovery*, pp. 73, 76–80, 86–7, 91 and 98; Mytum, 'Across the Irish Sea', p. 22.

houses, the former perhaps indicating sub-Roman 'romanisation' on sites where these are not found prior to the sixth century. There is slight evidence suggesting a reduction in the number of buildings to each farm, but overall, the known sub-Roman farm sites resemble (and are often on the same sites as) those of the Late Roman period. Most lower-status sites of the fifth- to seventh centuries in west and north Britain may have seen these changes, but the present sample is very small – the *cantrefi* of Wales imply thousands of contemporary *trefi*, but there are only a few, possibly lower-status, excavated settlements known from the whole of Wales.[6]

Our conclusions about lower-status farming settlements, therefore, can only be tenuous. But the distributional evidence mentioned above seems to indicate that, unless there is evidence to refute it, we may assume a general pattern of continuity in those parts of Britain unsettled by the Anglo-Saxons in the seventh century and beyond.

The evidence provided by texts and archaeology,[7] that sub-Roman society in Britain included a substantial class not involved in agricultural production, the secular élite (although not, perhaps, the clergy), suggests that a large agricultural surplus must have been produced to provide their food. If we envisage regular feasting and gifts of food, then this surplus would have had to have been even greater.

The British penitentials, probably datable to the sub-Roman period, indicate plentiful agricultural produce.[8] Even a penitent eats quite well, even by Late Roman standards, with dairy products as well as vegetables and eggs included in the penitential diet.[9] Presumably, if not undergoing penance, one ate better fare.

This impression is in accordance with the implications of an efficient agricultural economy, producing a large surplus, inferred from the existence of the secular élite. The construction of major 'public works' such as South Cadbury hill-fort's sub-Roman banks, and the Wansdyke (if this dates to this period) involved the removal of large numbers of workers from production for a long period of time, probably months.[10] This must, for similar reasons as those considered above, imply a substantial surplus (aside from its implications about royal control and resources).

From these strands of evidence I infer that the sub-Roman British economy was producing a large agricultural surplus, at least in the West Country, and probably elsewhere. If lower-status settlement continuity is also evidenced, then these settlements were presumably still producing agricultural wealth as they had been doing in the fourth century.

---

6   *Ibid.*, pp. 73, 75–6 and 78–9.
7   Dark, *Discovery*, pp. 7–14.
8   Bieler, *The Irish Penitentials*, pp. 61–73.
9   *Ibid.*, p. 61.
10   Dark, *Civitas*, p. 207.

That these sites are so hard for archaeologists to identify may be because they are very similar to Late Roman lower-status rural settlements, not because they were impoverished or lacking in a wide range of artefacts. If artefacts of this period sufficiently resembled those of the fourth century – and evidence suggesting that they did will be presented later in this paper – then such sites would not be recognisable in limited excavation and field survey no matter how numerous were finds of the fifth to seventh centuries. Textual evidence suggests that sub-Roman British settlements were not 'impoverished' either in terms of artefacts or the range of agricultural products available to their inhabitants, even if few traces of these artefacts and products survive today: Table 1 gives a list of some of those artefacts and agricultural products attested in textual and archaeological sources from fifth- to seventh-century western Britain. Obviously, the pastoral landscape in parts of modern Wales and northern England would not facilitate the recovery of distinctive artefacts by field-walking, even if these existed at all.

The writings of Gildas and Patrick also enable us to ascertain a few other inferences or observations about the sub-Roman economy. Gildas's reference in his *De Excidio* to transhumance is now well-known among specialists on Late- and sub-Roman Britain,[11] and Patrick lived in a *uillula* (a 'little villa' or 'little farm'), in Britain.[12] This shows that at least one element of the agricultural economy involved the movement of animals between summer and winter pastures, and the penitentials and Gildas's *De Excidio* show that crops, including wheat and vegetables, were also grown.[13] The sub-Roman economy was, therefore, apparently 'mixed', including both cultivation and pastoralism. This is the implication also gained from the sparse archaeological evidence.[14]

To return to Patrick's *uillula*. There seems to be conclusive evidence that in Britain, unlike Gaul, the 'villa'-economy, as observed by modern archaeologists, was disused by the mid-fifth century, probably by the early fifth century.[15] Although there seem to have been low-status farms at some villa-sites in the fifth century, no villa has produced evidence of high-status residence after that time.[16] Recent studies of the chronology of St Patrick's life favour a date in the later fifth century for his childhood.[17] If St Patrick lived in a *villula* as a child, he, therefore, did not live in what an

---

11 Winterbottom, *Gildas*, Gildas, *De Excidio*, 1.3; Wild, 'Wool Production' p. 119.
12 Hood, *St Patrick'*, Patrick, *Confessio*, 1.
13 Bieler, *The Irish Penitentials*, p. 13; Gildas, *De Excidio*, 1.3.
14 Alcock, *Economy*, pp. 67–82.
15 Alcock, *Economy*; Dark, *Civitas*, pp. 59 and 235; and *Discovery*, pp. 95 and 98; Dark, 'St Patrick's *uillula*'.
16 Cleary, *The Ending*, pp. 134 and 173–74; Dark, *High Status Sites*, pp. 200–201.
17 For a recent analysis supporting a later fifth-century *floruit* for St Patrick: Dumville *et al.*, *Saint Patrick*; and see references in note 15.

archaeologist today would call a 'villa'. This may, therefore, cast some light on the terminology of rural settlement in Late and sub-Roman Britain. A *uillula* was presumably not a hill-fort, sand-dune site or, probably, palisaded settlement.[18] In a recent paper, I have suggested that it may have been what modern archaeologists frequently describe as 'squatter occupation' inside a villa building.[19] Such a building would superficially resemble a villa from outside, and similarly humble structures were occupied by rural elites elsewhere in the Late Antique world.[20] The implications of this observation for the social archaeology of such settlements are far reaching, although there is no convincing evidence to support the view that even this type of villa occupation survived after the fifth century.

Another aspect of agricultural life in sub-Roman Britain, also illuminated by Gildas and Patrick, is the uncertainty resulting from raiding and famine. Gildas considered that there had been periods of both plenty and famine in the fifth century, and presents a sixth-century perspective on the insecurity of life on the land in the previous century.[21] This impression is also conveyed by Patrick, who was carried off by raiders but whose kin remained in Britain for him to return to later in life.[22] This implies some form of continuity of settlement, despite raids.

These textual sources are not especially suited for the establishment of a picture of the agricultural economy of Sub-Roman Britain, but they may be combined with the archaeological evidence to build the following interpretation. Every element of this interpretation can be supported by contemporary sources, but we must remember that our information is both partial and derived from different areas.

The sub-Roman agricultural economy consisted of mixed farming with a large surplus being regularly produced. Although occasionally disrupted by raiding, and probably climatic variation,[23] the continuity of production was maintained. The Late Roman settlement pattern survived into the sub-Roman period, although shifts of the exact location of settlements within the immediate locality occurred, but the villa-economy did not survive in its Late Roman form after the early fifth century. There is no direct western British evidence of widespread rural depopulation, nor of increased rural poverty after A.D. 400,[24] and there may have been periods of especial plenty as well as famine.

A further aspect can be added to this interpretation, if we adduce the

---

18 For such site-types see Dark, *Discovery*.
19 Dark, 'St Patrick's *uillula*', pp. 20–1.
20 Patrick, *Epistola*, 10.
21 Gildas, *De Excidio*, 1.14–1.21.
22 Patrick, *Confessio*, 23.
23 Randsborg, *The First Millennium*, pp. 23–29.
24 Arguable in contrast to that from other areas of Europe and the Mediterranean: Hodges and Whitehouse, *Mohammed*, especially pp. 33–48.

evidence of taxation. As Goffart and Wickham have pointed out, taxation played an important role in the transition from the Roman to medieval economies,[25] even if one would not want to agree with the interpretation of this transition by these scholars. Late Roman taxation was in two forms – 'in kind' and in coin. Taxation in (old) coin may have been maintained into the fifth or later centuries in the British west and north of Britain, but it is taxation in kind which is of most concern, as it closely relates to agricultural production.[26]

The Late Roman taxation system was certainly very harsh.[27] Even wealthy landowners, let alone the poor, feared taxation. It has been observed by Evans,[28] that the most noticeable aspect of the 'End of Roman Britain' in the early fifth century, to the lower-status farmers of remote parts of Britain, was probably the cessation of the weight of Late Roman taxation. Although sub-Roman rulers may have exacted regular taxes, this sudden reduction in taxation has been plausibly suggested as the cause of a fifth-century 'boom' in the agricultural economy.[29] Production was, it is argued, stimulated by the knowledge that less would be taken from the producer.

This is of relevance to sub-Roman agriculture because it implies a possible increased level of production after the Roman period, and, therefore, makes a reduction in production less plausible. It might also account for the indications of wealth found on lower-status sub-Roman settlements, such as Pant y Saer and Trethurgy.

The British kings, however, almost certainly taxed the agricultural population. Gildas may refer to this in his use of the term *annona*, the technical term for the tax 'in kind' of the Late Roman economy.[30] This was necessitated by the maintenance of the large élite already mentioned, and by their redistribution of agricultural surplus.

This element, therefore, combines with the model so far proposed to form an interpretation of the sub-Roman agricultural economy, which proposes not merely continuity, but agricultural wealth. Alongside this agricultural economy must be set the remainder of the productive industries, following the collapse of mass-production.

---

[25] Wickham, 'The other transition'; Goffart, *Barbarians and Romans*.
[26] Dark, *Civitas*, pp. 200–7.
[27] Goffart, *Caput and Colonate*.
[28] Evans, 'From Roman Britain'.
[29] Salway, *Roman Britain*, p. 457.
[30] Gildas, *De Excidio*, 1.25.

The Localisation of Production

Pottery production

The end of the Roman pottery 'industry' remains enigmatic in that well-dated assemblages are rare and the contextual evidence ambiguous.[31] On the one hand there seems a strong case for discontinuity, with the collapse of the mass-market in the early fifth century.[32] On the other hand there are quite a few instances, as at Heybridge in Essex or Shakenoak in Oxfordshire, of Romano-British pottery occurring in Anglo-Saxon contexts, found stratified alongside fifth-, and even sixth-, century Anglo-Saxon pottery, where this would not normally be considered 'residual'.[33] In my other contribution to this volume, I attempted to show that the stylistic conservatism of Late Romano-British pottery is explicable in terms of mass-production rather than decline, and it is possible that superficially Romano-British pottery might be, at least, fifth century in date, if typological conservatism outlasted mass-production.

The need is, however, for positive evidence of continuity and especially for the identification of well-dated fifth-century products. Given the dearth of well-dated fifth-century contexts, and the lack of typological change in the late fourth century, we might doubt that well-dated fifth-century pottery assemblages will be found.[34] It, therefore, comes as a surprise to find that a few well-dated instances implying the fifth- or sixth-century production of Roman pottery in Britain have already been discovered. It is puzzling to me why more attention has not focused upon my first piece of evidence, at least as a point for discussion.

The first example is the most compelling and the least well known. In the flue ashes of a Roman pottery kiln at Westwick Gardens, Lincoln, a complete stamped Anglo-Saxon pot was found.[35] The findspot was confirmed by excavation directed by no less an authority on Roman Britain, and its pottery, than Graham Webster. The identification of the pot was confirmed by J. N. L. Myres and is almost beyond dispute.[36] As Webster wrote at the time, 'the Saxon urn had been recovered from the flue. It seems a strange coincidence that this vessel should be placed in this position. The area round about was thoroughly trenched without finding a trace of either

[31] Fulford, 'Pottery Production'.
[32] *Ibid.*
[33] Drury and Wickenden, 'An Early Saxon Settlement'; Brodribb, Hands, and Walker, *Excavations at Shakenoak*.
[34] Fulford, 'Pottery Production', pp. 121–22.
[35] Webster, 'A Romano-British Pottery Kiln'.
[36] Myres, 'The Anglo-Saxon Pottery', pp. 87–88.

another urn or kiln'.[37] Moreover, the pot was found prior to the 'continuity debate' of the 1960s and 1970s and even if this were, by some intricate argument, felt credible then, is unlikely to be a 'plant' on the site. The pot, therefore, gives a *terminus post quem* for the ash deposit, and, therefore, for the last firing of the kiln.

This seems to be a clearcut instance of a Romano-British kiln, producing what Webster observed were characteristically fourth-century local products, used into the sixth century. There is no evidence of adaptation for domestic or other use from this well-excavated kiln, nor was there an adjacent Anglo-Saxon cemetery to explain the pot. However, it got into the flue, and one cannot rule out the possibility that it was fired in the kiln. It dates the final firing of that kiln to *terminus post quem* its own, at least sixth-century, date. It is, therefore, interesting that Myres has identified two other pots from Lincoln as, in one case, having a Roman form in an Anglo-Saxon fabric, and in another, an Anglo-Saxon form in a Roman fabric.[38] The Westwick Gardens kiln may be evidence of the sort of context in which such vessels might be produced.

Second, there are more apparent examples of Anglo-Saxon and Romano-British potters' interaction – for example, the mortarium (in an Anglo-Saxon fabric) found at Orton Hall villa and an Anglo-Saxon pottery stamp on an Oxfordshire Ware vessel found in the Barrow Hill cemetery, Oxfordshire.[39] The contemporary production of Anglo-Saxon and Romano-British pottery would readily explain such pots.

So, it seems that we must take a more open-minded view of those assemblages which seem to show Romano-British and Anglo-Saxon pottery in use together. The implications is that local 'Romano-British' kilns were in production – if only limited, occasional, production – and their products were distributed locally, in the fifth and sixth centuries.

The reason that there are not more dated fifth-century pottery assemblages from Britain is simply that there are not many well-dated fifth-century contexts. If we cannot date them by coins, or pottery, or other artefacts – given the relative imprecision of radiocarbon and archaeomagnetic dating – then we will never have a large number of such deposits.

There is one other piece of evidence, occasionally cited by critics of the suggestion of Romano-British ceramic continuity in the fifth and sixth centuries: the apparent absence of local pottery from sub-Roman sites in the north and west. This is, however, unfounded because recent work has made it quite clear that north and west British settlements never used the

---

37 Webster, 'A Romano-British Pottery Kiln', p. 214.
38 Myres, 'Lincoln in the Fifth Century', p. 87. Other 'sub-Roman' wares are known from early Anglo-Saxon cemeteries: White, *Roman and Celtic Objects*, p. 118.
39 Howe, Perrin and Mackreth, *Roman Pottery*, p. 10; personal communication, T. Briscoe, 1988.

same large amounts of pottery in the Roman period as their southern counterparts.[40]

Moreover, the consistent occurrence of calcite-gritted pottery on Welsh hill-forts of A.D. 400–700, noted by Knight,[41] requires explanation. It is true that for a few sites where an Irish cultural label may be appropriate (for example, Brawdy and Dinas Powys)[42] calcite-gritted pottery is absent, but it occurs where there may well be evidence of continuity from Romano-British occupation found: at Coygan, Dinas Emrys, Degannwy, and Dinorben.[43] This does not necessarily show that this pottery was made or used in the sub-Roman period, but it suggests that the argument that there is no potentially sub-Roman local pottery in Wales is incorrect.

The case in Cornwall is even more convincing. At Tintagel, local, superficially Romano-British pottery may have been in use alongside the (fifth-? and) sixth-century imported wares.[44] At Trethurgy, 'Romano-British' gabbroic pottery was seemingly in use, side-by-side with imported Mediterranean pottery, in the fifth and sixth centuries. As Henrietta Quinnell has written, 'At Trethurgy and at Grambla occupied throughout the fifth century A.D., there were no detectable changes in form, and it is only in the sixth century that Roman-type gabbroic pottery becomes scarce. The potting centres may have continued during the 5th century because they were less dependent on a monetary economy than kilns in other parts of the country'.[45]

In the West Country, organically-tempered pottery and other wares of probably fifth- and sixth-century date were perhaps successors to local Romano-British period products and fifth-century Black Burnished Ware forms have now been recognised.[46] Localisation, not collapse, would seem the most plausible explanation for the end of the Black Burnished Ware pottery 'industry'.

---

[40] Evans, 'From Roman Britain', p. 93.
[41] Knight, 'Pottery in Wales', pp. 9–10.
[42] Dark, *Civitas*, p. 193; and *Discovery*, pp. 138 and 143.
[43] Dark, *Discovery*, pp. 73 and 76.
[44] Thomas, 'East and West', p. 20; Morris, *Tintagel Castle*, pp. 9 and 13.
[45] Quinnell, 'Cornwall during the Iron Age', p. 129).
[46] Dark, *Civitas*, pp. 123–5; and *Discovery*, pp. 93 and 112. For fifth-century Black Burnished Ware, see Sparey-Green, in this volume. The recent argument by Hamerow, Hollevoet and Vince, in 'Migration Period Settlements', that organically-tempered pottery (which they refer to as 'chaff-tempered pottery') is a later sixth- and seventh-century introduction to west and north Britain (p. 16) can be refuted by the much earlier evidence from Crickley Hill and sites with imported Mediterranean pottery (Dark, *Civitas*, pp. 123–5), and these sites demonstrate its occurrence in what are probably fifth- and sixth-century British contexts outside of the Anglo-Saxon area of eastern England. As such, it seems unlikely that 'the cultural connections and date of the Somerset finds would probably be placed more firmly in the mid-Saxon period now than in 1974' (their note 37, p. 18).

The western British evidence is not conclusive, but, insofar as it indicates any conclusion, it would support an interpretation of continuing local pottery production and small-scale pottery use into the fifth and sixth centuries. We may conclude that the Romano-British pottery 'industry' did not collapse everywhere, and conclusively, in the early fifth century. Recognisably 'Romano-British' products seem to have been produced into the sixth century, but their market was now localised and the demand for them, or their capacity for production, was greatly reduced.

The end of the Roman irons-melting complex in the Forest of Dean is uncertain and the remaining iron-smelting centres of fourth-century Britain were within the area of Anglo-Saxon political control by the end of the fifth century. [47] In the west of Britain, the mining 'industry', however, can be seen to survive into the fifth to seventh centuries.

Mineral extraction

Almost all of Roman Britain's non-ferrous minerals were in the sub-Roman zone in the fifth and sixth centuries, yet these resources seem to have been used in the sixth and seventh centuries, as evidence of metalworking shows.[48] Unless all non-ferous metals used in sub-Roman metalworking were derived from scrap of pre-fifth-century date, or imported, it seems likely that mineral extraction occurred in west and/or north Britain in this period. Most of these resources had been exploited in the fourth century, as textual epigraphic and archaeological data attest.

As Penhallurick[49] has shown there is a little textual and archaeological evidence to suggest that tin-extraction continued in Cornwall after A.D. 400, perhaps into the seventh century. This seemingly still used Romano-British mineral workings.

In Wales there is far less evidence one way or the other. It would certainly be possible to interpret the Draethen comb as indicating sub-Roman activity in the lead mine there, and the evidence from Lesser Garth Cave has been taken by Campbell to suggest mineral extraction.[50]

Among the clearest evidence for the continued exploitation of western Britain's mineral wealth is the distribution of imported Mediterranean pottery in Britain. This is most conveniently explained by contact between the mineral-rich areas of sub-Roman Britain and Byzantine traders,[51] as the majority of these imports are found in the mineral-producing areas of Late Roman Britain. There may have been other, diplomatic,[52] reasons for

---

47 Dark, *Civitas*, p. 219.
48 Jones and Mattingly, *An Atlas*, Map 6:1 on p. 179.
49 Penhallurick, *Tin.*
50 Edwards and Lane, *Early Medieval Settlements*, pp. 67 and 86–7.
51 Thomas, 'East and West', pp. 26–27.
52 On direct contacts between Britain and Constantinople in the sixth century, see: Fulford,

Byzantine voyages to Britain, but the argument derived from the association between imported wares and Late Roman mining areas, seems strong enough to form evidence for the continued mining of deposits exploited in the Roman period. As Knight has observed, this is also true of Spain, where early Byzantine pottery occurs in the mineral producing areas, and there, too, both trading and diplomatic contacts may have been combined.[53] Britain and Spain were, it should be noted, the only early Byzantine sources of tin, despite the large scale production of copper-alloy artefacts in the Byzantine Mediterranean.[54]

There does, then, seem to be sufficient evidence to support, although not to prove, the interpretation that Romano-British mines remained in use into the fifth and sixth centuries. This, once again, seems to be a case of economic continuity, involving reduced and localised production.

Other industries

The pattern of reduced but continued production evidenced by pottery and mineral extraction may be applicable to other 'industries'. The strongest evidence for this comes from Droitwich.[55] This Romano-British small town was apparently dependent on salting and the site was, again, a salt-producing site by the seventh century, as textual evidence shows. Recent, excavation has filled the gap between these two phases of activity by the discovery of small-scale sixth-century salt production at the site. This is well dated by radiocarbon and associated ceramics, including stamped Anglo-Saxon pottery. This need not indicate an Anglo-Saxon community at the site, merely contact, not necessarily direct, with an Anglo-Saxon area. Elsewhere in western Britain, sub-Roman British communities used a small number of Anglo-Saxon artefacts.[56] The evidence from Droitwich, therefore, may indicate once again, small-scale continued sub-Roman production at a Late Roman 'industrial' site. It is interesting that the production of salt at Droitwich may have begun as early as the pre-Roman Iron Age, hinting at an even longer continuity of production at this site.[57]

'Byzantium and Britain'; Dark, *Civitas*, pp. 209–13 discusses the diplomatic character of these contacts. See also Anne Bowman in this volume.

[53] Jeremy Knight in this volume; Dark, *Civitas*, p. 209–13.

[54] Thomas, 'East and West', p. 27; Fulford, 'Byzantium and Britain', p. 4.

[55] The account of the site is derived from Burnham and Wacher, *The Small Towns*, pp. 211–17; Hurst, 'Major Saxon Discoveries'. See also Woodiwiss, *Iron Age*.

[56] Cleary, *The Ending*, p. 201.

[57] Morris, 'Prehistoric Salt Distributions', pp. 336–79.

Conclusion

There is, therefore, a convincing case to be made for the localisation rather than collapse of Romano-British 'industry' and a reduction in scale in its production. Mass-production and regional marketing had ceased in the early fifth century. However, the only 'industry' which seems to show evidence of sudden rapid decline in its local production is iron-smelting. Perhaps this was because it was integrated more fully with urban life or the inter-provincial market.

The archaeological and historical evidence, although meagre, consistently favours continuity of low-status settlement and production into the fifth to seventh century. This is, as we have seen, consistent with the material available relating to local 'industry' and in contrast to that for large-scale villa-based production. Despite the disappearance of the villa-system at the start of the fifth century, the estate structure of sub-Roman Britain may have survived into the sub-Roman period. Tenurial continuity may have formed a basis for survival of low-status sites, while those directed at the market economy may have been replaced by new site-types, or have disappeared from the archaeological record.

The rapid collapse of Romano-British economy was a collapse of the proto-industrial market. As mass-production and long-distance trade within Britain ceased to be viable, the aspects of production directed toward that economy were, themselves, no longer viable: their collapse was sudden and comprehensive. But this was a collapse of mass-production, not of production itself. While there ceased to be mass-production for urban or distant markets, local production continued into the fifth and sixth centuries. As with so much of romanised life in Britain, the collapse occurred, not in the early fifth, but in the sixth and seventh centuries, and sometimes not even then. Where demand was still there, and technology and communications available, production continued.

In most of the area remaining in British control in the fifth to seventh centuries, the use of mass-produced artefacts was limited even in the fourth century. The local Romano-British economy of these areas had not been as completely integrated into that of the major towns and villas as was that in what, by the sixth century, was the Anglo-Saxon east. Consequently, we might expect that the collapse of these aspects of the Romano-British economy would have had more limited impact on that of western Britain than on agricultural production in eastern England.

The interpretation presented in this paper has been one of localisation in manufacturing, and agricultural continuity. This should not obscure the fact that the Late Roman economy had ceased to operate as a proto-industrial system in the early fifth century, nor should it obscure the collapse of the larger urban population concentrations, of the villa system, of inter-regional large-scale trade, or of mass-production. When Esmonde-Cleary[58] and others have considered the end of the Romano-British economy, it is these aspects that they have observed, not the local market and the small-scale producer.

The end of the Roman economy in Britain is, therefore, drawn out over centuries depending upon the scale of production and type of manufacture, or agriculture, considered. In one sense it is quite accurate to say that the economy of Late Roman Britain ended in the early fifth century, in another sense it did not end until the seventh century, if then. This interpretation is closer to that usually proposed for the economic history of the Late Antique world[59] as a whole than are conventional views of the end of the Romano-British economy, and now also has more evidence in its defence.

Table 1

British products of the fifth to seventh century attested or implied by textual and archaeological sources, showing that, while sites may have had access to a wide range of artefacts and agricultural products, few of these can be expected to be found in excavations or surveys aimed at examining lower-status settlements.[60]

Key
** Evidence potentially surviving on low-status sites with acidic soils
* Evidence potentially surviving on low-status 'dry' sites without water-logging.
Underlining is used for evidence likely to be specific to either secular élite or religious contexts, so unlikely to be found on lower-status secular settlements.

** Pottery vessels
** Ceramic spindle-whorls and loom-weights
** Glass beads
** Iron domestic artefacts
** Iron ploughshares and other iron agricultural tool parts

---

[58] Cleary, *The Ending*, pp. 154–57.
[59] Hodges and Whitehouse, *Mohammed.*
[60] The textual sources used are Bieler, *The Irish Penitentials*, pp. 60–73; Gildas, *De Excidio*; and Patrick, *Confessio* and *Epistola*. The archaeological sources used are the sites ascribed to the period A.D. 400–700 in Dark, *Discovery*, pp. 46–50, 67–98.

** Iron knives and their wooden or bone handles
** Iron tools and their wooden or bone handles
** Copper-alloy or iron, drinking, eating, or storage vessels
** Iron and copper-alloy jewellery
** Spears
** Buckets
** Querns and other grinding-stones
** Polishing stones and other stone tools
** Roofing slates
** Gaming boards and pieces of stone or bone
* Meat beef, pork, lamb, wildfowl, chicken, game animals, fish
* Bone combs and other bone artefacts
Salt
Bread
Milk
Dairy products, such as cheese and buttermilk
Vegetables
Beer
Leather shoes and clothing
Leather horse-trappings
Leather domestic artefacts?
Ships/boats
Rope?
Woollen cloth and possibly linen
Dyes?
Wooden domestic artefacts?
Wooden furniture
Wooden agricultural tools
Carts
Church liturgical artefacts
Sculptured stones and inscriptions
Glass vessels
Gold and silver artefacts
Manuscripts
Ink
Writing implements
Iron swords
Shields and helmets
Secular élite ceremonial artefacts

IV

CARGOES IN TRADE ALONG
THE WESTERN SEABOARD*

Jonathan M. Wooding

The very few studies to date of western coastal trade in early mediaeval Europe have concentrated largely upon the evidence for contacts in general, or upon the evidence for commerce. Beyond this, they have concentrated upon defining trade in terms of a single, characterising, cargo – most particularly wine.[1] The assumption that there were contacts whose specific purpose was overseas trade, rather than simply travel, is a reasonable one: *Cormac's Glossary*[2] refers to 'Gaulish merchants' (*cennaigi Gall*); Jonas refers to *Scottorum commercia*)[3] at Nantes in the seventh century, and the *Vitas Patrum Emeretensium* refer to *negotiatores Graecos*[4] sailing to Mérida in the sixth century. A range of other texts also imply trading voyages. However the commercial and maritime dimensions of this trade have not been studied as an integrated whole. Historians and archaeologists whose primary concerns are the economic and social values of goods, or the cultural implications of movements of people alongside of their circulation (such as scholars who travel on trading ships), seem to neglect the analysis of what Marx termed the 'vascular systems': the integrated study of the ships and containers used to transport goods.[5] Most of our surviving evidence for trade goods in this period is within this context. As we shall see, it is mentioned in association with ships and their cargoes, rather than use-contexts. Upon the vestigial traces of these 'vascular systems', in the form of the scattered evidence for cargoes and their points of origin and destination, hinge influential theories of cultural exchange which colour the

* This paper was first presented at a conference in Perth, Western Australia, in 1987. I would like to thank Lynette Olson, Leslie Alcock, Tim Runyan, and Oliver Padel for reading the earlier version and making helpful suggestions. I would also particularly thank Ewan Campbell and Peter Hill for much helpful discussion.
1   See most recently Thomas, '*Gallici Nautae*', pp. 16–17; Alcock, *Economy*, pp. 89–90.
2   Stokes, *Three Irish Glossaries*, p. 19.
3   Jonas, *Vita Columbani*, I.23 (ed. Krusch), p. 97.
4   *Vitas Patrum Emeretensium*, IV.3 (ed. Garvin, p. 168).
5   Marx, *Capital*, Book V, Chapter 1.

interpretation of these data, and which necessitate a full critical treatment of them in their own right.

The conflicting theories of Zimmer, Hillgarth and James upon the origin points of continental influences in the culture of early Christian Ireland (they favour the Aquitaine, Spain and the Loire valley, respectively[6]), serve to illustrate how even subtly different readings of the same evidence for trade routes and the scale of trade can exert great influence in cultural studies. Hillgarth has recently stressed that the question of routes may be 'secondary to the question of reception'[7], but it is clear that both can significantly inform cultural arguments. Where established trading links may carry cultural practitioners in no way can be seen to limit their subsequent theatres of activity, as James highlights in discussing the seeming paradox that most Irish churchmen worked in east Francia, not western Gaul,[8] but it may still be an influential factor. Hillgarth and Wallace Hadrill, in highlighting deliberate recruitment in the western Gaulish church, both of Gaulish and Irish churchmen, for the German mission by the Frankish crown, throw the emphasis back on the importance of the direct links between Ireland and western Gaul, which brought the Irish into the sphere of the western Gaulish church.[9] Dáibhí Ó Cróinín, by restating the Irish starting point of Willibrord, in the face of those who see a fully Northumbrian character in his mission to the Continent, has also reinforced the importance of studying exactly which routes travellers took in this period.[10] Questions of scale and chronology in the use of sea routes are obviously important here and are fundamentally influenced by assumptions which have been made concerning cargoes and the character of shipping practices.

Most of the documentary sources relating to western seaboard trade in the period A.D. 400–800 were discussed by Heinrich Zimmer in his monumental study: 'Über direkte Handelsverbindungen Westgalliens mit Irland im Altertum und frühen Mittelalter'.[11] Most subsequent studies have relied upon the core of references to trade assembled in that study.[12] Moreover most, to their detriment, also too readily adopt Zimmer's conclusions on the character of the cargoes carried. Zimmer's overall model depended upon sources which we should no longer take at face value. More significantly, however, he tied his interpretation of the sources to a controversial cultural thesis and did not take objective account of the evidence for

---

6 Zimmer, 'Über Direkte'; James, 'Ireland and Western Gaul'; Hillgarth, 'Ireland and Spain'.
7 Hillgarth, 'Ireland and Spain', p. 16.
8 James, 'Ireland and Western Gaul', p. 380.
9 Hillgarth, 'Modes', p. 323; Wallace-Hadrill, *The Frankish*, pp. 143ff.
10 Ó Cróinín, 'Rath Melsigi', pp. 30ff.
11 Zimmer, 'Über Direkte'.
12 E.g. Lewis, 'Le Commerce'; Doherty, 'Exchange and Trade'; James, 'Ireland and Western Gaul'.

cargoes in the more reliable sources. Subsequent users of his material do not seem to have appreciated this fact fully. This has had the result of encouraging belief in the existence of larger scale contacts, from an earlier date and emanating primarily from a less likely region (south-west Gaul) than an impartial reading of the evidence would suggest.

Zimmer had a particular interest in proving the existence of contacts between the Bordeaux region and Ireland as early as the fifth century A.D. His views were based upon a discursive note in a glossary, of mostly different character to this entry, in a manuscript (Leyden Voss. Lat. F.70, f. 79) no earlier in date than the eleventh or twelfth century. This note he took to refer to an exodus of scholars from the Continent in the fifth century: '. . . all the *sapientes* on this side of the sea took flight and in the lands overseas, that is in *Hiberia* [sic] and wherever they went, greatly increased the learning of those regions'.[13] The problems of this passage are manifest. The exodus of *sapientes* might refer to a loss of wise leadership as much as the departure of classical scholars. *Hiberia*, though the stem used by Patrick and Columbanus,[14] is still only questionably equated with *Hibernia*. The manuscript is late. Zimmer interpreted this very doubtful and unspecific comment as describing an exodus of *rhetorici* from the schools of Bordeaux to Ireland.[15] These particular locations he adduced from Irish references to Ausonius, the possible fifth-century Aquitanian connexions of the Irish influenced scholar Virgilius Maro Grammaticus (now seen, on the basis of his use of Isidore, to be at least seventh century in date),[16] and what Zimmer thought to be the general commercial significance of Bordeaux which he compared, in a dramatic passage, to the Hamburg of his own day.[17]

Zimmer proposed a wine trade of considerable scale between Ireland and Gaul as the vehicle for this cultural exodus. This hypothesis was supported by the numerous references to wine consumption in the Ulster Cycle tales and some further references suggesting trade with Gaul, with or without wine. These were all conflated with Giraldus Cambrensis' twelfth-century reference to the prolific consumption of Gaulish wine in Ireland.[18] A perception of the evolving character of trade across this period was submerged beneath an exaggerated image of its scale and the differences between distinct phases of contact were obscured by Zimmer's rather sweeping hypothesis.

---

13 'omnes sapientes cismarinis fugam ceperunt et in transmarini videlicet in Hiberia et quocumque se receperunt, maximum profectum sapientiae incolis illarum regionum adhibuerunt', text most recently reprinted in Herren, 'Some New Light', p. 39.

14 *Confessio* XVI (ed. Hood, p. 25); Columbanus, *Epistolae* II (ed. Walker, p. 22).

15 This thesis is best summarised in Meyer, *Learning in Ireland*.

16 Herren, 'Some New Light'; Herren, 'On the Earliest'.

17 Zimmer, 'Über direkte', III, p. 591.

18 *Ibid.*, II, pp. 430ff; *In Topographia Hiberniae* II (ed. O'Meara, 'Giraldus Cambrensis', p. 121).

This model, in which Zimmer read a particular complexion into his sources, has exercised an influence in economic and social studies far out of proportion either to its reliability in general, or its acceptance in the sphere of cultural studies. Zimmer's model tackled broad questions of cultural continuity and the role of such continuity in the formation of the culture of the Middle Ages, in a similar vein to Pirenne's maritime continuity model for Mediterranean civilisation. Much of its documentation remains of value, but its broad framework is inevitably dated. Ironically, whereas Zimmer's central cultural thesis has long been abandoned, the supporting thesis of wine trading is still guardedly accepted by most archaeologists and historians as central to early mediaeval trade with Gaul[19] and finds of Gaulish material in Britain and Ireland are usually brought under the label of the 'wine trade'. The sources which refer to early wine trading between Gaul and the Irish Sea basin, and to links with Bordeaux, are amongst the least reliable sources for cargoes. The 'merchants with Gaulish wine' (*mercatores cum vino Gallorum*) who, in the Latin *Vita Kyarani*, sail up the Shannon to Clonmacnoise in the middle of the sixth century,[20] are far more likely to reflect the regular wine trading with Gaul around the period of the earliest text of the *vita* (*ca* twelfth century), than any sixth-century activity. Other specific references to wine from Gaul in the Irish Sea basin before the ninth century are from vernacular tales, for example the *fín Gall* mentioned in *Tochmairc Emire*.[21] These tales are not securely datable to before the eighth century, however, and Mallory has recently given cause to cast doubt upon the early date of any of their material descriptions.[22] Likewise what we may make of the reference, to the death of Muirchertach Mac Erca in the early Irish equivalent of a butt of Malmsey,[23] must remain an open question, as it is ascribed to a date which is just before the period for which we accept the annals as likely to be contemporary witness, and is hence likely to be a later addition. None of this must lead us to doubt that there was wine being consumed in Ireland. Adomnán, in the late seventh century, describes 'wine which is necessary for the most holy mysteries',[24] as it is everywhere, but where this wine came from is very unclear and we should not, for example, overlook Bede's reference to vines

---

[19] See note 1, above; also, James, 'Ireland and Western Gaul', p. 383; Doherty, 'Exchange', p. 77; Hillgarth, 'Ireland and Spain', p. 16.
[20] *Vita Kyarani* XXXI (ed. Plummer, *Vitae*, vol. I, p. 214).
[21] Meyer, 'The Oldest', p. 443.
[22] Mallory, 'Silver', pp. 57–9.
[23] *Annals of Ulster, s.a.* 534: 'Demersio Muirchertaig filii Erce .i. Muirchertaigh mc. Muireadaidh mc. Eoghain mc. Neill Naoighiallaigh in dolio pleno uino . . .' (ed. Mac-Niocaill and Mac Airt, pp. 70–1).
[24] 'ad sacrosancta misteria necessarium . . . vinum', Adomnán, *Vita Columbae*, I.28 (ed. Anderson and Anderson p. 196).

growing in Ireland itself.[25] The point is that we cannot find evidence of consumption such as would support a 'wine trade'.

We search in vain for the earliest reliable sources, such as the early Irish laws, for references to wine consumption. Amongst many references to ale and mead, the only references to wine all derive from commentaries on one text, the lost text *Muirbretha* (*'Sea Judgements'*) which describes wine as one among many goods which might be found in a wrecked ship.[26] Even the wisdom text *Tecosca Cormaic*, which also mentions wine, can be shown to be most likely quoting the *Muirbretha*.[27] Jonas, writing in the late seventh century in a continental milieu where wine was readily available, states that the Irish, like most northern Europeans, had a preference for ale.[28] Though there may have been wine imported to Ireland, there is thus no suggestion that importation of large quantities of wine was a *raison d'être* of trade, as seems commonly to be accepted. Zimmer's 'wine trade' was a seductive image, invoking not only modern tastes, but the stereotypes established by Diodorus's and Polybius's descriptions of continental Iron-Age Celtic elites 'greedy for wine'. These must not be confused with insular Celtic tastes of the period A.D. 400–800.

We must consider each individual reference to trade on its own merits, not attempting to fit it within an anachronistic model, as Zimmer did by beginning his study with Giraldus' references to the 'superabundance' of French wine in twelfth-century Ireland and forcing this model back over the earlier evidence. No single model can explain the diverse references to several centuries of trading activity. A range of goods and nationalities were involved in commerce.

Adomnán has left us an account of a sixth-century voyage from Gaul to Scotland. In the *Vita Columbae*, the saint fortells of a disaster abroad, saying: 'And before the year is out Gallic sailors, from the provinces of Gaul, will tell you the same.'[29] Some time later, such news is brought by 'the master and sailors of a ship' (*nauclerum et nautas adventantis barca*) arriving in the 'chief place of the district' (*caput regionis*).[30] The use of the word barca is evidently to denote a commercial ship. It is unknown

[25] Bede, *Historia Ecclesiastica*, I (ed. Colgrave and Mynors, p. 20).

[26] Binchy, *Corpus*, p. 315.28.

[27] *Tecosca Cormaic*, I.25–8: 'Bárca do thocor i port | Allmaire sét | Murchuirthe dílse: Inviting barks into harbour, Importing treasures from overseas, Forfeiture of sea waifs' (ed. Meyer, 1909, pp. 2–3). These are the topics covered by *muirbretha* in the passages bearing that name in *Di Chetharslicht Athagabála* (e.g. ed. Binchy, *Corpus*, p. 369.2–369.8, named as *muirbretha* at p. 388.18) and the *Bretha Étgid* (e.g. ed. Binchy, *Corpus*, pp. 314.17–315.28, named as *muirbretha* at p. 314.17).

[28] *Vita Columbani* I.16 (ed. Krusch, p. 82).

[29] 'Et antequam praesens finiatur annus gallici nautae de Galliarum provinciis adventantes haec eadem tibi enarrabunt', *Vita Columbae* I.28 (ed. Anderson and Anderson, p. 262).

[30] *Ibid.*, I.28 (p. 264).

elsewhere in Adomnán, but is explicitly designated with a commercial context by Isidore, whom Adomnán certainly has as a source.[31] The *Tecosca Cormaic* (*ca* eighth-century) uses the same word to describe a merchant vessel, where a king: 'invites barcs into port, with overseas treasures'.[32] The *Vita Filiberti* (ninth-century, from an eighth-century original) tells of a seventh-century scene where: 'Irish ships, with a diversity of goods aboard, put in at the island and provide the brethren with an abundance of shoes and clothing'.[33] Trade is not specified, but ships are expected to appear with gifts in saints' *vitae*[34] and the Irish ethnicity of the ships may be to emphasise the Irish connections of St Filibert's monasticism. However, the ships might be a regular appearance and the cargo typical. Noirmoutier was a commercial centre of some note. In the *Vita Filiberti* the saint extols the virtues of monastic commerce.[35] The ninth-century *Miracula* of St Filibert link the monastery with production of salt, which is traded by sea and along the Loire,[36] and charters establish the existence of a fair where wine was traded.[37]

This connexion of western Britain and Ireland with the Loire estuary seems to have been relatively frequent. In Jonas' *Vita Columbani*, Columbanus is put on board a ship in Nantes which is involved with *Scotorum commercia*.[38] When Dagobert II was to be exiled in the mid-seventh century, the conspirator entrusted with the task of sending him abroad was Bishop Dido of Poitiers, who arranged his exile to Ireland.[39] The route is not specified, but again a western Gaulish connexion is involved. In the *Vita Wilfridi*, *navigantes* convey news of Dagobert II back to Gaul.[40] There are other suggestions of an Irish link with western Gaul.[41] The link is consistently more northwestern than Zimmer believed, however, with the Loire estuary and Poitou, not Bordeaux, the primary focus, at least in such sources as we have.

The words of the texts should be examined carefully where they relate to potential cargoes. The *Vita Filiberti* lists shoes and clothing as a ship's cargo; there is no mention (contra Hodges)[42] of wine as a return cargo. The

---

[31] Isidore, *Etymologiarum* XIX.19: 'Barca est quae cuncta navis commercia ad litus portat' (ed. Lindsay).

[32] See note 27.

[33] 'Scothorum navis diversis mercimoniis plena ad litus adfuit, qui calciamenta ac vestamenta fratribus larga copia ministravit', *Vita Filiberti* XLII (ed. Levison, p. 603).

[34] Cf. the *Vita Kyarani*, above.

[35] *Vita Filiberti*, XXIII (ed. Levison, p. 596).

[36] Doeheard, *The Early Middle Ages*, p. 156.

[37] *Ibid.*, p. 156.

[38] *Vita Columbani* I.23 (ed. Krusch, p. 97)

[39] *Liber Historiae Francorum* XLIII (ed. Krusch, p. 316).

[40] Eddius, *Vita Wilfridi* XXVIII (ed. Levison, p. 221).

[41] Kenney, *The Sources*, pp. 489–99; James, 'Ireland and Western Gaul', pp. 378ff.

[42] Hodges, 'Some Early Medieval', p. 241.

crucial point is that a 'diversity of goods' is mentioned. Similarly, the 'Irish commerce' of Jonas is suggestive of non-specific trade, probably with ships carrying a variety of goods to more than one destination – something like a modern 'tramp steamer'. Commentaries on the lost Irish legal text *Muirbretha* give a broader picture of the diversity of wrecked ships' cargoes and a range of goods involved in overseas commerce: 'Hides and iron and salt . . . foreign nuts and goblets and an escup of wine or honey, if there is wine or honey in her.'[43] Other recensions of this commentary add 'gold, silver,[44] furs[45] and British horses'.[46] In one case the *escup* phrase is reversed to read: 'an *escup* vessel of honey or wine if honey and wine be in her'.[47] Hence wine is neither ahead of honey as trade good, nor seen as a ubiquitous element of a cargo.

The early date of the detail in these commentaries cannot be taken for granted. The 'canonical' phrases which they supplement are unspecific as to the goods which are found on the shore, which doutless varied across time. The fact that lists of cargoes, and not the surviving 'canonical' text, are what is quoted in the legal glossaries, however, does suggest an early date for some elements of the commentaries themselves, or that the material from the commentaries is lifted from other passages of canonical text which no longer survive. The latter would certainly fit with the *Cormac's Glossary* reference, which states that the term *e(p)scop* was used in the *Muirbretha* itself.[48] It is sufficient to say that they are potentially early material which demonstrates diversity in cargo composition. That alone is sufficient basis for questioning Zimmer's equation of the early sources with Giraldus' implicit 'wine trade'.

This discussion in the commentaries obviously involves both potential import and export cargoes. Hides and honey are local produce. The *Vita Filiberti* suggests that leather goods had a market in Gaul.[49] Saxon merchants from Quentovic trade in honey at St Denis, in a probably tenth-century forged charter.[50] Hodges infers that this honey was ultimately from

---

43 'seichida ᚊ iarann ᚊ saland . . . cno gnae ᚊ cuirnd ᚊ, escup fina no mela ma ta fin mil indti', Trinity E 3.5 (ed. Binchy, *Corpus*, p. 315.26–8).

44 'masa or [no] airget [no] allmhaire set ᚊ set foraicce se scripla do masa iarand [no] sechedha ᚊ escub meala [no] fina ma ta mil [no] fin indte', RAWL. B 506 (ed. Binchy, *Corpus*, p. 139.32–4).

45 'clúman', Trinity H.5.15 (ed. Binchy, *Corpus,* p. 2155.20).

46 'Gaillti .i. laire breathnacha no cno g[n]ae ᚊ cuirnd ᚊ buabhaill, etc.', *O'Davoren's Glossary* (ed. Stokes, *Three Irish Glossaries*, p. 95).

47 See note 44.

48 See note 52 for *Cormac's Glossary* text. On the possible early date of commentaries see Binchy, 'A Text', pp. 72–80.

49 *Vita Filiberti*, XLII (ed. Levison, p. 603). Also note the references to a clothing trade in Gaul, Doehard, *The Early Middle Ages*, pp. 160–1.

50 *Diplomata Spuria* no. 23 (ed. Pertz, *Diplomata*, p. 140).

England.[51] The existence of a trade in honey in Gaul at the end of the first millennium A.D. is at least suggested. Honey might, accordingly, have also been exchanged between Ireland and western Gaul.

Wine is likely enough to have been an import, though here only amongst other goods, not as a characterising cargo. *Cormac's Glossary* interprets the *Muirbretha* reference further on this point: '*Epscop (sic) Fina:* in the *Muirbretha*, i.e. a vessel for measuring wine amongst the merchants of the Gauls and Franks.'[52] It is satisfying here to note that this specifies 'merchants' (*cennaigi*), definitely indicating trade, and not 'wine-merchants'. It is tempting to see the use of a measuring jug (escup: note the glossary's epscop is likely a play on words: drunken bishops?[53]) as indicative of trade only in small amounts of wine, not shiploads of many barrels, as suggested by some scholars. Adomnán makes reference to a 'Gaulish pint',[54] but this may be a phrase from the Gaulish Bishop Arculf, so it is unclear whether his Insular audience accepted it as a common measurement.[55] *Escup* itself is likely to be a local word, not a Gaulish borrowing.[56] There is no evidence of barrels or casks in any relevant context. Thomas' reference to Adomnán's metaphor of 'wine oozing from a cask',[57] is actually to nothing more specific than 'cracks' (*rimulas*) in a 'large vessel (*pleni vassis*),[58] which could just as easily be ceramic.

The reference to salt in the *Muirbretha* commentaries brings to our attention an underrated trade good. Salt was certainly exchanged in 'Celtic' Britain in the Iron Age, where 'Very Coarse Pottery' represents containers for its transportation. In Ireland, place-names for coastal salt-workings are mostly English in origin, rather than Irish.[59] This, along with evidence that English salt (*salann Saxanach*[60]) was imported into mediaeval Ireland, suggests that early mediaeval Ireland did not produce salt on any appreciable scale. Evidence for contacts with Gaul, in particular Noirmoutier, a salt trading centre, assume greater importance in this connexion with salt as a potentially major, if not a characterising, cargo. The social basis for trading in salt is not impossible to explain. It might seem logical that any sea-girt region would simply produce its own salt. An historical sense is necessary

[51] Hodges, *Dark Age Economics*, p. 127.
[52] 'EPSCOP FINA isna Muirbrethaib .i. escra tomais fína le cennaigib Gall 7 Frange' (ed. Stokes, *Three Irish Glossaries*, p. 19).
[53] *Viz* 'Epscop .i. onni is episcopus', *Ibid.*, p. 19; Zimmer, 'Über direkte', II, p. 441ff. It is 'Eascop fina' in O'Davoren's Glossary (ed. Stokes, *Three Irish Glossaries*, p. 82).
[54] 'sextarii Gallici', Adomnán, *De Locis Sanctis* I,7.1 (ed. Meehan, p. 50).
[55] I would like to thank Ewan Campbell for drawing my attention to this reference.
[56] Though ultimately a loan-word through British. See D. A. Binchy, review of Jackson, p. 291.
[57] Thomas, 'Imported Late-Roman', pp. 252–3.
[58] Adomnán, *Vita Columbae*, epilogue to Book I (ed. Anderson and Anderson, p. 322).
[59] Scott, 'Some Conflicts', pp. 115–16.
[60] *Aislinge Meic Conglinne* (ed. Meyer, p. 62).

here, however: Ireland may have been less likely to initiate subsistence extraction of salt if large quantities of salt only became necessary for the first time in the early Christian period. It may be possible to trace changes in eating and cooking habits, with communal killing and immediate consumption of meat giving way to killing and storing of individually owned beasts, for which salt would be necessary.[61] The references to salt,[62] and salted meat,[63] in a text such as *Críth Gablach* (early eighth century) might suggest this. If Ireland did not possess salt industries from prehistory, economic structures of the fifth–ninth century may not have accommodated their foundation. Do the place-names suggest that this waited upon the much later arrival of an English bourgeoisie?

The range of goods involved in commerce is diverse and wine is not accorded any central status. A similar diversity of trade goods, indeed much the same range, is mentioned in Merovingian commercial sources – especially those charters and saints' *vitae* which depict relations between the Frankish crown and the church, including the monastic successors of Columbanus, such as Filibert.[64] These texts also discuss trade in dyes,[65] not mentioned in Insular texts, but attested archaeologically in finds such as the piece of orpiment found at Dunadd, a colouring matter used in Insular manuscripts.[66]

This evidence may also in time provide further clues as to the political or social networks which utilised the 'tramp steamer' trade pattern. The commentaries on the *Muirbretha* describe a case where a ship may be 'directed towards a certain person'.[67] Does this imply that goods were ordered in advance, such as when Alcuin orders goods to be bought in Gaul to be shipped to York?[68] Monastic contacts might be responsible for communicating demand for goods, or orders. This need not imply regular monastic backing of trading voyages. Rather, shipowners might be general carriers who seek patronage or regular custom from monasteries and in ports sponsored by monasteries. Secular authorities might also provide such patronage, however, as in the *Vita Columbae* a man must leave Iona and travel to the *caput regionis* to meet ships from abroad.

The distribution of the ceramic known as E-ware increasingly seems to

---

61 Wooding, 'What Porridge', p. 15.
62 *Críth Gablach* XV, l. 190 (ed. Binchy, p. 8).
63 *Ibid.*, ll. 270, 300, 350, 381 (ed. Binchy, pp. 11, 12, 14, 15).
64 *Vita Filiberti* V (ed. Levison, p. 587).
65 Hodges, *Dark Age*, p. 127. Also see the charter cited in note 50.
66 E. Campbell, 'A Cross-Marked Quern', p. 113.
67 'Where she [the ship] is directed to a certain person' ('in tan tainic fo thomus duine airithi hi'). Also note the phrase 'where she is directed towards a certain tuath' ('in tan tainic fo tomus tuaithi airithi hi') in the same commentaries (ed. Binchy, *Corpus*, p. 315.24–5 and 315.17).
68 *Epistolae*, 8 (ed. Dümmler, p. 33).

reinforce these conclusions, though we must remain aware of the the influence of historical models upon research into E-ware, which could make this point slightly circular.[69] E-ware is a coarse domestic pottery in the form of cooking pots (Ei), beakers (Eii), dishes (Eiii) and pitchers (Eiv). The ware is unglazed, and rarely decorated in any way. It is not a container-type ceramic and clearly was exchanged for functional use, rather than for any valuable contents.[70] It is found on some seventy-odd British and Irish sites,[71] with the greatest concentration of finds in Scotland and Northern Ireland. The wide range of sites and relatively small numbers from individual sites may reflect the nature of excavation practices, but also tends to discourage belief in the idea that E-ware formed the central element of cargoes to any particular region, which is perfectly consistent with the evidence for the 'tramp steamer' model of commerce outlined above. The plainness of E-ware makes it an unusual candidate for long-distance trade, again underscoring the point that it is unlikely to have formed the central element of cargoes. We should not overlook Pucci's point that plain pottery may be a luxury good if it is imported,[72] nonetheless attempts to prove from a literary reference that E-ware was a luxury good have a strained air.[73] It remains easiest to see E-ware as having been carried as a subsidiary to more valuable trade goods, though this does not necessitate that we follow Thomas[74] in assuming that this trade centred on wine, rather than the range of equally valued goods discussed above. The persistent association of E-ware with wine has also led to a failure to appreciate E-ware as a trade-good in its own right.[75]

The concentration of finds in the north of the Irish Sea basin ties in with Adomnán's reference to Gaulish ships going as far north as Dalriada.[76] If the wares were transhipped in the south of the Irish Sea the distribution would surely be larger at that point (as is the pattern with the sixth-century Mediterranean wares, discussed below), even allowing for the unevenness of excavation activity. That E-ware is a relatively homogeneous ceramic type would suggest that a single continental port was regularly involved in the voyages which brought it in. Close parallels for E-ware have been located in Herpes[77] and Chadenac (Charente), and Tours (Touraine),[78] so

---

[69] E.g. Peacock and Thomas, 'Class E', p. 39.

[70] See Wooding, 'What Porridge', p. 13.

[71] Thomas, *A Provisional*, pp. 20–24, to which must be added a large number of more recent finds, mostly unpublished.

[72] Pucci, 'Pottery', p. 110.

[73] Mytum, 'High Status Vessels', p. 377; Wooding, 'What Porridge', p. 14.

[74] Thomas, *'Gallici Nautae'*, pp. 16–17.

[75] Wooding, 'What Porridge', pp. 12–17; reaffirmed by Thomas, *'Gallici Nautae'*, p. 8.

[76] *Vita Columbae* I.28 (Anderson and Anderson, p. 262).

[77] British Museum, Delamain Collection, nos. 1905 5–20: 176, 178, and esp. 179.

[78] Randoin, 'Essai', p. 107, catalogue no. 18; Giot and Querre, 'Le Tesson', p. 99.

E-ware also seems to hint at a Loire estuary connexion so far, although we must remain open-minded on this point. Site chronology at Clogher (Tyrone),[79] Whithorn (Dumfries and Galloway)[80] and other sites including the sequence at Tours,[81] in France, seems to indicate that E-ware is a largely seventh- century phenomenon.

That much of the evidence seems to suggest a mostly seventh-century *floruit* for links between Gaul and the Irish Sea basin must be set against our comparative lack of sources for the sixth century. When we turn to the question of the evolution of western sealanes commerce, however, once we step aside from the model followed by Zimmer there is no reason to assume a long continuity to the Gaulish connection. Zimmer was at pains to stress continuity from the Roman period. In doing so he conflated sources which we can now clearly distinguish in reference. Strabo's first-century descriptions of a trade between western Gaul and Britain can now, on the evidence of archaeology, be seen only to have extended into the English Channel, not the Irish Sea.[82] Caesar, indeed, had been unable to find merchants who knew anything of the western coasts of Britain,[83] despite his extensive employment of western Gaulish fleets.[84] In later centuries, Roman writers remained ignorant of the correct distance of Ireland from Gaul.[85]

For the fifth century there is no reliable evidence for direct links between Gaul and the Irish Sea basin. The story of St Patrick's escape to a land three day's sail from Ireland could refer to Britain, as much as Gaul, and requires a definite reading of an ambiguous passage to decide which.[86] It is also correct to reject the idea that the manuscript variant *canes*[87] indicates that the ship's cargo was hounds (which does not mean we should overlook the possibility that such were traded, as Strabo and Symmachus both identify hounds as a British export prized in the Empire[88]). The vague suggestion that St Germanus set off westward to get to Britain from Auxerre requires considerable stretching to indicate an Atlantic voyage and Palladius's, clearly closely related, journey to Ireland two years later, in 431, is equally likely to have been through Britain, where Saxon conquest had not yet

---

[79] Warner, 'The Clogher', pp. 37–8.
[80] Hill, *Whithorn*, pp. 4–7.
[81] Randoin, 'Essai', p. 107 and pers. comm.
[82] Cunliffe, 'Relations', pp. 4–8.
[83] *Bellum Gallicum*, IV (ed. Edwards, 1979, pp. 204–6).
[84] *Ibid.*, III (p. 153).
[85] Killeen, 'Ireland in the Greek', pp. 209–13.
[86] *Confessio*, XXIII (ed. Hood, p. 27).
[87] *Ibid.*, XIX (pp. 26 and 40).
[88] See Crawford ('Western Seaways', p. 193), for an especially imaginative example of speculation on this point. For Classical references to British hounds: Strabo, *Geographica* IV.5.2 (ed. Jones, pp. 254–5); Symmachus, *Epistolae* II.77 (ed. Seeck, p. 65).

interfered with the overland routes and where St Germanus had already initiated contacts.[89]

There are no grounds for seeing the trade of the sixth century and later as continuing significantly earlier patterns. Attempts to see archaeological continuity should be treated with care. There is no overlap between African Red Slipware series in Roman Britain and the types found in western British sites.[90] Thomas's suggestion that the fourth century French *éponge* pottery imported to south-western Britain from western France, 'prefigures' E-ware[91] ignores the fact that E-ware is found principally in Ireland and Scotland (where no *éponge* pottery is found) and is primarily seventh century in date.

Further work will be needed to clarify the sixth-century evidence, which has important implications for the causation of contact. On the strength of the quantity of E-ware pottery in Northern Ireland Nieke and Duncan have raised the hypothesis that the pattern of commerce between Gaul and Ireland might have been influenced by monastic contacts through the familia of Columbanus,[92] not the opposite as is usually assumed. In the light of the involvement of Gaulish monasteries in commerce, such an model would seem to deserve greater consideration than it has so far received. Much then depends upon whether E-ware is as early as sixth century in date. If such contact were of a 'tramp steamer', character it might also be simply escalated or re-routed by monastic connexions. The appearance of E-ware in Insular assemblages may only represent one of these changes to pre-existing trade patterns.

The evidence of the pottery known as D ware may suggest a sixth-century link between the Irish Sea basin and Gaul. It is a regular western-Gaulish type, where it is known as *sigillées paléochrétienne grise*. But in Britain its distribution is very limited.[93] That it was long considered to be a Bordeaux product[94] has been held to support the connexion proposed by Zimmer, but French scholars now suggest that the Saintonge or Touraine may be equally likely.[95] In any event the amounts involved in this distribution are not so great as to be certain evidence that ships' cargoes were reaching western Britain. It sits within a range of evidence for contact between Britain and a Roman-Christian milieu on the Continent, centring on the sixth century and

---

[89] Thomas, *Christianity*, pp. 301–2.

[90] Thomas, *A Provisional*, p. 4; Bird, 'African', pp. 272–5.

[91] Thomas, *A Provisional*, p. 4.

[92] Nieke and Duncan, 'Dalriada', p. 15.

[93] Some seven sites in all: Congresbury and South Cadbury (Somerset), Mays Hill (Isles of Scilly), Dinas Powys (Glamorgan), Longbury Bank (Dyfed), Whithorn and the Mote of Mark (Dumfries and Galloway, and Dunadd (Argyll). The finds from Tintagel and Clogher are now discarded.

[94] Campbell, 'The Post-Roman Pottery', p. 125.

[95] J. Santrot, pers. comm.; B. Randoin, pers. comm.

exclusive of Ireland.[96] This represents some discontinuity with the seventh-century pattern evinced by E-ware, which centres on Ireland and Scotland. This may only serve to stress that a range of different voyages are likely to have occurred and that we should not adopt overly reductionist approaches to all evidence of contact with Gaul. The *Vita Filiberti* mentions *naves Britannici*[97] as well as Irish ships. The pottery itself, as durable evidence, may also only indicate a small part of traffic which was mostly in less durable goods.

Another sixth-century phase of ceramic activity causes us to think in entirely different terms regarding trade, cargoes and destinations involved in voyages. Where E-ware seems to be a ceramic of little weight, almost certainly a subsidiary cargo and not a container, the amphorae and dishes of Mediterranean origin, found in their greatest quantities at Tintagel,[98] on the other hand bear witness to definite shiploads of cargo in bulk. These cargoes consist of the well known eastern Mediterranean amphora types: Bi (henceforth class 43, after Peacock and Williams, probably wine jars made in Greece); Bii (henceforth class 44, probably oil jars from Asia Minor); Biv (class 45, probably wine jars from Asia Minor); and Bvi (class 49). Accompanying these are a range of tablewares of eastern Mediterranean (Phocaean Red Slipware, henceforth PRS) and north African origin (African Red Slipware, henceforth ARS) and a very small quantity of African amphorae.[99] The discovery of assemblages in Portugal with a similar range of tablewares and amphorae,[100] and their absence from western French sites, indicates clearly that these wares were carried by sea direct from the Mediterranean to western Britain and Ireland.

It would be easy to fall into the trap of considering the wide date range of each of these types, ubiquitous in the Mediterranean, as indicative of several phases of importation. Miller, for example, does this[101] and other scholars have suggested the irreconcilable character of the evidence to a single phase. The need here is to take a different approach and consider the entire British and Irish assemblage in combination. It emerges on doing so that class 43 and 44 amphorae make up together nearly 90% of the amphora finds.[102] Two other classes of amphorae from the eastern Mediterranean are involved. The African element is very small, only around 20%,[103] and much

---

96 E.g. Knight, '*In Tempore*', pp. 60–2.
97 *Vita Filberti* XL, XLI (ed. Levison, p. 603).
98 Thomas, *A Provisional*, pp. 6–18.
99 Peacock and Williams, *Amphorae*, pp. 182–9; Hartgroves and Walker, 'Excavations', pp. 24–5.
100 Prieto, 'Algunos'; Keay, *Late Roman Amphorae*, p. 655.
101 Miller, 'Hiberni', p. 317.
102 In Britain, however, class 43 makes up 35% of total finds and class 44, 54%. At Yassi Ada the ratio is 12%:71%.
103 Thomas, 'The Context', p. 12.

of this is made up of dishes, not of the amphorae which would be the core of any cargo. It is important then to stress that the most convincing model is of eastern Mediterranean ships, with a heavy cargoes of amphorae, calling at an African port and taking on a small amount of further goods. Neither a 'tramp steamer' model, nor a transhipment of cargo in Africa explains these proportions. That dipinti and graffiti testify to handling of the cargoes by both Greek and Latin speakers does not invalidate the basic conclusion that the ship was from a Greek-speaking zone.[104] A similar mixture of graffiti is seen on a western Mediterranean ship sunk at Fos-sur-Mer.[105] Ships' crews and stevedores may have been an ethnically mixed bunch.

A ship which sank off Yassi Ada in Turkey in 625 provides evidence upon which to construct a cargo model for the British finds. The Yassi Ada ship contained some nine hundred amphorae – all but a handful being either class 43 or class 44[106] and the remainder being a variety of tablewares and amphora types for use on board ship. Here then is an assemblage which proves that the British materials are likely to represent composite cargoes rather than a long period of trade with variety representing change across time. However both Alcock and Thomas see difficulties in the comparison of the British assemblages with Yassi Ada, in that the latter shows greater standardisation of forms amongst classes 43 and 44 than is seen in Britain. There may be good reason not to overemphasise the similarities, as the Yassi Ada voyage is a century later and working within the east. Nonetheless, its comparability as a mixed, bulk cargo of amphorae, made up of predominantly two types, the same as predominate in Britain, seems compelling. The later date probably accounts for the greater standardisation of forms along with the amphorae coming from a different kiln (Black Sea) to the British finds (Aegean). Alcock underemphasises the variety demonstrated by Bass amongst the amphorae[107] and Thomas correctly dismisses the idea that this proves that the wares were transhipped at an intermediary point,[108] such as Africa or Portugal – though he seems to misinterpret Alcock's comments on the variety present as being to the number of individual types, rather than variety within types.[109] His suggestion that the British cargoes were thus a 'mixed bag' is hence probably an overstatement.

The published volume of finds from the Avenue du Président Habib Bourguiba site in Carthage also provides excellent comparative evidence. The eastern Mediterranean wares on that site have a definite *floruit* in a

104 Thomas, *A Provisional*, pp. 13–14.
105 Reith, 'Research', p. 416.
106 Bass and Van Doorninck, *Yassi Ada*, pp. 156ff.
107 Alcock, *Economy*, p. 90.
108 Thomas, 'The Context', p. 12.
109 *Ibid.*, p. 12. The point here is that the British cargoes date from a period when earlier types (Class 45 and Class 49), were giving way to Class 43 and Class 44. Such overlap did not exist at the time of Yassi Ada, hence the cargo is more homogeneous.

longer sequence of western and African types, this intrusive presence dating from the late-fifth/early-sixth century, cognate with the eastern Mediterranean interest which culminated in Justinian's reconquest.[110] Outside the Straits of Gibraltar an extension of this phase is equally becoming clear. African Red Slipware had been traded to Iberia throughout the Late Roman period into the fifth century. A revival around 500, however, is discontinuous with this earlier phase. In this later *floruit* the accompanying presence of PRS form 3 indicates importation by eastern Mediterranean ships, travelling via Africa. This phase was long misdated, however, on the strength of the historical misdating of Conimbriga which truncated the fifth-century phases into the period before the 'destruction' of the site in 465–8. This misdating affected Forms 91–104 of ARS right across the board.[111]

The British and Irish finds, their context thus established, represent the short-lived extension of a known pattern of eastern Mediterranean trade in the Atlantic for a brief period around the beginning of the sixth century. This is clearly an innovation, discontinuous with Roman traffic – most likely linked with Justinian's 'reconquest'.[112] Its obvious opposition to the Pirenne thesis is relevant here: this is not the heavyweight, capital-based trade of the Roman period, but doubtless the entrepreneurial type of the *Rhodian Sea Law*[113] involving the sort of small cargoes carried by the Yassi Ada ship. In the late-sixth-century *Vitas Patrum Emeretensium*, negotiatores Graecos come to Mérida, in Spain – where there seems to have been a Greek enclave – for more than just commercial purposes.[114] It is satisfying that trade and Greek nationality are specified here. Investigation of the Yassi Ada material brings other important details on cargoes. A round sherd of reworked class 43 pottery, found at Congresbury,[115] seems to be an amphora stopper of the type found at Yassi Ada.[116] It is telling evidence that at least one full amphora was brought to Congresbury, almost certainly unopened from the eastern centre where it was originally filled. Such finds may be of considerable importance in archaeological chronology, when we consider the possible residual value of the amphorae as storage jars. Where we find the stoppers, we may well find the event of the actual first opening of the jar, as the sealing of the stopper in again with wax may be seen as less likely in subsequent use, where a less cumbersome stopper would be more likely.

What the amphorae contained is still unknown. Wine and oil are the most likely substances. In this connexion we should not neglect the witness of

---

110 Fulford and Peacock, *Excavations*, pp. 258–61.
111 Hayes, *Supplement*, p. 521; Fulford and Peacock, *Excavations*, p. 114.
112 Fulford, 'Byzantium and Britain', pp. 1–5.
113 Van Doorninck, 'Byzantium, Mistress', p. 139.
114 See note 4, above; Collins, 'Mérida', pp. 203–4.
115 Rahtz, 'Pottery', p. 110, fig. 3, no. 20.
116 Bass and Van Doorninck, *Yassi Ada*, pp. 160–1.

Gildas that these were prized symbols of Romanitas.[117] Wine may have had a market in western Britain on the strength of this, a more likely explanation than any notion of residual tastes, now rightly dismissed by Thomas.[118] Oil was prized in northern Gaul for church lamps[119] and so may also have been in Britain, though tests for oil residue on British finds have so far been negative.[120] Whatever the needs of the local market, there is no question that the contents of the ships were unloaded and consumed. What did the ships carry as return cargo? The overwhelming focus of the distribution of the wares upon Cornwall, Devon and Somerset makes tin the best candidate. As the amphorae were clearly unloaded along with their contents, a cargo of considerable weight would be required to re-ballast the ship for the return voyage. Tin ingots fit this model perfectly. Stephanos of Alexandria in the seventh century termed tin the 'British metal'.[121] Much quoted also is the miraculous story, in the *Life of St John the Almsgiver*, of the ship's captain who, 'falling on evil days', enters the service of the Church and, when blown by storm to Britain, returns with a cargo of tin, which is miraculously transformed into silver.[122] This story further indicates the consciousness of tin as a British product, possibly derived from Classical references. This may explain why such a long-distance venture was attempted and the likelihood is then that the return cargo was of a single-element character. The frequent literal interpretation of this story is mistaken: the Church did not necessarily back such voyages.[123] The feature of the captain in service of the Church is a topos made more poignant by the fact that the *naukleroi* were normally 'free traders'. It is this latter notion which may explain the adventurous quality of the voyage to Britain. Most of all, however, it should serve to stress the unlikelihood of continuity in this commerce.

In conclusion, the intrusive, short-lived, character of this sixth-century phase and the large cargoes involved, carry no implications for the diversity of cargo and destination which seem to characterise traffic between Gaul and the Irish Sea basin in the sixth and seventh centuries. The reductionist search for continuity of traffic, initiated by Zimmer, can only be seen as having obscured the diversity of goods and routes used in several phases of commerce.

---

117 Gildas, *De Excidio* VII (ed. Winterbottom, p. 91).
118 Thomas, 'The Context', p. 11.
119 *Vita Filiberti* XXXVII (ed. Levison, p. 602).
120 'The Context', p. 21.
121 Penhallurick, *Tin*, p. 10.
122 Dawes and Baynes, *Three Byzantine*, pp. 216–18. This episode is no doubt influenced by the story of Colaeus of Samos (Herodotus, *Histories* IV.152, ed. Godley 1926, 352–3), though it may still reflect a contemporary interest in Britain.
123 *Viz* Brown, *The World*, p. 156.

V

THE ARCHAEOLOGICAL EVIDENCE FOR EXTERNAL CONTACTS: IMPORTS, TRADE AND ECONOMY IN CELTIC BRITAIN A.D. 400–800

Ewan Campbell

There is abundant archaeological evidence which shows that Celtic Britain and Ireland were not isolated from the mainstream developments of continental Europe in the 'Dark Ages', here taken to be the period *ca* A.D. 400–800. This physical evidence, consisting mainly of pottery and glass imported from the Mediterranean and north-western Europe, can be shown to be the result of regular and sustained maritime-trading connections which would have provided a ready-access route for more perishable cargoes such as manuscripts, textiles and, of course, people carrying their knowledge and beliefs. Although the physical evidence is almost entirely for the movement of goods from abroad to Britain, the importance of the necessary reflux of shipping in exposing continental Europe to British and particularly Irish culture should not be forgotten, though it is outside the scope of this chapter.[1]

The Celtic west, unlike Anglo-Saxon England, has virtually no documentary evidence which throws any light on the economic basis for, or mechanisms of, these trading-contacts, and consequently the archaeological interpretation of the evidence is essentially of a pre-historic nature. Some comments on the apparent differences, in terms of economic development, between the two areas will be made in the final section of this chapter, after a discussion of the imports in the 'Celtic' areas.

The imported pottery and glass can be divided into two groups, each with distinct regions of provenance and chronological range, and each having different distributions in Insular contexts. The earlier of these groups comprises Mediterranean pottery, mainly from the Aegean area but with a smaller component from North Africa, while the later group is composed of pottery and glass from north-western Europe. These two groups of imports, here for convenience termed the 'Mediterranean' and the 'Continental', are the products of quite different trading-systems, each of which

---

[1]   See, for instance, Whitelock *et al.*, *Ireland.*

has potentially different socio-economic bases. It is important to look at the imports in terms of these two general trading-systems rather than in terms of particularised distributions of individual types of pottery, as it is the history of these systems which may give some insight into the changing economic conditions within north-west Europe in the immediately post-Roman centuries.

In the absence of any documentary evidence for the identity of merchants, types of cargo, or trade-routes, any interpretation based solely on the provenance of the imports must be simplistic. Recent work on the documentary evidence for trade in the later mediaeval period has shown that the routes taken by pottery between its production area and eventual findspots were affected by complex patterns of cabotage trade, warehousing and re-export.[2] There cannot be an *a priori* assumption that pottery imports from a given source indicate direct trade with that area, though evidence will be presented which suggests that such direct links did exist in the Dark Ages.

The view of imported material presented here is a brief summary of the conclusions of a detailed study of all the imported pottery and glass from Dark Age sites in Britain and Ireland.[3] This study included analyses of the typology, chronology, taphonomy and function of the imports along with a comparative study of the sites and contexts in which they are found. Previous work has tended to concentrate on discussing problems of chronology and provenance, and in listing examples of different types of ware.[4]

The Mediterranean imports

The Mediterranean imports consist of a variety of types of amphorae and fine red-slipped tablewares, many of which recent research has succeeded in localising. The major production-area in terms of imports to Britain was the north-east Mediterranean, which produced the following amphora types: Bi, with its distinctive combed decoration, from the Argolid region of Greece; Bii, with tegulated ribbing, possibly from a number of sources around Asia Minor; and Biv, small micaceous *lagaenae* from the Sardis area of western Turkey. This last area also produced Phocaean Red Slipware dishes, often decorated with rouletting and stamped zoomorphic or religious motifs.

The amphorae are not closely datable in themselves, as similar forms tended to be produced over several centuries, and fabric differences indicate

---

[2] Allan, 'Some post-medieval'; Evans, 'Reflections'.
[3] For full details of the evidence presented here see Campbell, *Imported*; 'Trade'.
[4] For example Thomas, 'Imported pottery'; 'Imported Late-Roman'; *A Provisional List*.

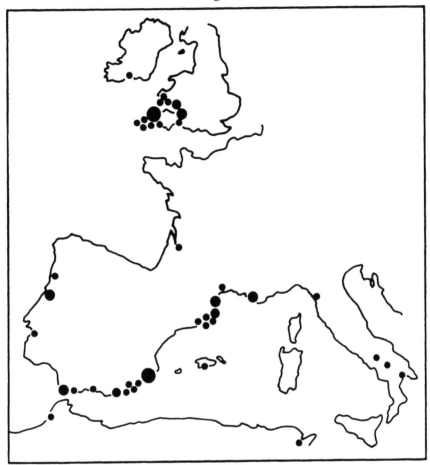

*Figure 1. Distribution of Phocaean Red Slipware in western Europe.
Size of symbol proportional to number of vessels.*

a number of production-centres for each 'type'.[5] However, these four wares
form a 'package' of pottery types which are found in association with each
other in areas outside the eastern Mediterranean, such as Iberia and Britain.
This enables the whole package to be dated from the fine slipwares whose
chronology is well established.[6]

In Britain the Phocaean Red Slipware gives a maximum date-range for
the Aegean imports of A.D. 475–550, with a *floruit* in the first quarter of
the sixth century. Small numbers of amphorae and finewares produced in

5 In Britain there is wide variation in the Bii fabric and at least two Biv fabrics, while at
least four Biv fabrics are known in the Mediterranean (G. Sanders, pers. comm.).
6 Using the chronology of Hayes, *Late Roman*.

the Carthage region of North Africa are also found in Britain, although in any quantity only on the key site of Tintagel, Cornwall. These can be dated, again by the finewares, to the second quarter of the sixth century.[7]

A number of questions are raised by the presence of these Mediterranean wares in Britain: are the imports the result of trade or merely casual contact; if it is trade, was this direct contact with the eastern Mediterranean; and what commodities were being exported from Britain? The only means of answering these questions lies in an analysis of the distributions and site-occurrences of the imports.

An overall view of the distribution pattern of the Aegean group of imports, outside of the eastern Mediterranean, where they are widespread, has to be based on occurrences of the distinctive Phocaean Red Slipware dishes, as the amphorae have not tended to receive critical study until recent years (Figure 1). The distribution shows three major concentrations, in north-east and south-east Spain, and in south-west Britain, with a scatter of occurrences around the Atlantic coast of Iberia. What is important about this distribution is that the number of vessels from British and Spanish sites is of the same order of magnitude, although the Spanish sites are considerably closer to the source of the pottery. This type of distribution differs from the normal case where the number of vessels diminishes in relation to distance from source, and clearly shows that contact was directed at these specific areas in Spain and Britain. This in itself is evidence for trade rather than casual contact, and this is reinforced by the fact that the Aegean package of wares is found on most of the sites where Phocaean Red Slipware is found. If the distribution of these wares was the product of some form of coastal 'tramping' trade one would expect a variety of mixed wares to be carried, with local products picked up *en route* gradually replacing the Aegean wares at increasing distance from the production-area. The coherence of the Aegean package of wares at sites such as Tintagel or Dinas Powys (Glamorgan), some three thousand kilometres from their source, is clear evidence of direct trading-contact between the areas. This conclusion is supported by the work of Michael Fulford who advances a historical explanation for this expansion of trading from the eastern Mediterranean, relating it initially to a relaxation of Imperial control following the Vandal invasions of Iberia and North Africa, and coming to an end with Justinian's reconquest of the area in the mid-sixth century.[8] Trade implies regular contact, but it has been argued that the small quantity of Aegean imports in Britain resulted from no more than a single voyage of an adventurous, or wayward, Byzantine merchant-vessel.[9] This argument is based on the evidence of the Yassi Ada wreck excavated from a site near Bodrum,

---

7 Using the chronology of Fulford and Peacock, *Excavations*.
8 Fulford, 'Byzantium'.
9 Alcock, *Economy*, p. 90.

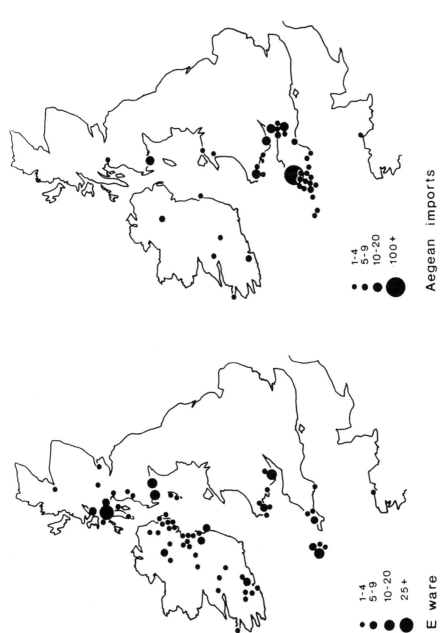

Aegean imports

1-4
5-9
10-20
100 +

E ware

1-4
5-9
10-20
25 +

Figure 2. Comparison of distribution of Mediterranean and Continental imported pottery vessels.

Turkey, which was an early seventh-century trading-vessel carrying a cargo of many hundred Bi and Bii amphorae.[10] However there is abundant evidence from other wrecks in the Mediterranean that pottery was never more than a minor component of cargoes[11] and it can be assumed that other, higher value and more perishable, wares such as silks were the main item of trade. The stratigraphical evidence from Carthage, at least, shows that there was a considerable and continuing volume of trade with the eastern Mediterranean throughout the period in question.[12] The date-ranges of the forms of Phocaean and African Red Slipware found in Britain span a considerable period, which, even stretching the known limits to their extremes, could not have occupied a time span of less than A.D. 500–525, showing that trade must have been a continuing process. In total, this evidence points to a regular and sustained maritime-trade between the Byzantine empire and south-western Britain in the early sixth century, a trade which was an extension of attested large-scale commercial contacts with North Africa and Iberia.

Whatever encouraged Byzantine merchants to leave the relative security of the Mediterranean basin to venture across the Bay of Biscay, the dynamic must have been a search for particular commodities to import, rather than for new outlets for eastern products, otherwise there would have been no need to travel as far as Britain. The only indication of what was being sought lies in the detailed distribution of the imports in Britain (Figure 2). There are two concentrations, one in Cornwall, and the other in Somerset with outlying sites along the South Wales coast, and a scatter further north which represent redistribution from centres in the south-west. These concentrations coincide so closely with areas of metalliferous deposits, stream-tin in Cornwall, and lead/silver ores in the Mendips, that the search for these metals must be assumed to be the driving force behind the Byzantine trade.

A number of other lines of evidence support this conclusion. There is now scientific evidence that tin was being produced in Cornwall at this period, and this is almost the sole area in Europe, North Africa or the Near East.[13] There is some evidence for production in Brittany and further Byzantine imports can be expected in this area to supplement the single findspot known at present.[14] Isotope analysis of metal objects from Carthage has shown the presence of British lead in a few items, suggesting that lead was indeed carried back to the Mediterranean.[15] Lead, although not as rare as tin, is not a common metal in the Mediterranean region and it was

10 Bass and van Doornick, *Yassi Ada*.
11 Parker, 'Shipwrecks'.
12 Fulford and Peacock, *Excavations*, pp. 258–62.
13 Penhallurick, *Tin*, pp. 212, 234.
14 Fleuriot and Giot, 'Early Brittany', p. 114; Giot and Querre, 'Le tesson'.
15 Farquhar and Vitali, 'Lead isotope'.

probably worth collecting having made the voyage to Britain primarily for tin. It is possible that other metals, such as copper and gold from Ireland, were also collected but there is no evidence for this other than outliers of Byzantine imports in the Cork region. Tin cannot be considered as a precious metal in this period, but it was necessary for the production of bronze, brass and pewter items, including low denomination coinage, and its scarcity would have attracted the attention of merchants, and possibly even imperial procurators of minerals.

The implications of this suggested trading-pattern are considerable. In return for these British metals[16] Byzantine merchants would have supplied amphorae containing wine, olive oil, and a host of other exotic commodities, as well as the other perishable items mentioned above. A sustained trade would have provided a route for travellers and it is possibly no coincidence that the introduction of cenobitic monasticism to the relevent parts of the south-west of Britain may coincide with the date of the earliest imports.[17] The influence of the Byzantine art-motifs of the stamped pottery on contemporary design in Britain and Ireland has been described by Charles Thomas.[18] In social terms the concentration of imports on fortified sites such as Tintagel, Cadbury Congresbury, Dinas Powys and South Cadbury illustrate a concentration of political power which may be related to control over the export of the metals sought by overseas merchants. The emergence of these forts from the obscure conditions of the immediate post-Roman period again seems to coincide with the arrival of the first imports, although in this case a direct connection is unlikely as forts also appear in areas outside the south-west. However, it is arguably only in south-west England that these forts do not survive into the seventh century and it can be argued further that the sudden removal of the market for metals may have led to a breakdown in the social ties which had been built on control of access to foreign luxuries, with a subsequent collapse of central authority. While in other British areas kingdoms developed throughout the pre-Norman period, there is little evidence for centralised kingship in Dumnonia after the sixth century.

The concept of a tin-trade between the Mediterranean and south-west Britain is of course not a new idea, and it follows on from the putative prehistoric trade documented in early textual sources, and from the known Roman-period exploitation of the same resources. The evidence for a discrete period of this trade in the sixth century now seems undeniable, and the consequences perhaps more wide-ranging than has been appreciated in the past.

---

16 It is surely no coincidence that tin was referred to as 'the British metal' in a seventh-century Egyptian document according to Penhallurick, *Tin*, p. 237.

17 Olson, *Early Monasteries*, p. 105, although France is a more likely source..

18 Thomas, 'The earliest'.

The Continental imports

The Continental group of imports consists of black-slipped tablewares, white coarseware containers and tableware, and glass drinking-vessels. Unlike the Mediterranean imports no production-sites have been discovered, and therefore the chronology and provenance of the wares are still matters of debate, but again two sub-phases of importation can be distinguished, the earlier of D-ware and glass, the later of E-ware and glass.

The earlier phase includes black-slipped greywares, formerly known as Tintagel Class D-ware, comprising of mortaria, stamped and rouletted shallow dishes and rarer bowls along with glass vessels, mainly drinking beakers. The D-ware, which is ultimately of Late Roman origin and the *derivées sigillées paléochrétiennes* of French authors, can be shown to belong to the Atlantic Group defined by Rigoir. This is believed to have been produced in the Bordeaux area, although other production-centres in the Loire valley and elsewhere are likely.[19] These wares can be broadly dated to the sixth century, but are so rare on British sites that they will not be discussed further here.

The glass vessels until recently have been of even more problematic origin.[20] They consist mainly of conical drinking-beakers, often decorated with opaque white decoration in the form of horizontal bands or sometimes vertical-running chevrons, with occasional bowls. The glass is of high quality, usually colourless or pale yellow, but with a few deeply coloured green, blue, brown and red vessels. Apart from a few vessels of distinctively Anglo-Saxon manufacture,[21] these glass vessels are not matched in the extensive collections of glass vessels from pagan Anglo-Saxon graves, or from Frankish cemeteries in northern France or the Rhineland. Recent evidence from Bordeaux has shown manufacture of glass vessels from the Late Roman period to the seventh centuries, with similar types of glass being produced.[22] It is, therefore, likely that much of the imported glass comes from this region of western France. In distribution and stratigraphical context it is associated with D-ware, but also with and E-ware, and can be assigned to the same date-range, with a *floruit* in the sixth century but continuing into the seventh. The Insular distribution is similar to that of E-ware except that it overlaps into south-western areas, supporting the suggestion that some of the glass pre-dates E-ware and the desertion of the major south-western fort-sites (Figure 3).

---

19 Rigoir *et al.*, 'Les derivées'; S. Soulas pers. comm.
20 For a recent discussion and division into groups see Campbell, 'A Review'; 'New Evidence'.
21 Campbell, 'A blue'.
22 Foy and Hochuli-Gysel, 'Le verre', fig. 14.

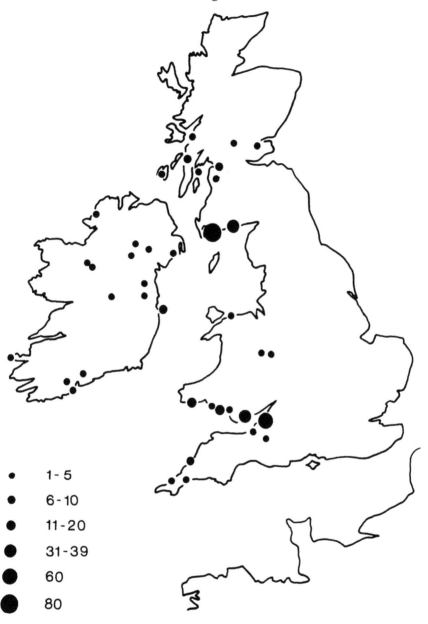

●	1- 5
●	6-10
●	11-20
●	31-39
●	60
●	80

Figure 3. Distribution of imported Contental glass vessels.

The most widespread of all the post-Roman imports is Thomas's Class E-ware, a coarsely-gritted plain white or grey ware, which consists mainly of jars and beakers with lesser amounts of jugs and bowls. The vessel-forms are of Frankish derivation of the type found widely in the Merovingian cemeteries of France, but the particular fabric and vessel-forms are unrepresented in the collections from these cemeteries. A combination of geological and typological evidence suggests a source in one of three areas: the lower Seine around Rouen; the lower Loire valley or Vendée; or the Charente. A wide variety of evidence from Britain and Ireland combines to show that E-ware was traded from the later sixth to late seventh centuries, with a *floruit* in the early seventh century. The Insular distribution, concentrating on coastal sites around the Irish Sea and western Scotland, lies mainly to north of the earlier Mediterranean imports, with overlap only along the South Wales coast (Figure 2). The seventy or so sites have produced more than two hundred E-ware vessels.

Before the author's study of the Continental imports, E-ware was considered to be a 'robust kitchenware', imported to alleviate a lack of locally-produced cooking-ware,[23] while the glass was considered to be scrap intended for use as cullet.[24] Neither of these views can be upheld after detailed examination of the vessels. Examination of sooting patterns and internal deposits shows that the commonest E-ware vessels, the jars, were not used primarily as cooking vessels, but as general purpose containers for a variety of commodities. There was, however, sporadic secondary recycling of the empty jars for a variety of purposes. In this sense they are the equivalent of the earlier amphorae in not being imported as pottery but as ancillary containers. The commodities traded, in general, can only be guessed at, but scientific analysis of the interiors of a few vessels has revealed the presence of a reddish purple dyestuff derived from Dyer's madder (*Rubia tinctorum*), a plant not native to Britain.[25] Contemporary Irish textual sources mention other foreign commodities which might have been carried in these vessels: honey, spices, exotic nuts, and sweetmeats.[26] Recent corroboration of this hypothesis comes from two Scottish sites which have produced seeds of coriander and dill, plants known to have been produced on royal estates in Aquitaine around A.D. 800, in contexts associated with madder-stained E-ware.[27] However, as with the Mediterranean imports, these goods were probably a minor part of any cargo, which would have consisted of bulk commodities such as salt and/or

[23] Thomas, *A Provisional*, p. 20. Most of the Celtic areas were aceramic throughout the pre-Norman period.
[24] Alcock, *Dinas Powys*, pp. 52–3.
[25] Analysis by Penelope Walton Rogers, Textile Research Associates, York.
[26] James, *The Franks*, p. 189 ; O'Mahaney and Richey, *Ancient Laws*, p. 427.
[27] Buston crannog, A. Crone, pers. comm; Whithorn Priory, P. Hill, pers. comm.

wine. Both of these were major exports from western France in the later mediaeval period. There is one written reference which might refer to the E-ware trading-system, a charter of St-Denis Abbey, Paris, which mentions the export of wine, madder and honey.[28] This charter purports to be of the early seventh century, but although it is almost certainly a forgery of the ninth century some features suggest it may be based on an earlier document. Whatever the date, the interesting feature is the mention of three commodities possibly involved in the E-ware trade and the confirmation that madder was exported from France in the early Merovingian period.

As far as the glass is concerned, detailed examination of the abundant material from Dinas Powys has shown that sherds from individual vessels are found in discrete stratigraphical and distributional groupings. This enables some vessels to be reconstructed sufficiently to show that they must have been broken on the site and in use as complete vessels. Other evidence shows that the sherds from these vessels were collected and melted down, but this was recycling of material broken on site rather than material specially imported as sherds. Similar evidence is now known from Cadbury Congresbury and Whithorn, and it must be assumed that the glass sherds found on other Celtic sites could also be derived from complete vessels. The conical beakers did not have a large capacity, and would have been used to drink the wine which, it is suggested, was imported as part of the E-ware trading-system. There are, of course, numerous references in the 'Celtic' literature to royal feasting-halls where wine was drunk from glass vessels.[29] In recent years these references have been viewed either as anachronisms or poetic licence, but the archaeological evidence now shows that this need not be so, and we can reinstate the Celtic aristocracy into their richly-coloured garments, and restore to them their foreign wines drunk from glass vessels.

Unlike the Mediterranean imports, the later imports are not directed at any specific region, giving no indication of the nature of the commodities exchanged for the imports except that they must have been widespread and organic. There are a few contemporary textual sources which suggest possibilities such as finished leather-goods,[30] but otherwise one can only speculate on the inclusion of items such as furs and slaves. Archaeological evidence indicates large-scale production of leather-goods at sites with

---

28 *Monumenta Germania Historica, Diplomatum Imperii 1* (ed. Pertz, p. 140). Professor John Percival, U.W.C. Cardiff, kindly supplies the following translation of the relevant passage in a difficult text: 'And may you our *missi* know from this market [St-Denis] and at all the cities in our kingdom, especially at Rothomo port [Rouen] and Wicus port [Quentovic], those who come from beyond the sea to buy wines and honey or *garantia* [madder] . . .'

29 Jackson, *Gododdin*, pp. 34–5.

30 Finely decorated leather shoes and satchels are known from Celtic contexts. For the documentary evidence see James, 'Ireland and western Gaul'.

E-ware such as Dinas Powys, and Loch Glashan, Argyll, lending some
support to the documentary evidence.

The only specific references to the identity of the traders mention Gallic
merchants in Scotland and Irish ships at the mouth of the Loire. This might
suggest a two-way trade, but consideration of the ceramic evidence supports
the view that the E-ware trading-system was controlled by Merovingian
merchants. The forms and fabric of E-ware are so consistent that a single
source area is indicated. If 'Celtic' merchants were visiting the Continent,
a wide variety of imported pottery-types would be expected to occur,
showing contact with a variety of regions.[31] While there may well have been
two-way contact, the goods associated with E-ware are likely to have been
exported from one specific area of France, under the control of local
merchants.

Celtic and Anglo-Saxon economies

Any discussion of trade in the 'Celtic' west must include a consideration of
the economic system which produced the surplus necessary to sustain the
trade, and here it is illuminating to contrast the developing economy of
Anglo-Saxon England with that of the western areas. It is generally assumed, though rarely articulated, that the 'Celtic' areas were economically
undeveloped, and there is evidence to support this view in the lack of the
coin-based market-economy, towns, or merchant classes found in Middle
Saxon England.[32] Where these appeared in the west it was only under the
influence of Norse, or later Norman, intruders. However, in the sixth and
seventh centuries a different picture emerges, and one which has tended to
be ignored in general accounts of the period.[33]

In the early sixth century, as we have seen, there was a sustained maritime
trade between the Mediterranean centre of the Byzantine empire and
south-western Britain. This trade was linked to the control of exploitation
of mineral resources, and their concentration at fortified centres. As a
society undoubtedly with some literate members, this trade made western
areas open to influences of religion, art and thought contemporary with
those at the heart of the Empire. In contemporary Anglo-Saxon England
there were also Mediterranean imports such as bronze Byzantine bowls,

[31] At Middle Saxon Southampton almost one hundred imported fabric types are recorded:
Timby, 'The Middle Saxon pottery'.
[32] For a recent view of the Anglo-Saxon economy see Hodges, *The Anglo-Saxon*. Doherty,
'Exchange', attempts to redress the balance as far as Ireland is concerned, but most of
his evidence relates to the eighth century or later.
[33] For example, the maps of trade to Britain in Hodges, *Dark Age*, Figure 5, omit the
contemporary western evidence entirely.

cowrie shells and amethyst beads,[34] but these arrived overland in piecemeal fashion and not by direct contact. There is as yet no comparable archaeological evidence for centralisation of trade or seats of power although, of course, this was the period of the emergence of the Anglo-Saxon kingdoms.

In the later sixth and seventh century the 'Celtic' west was again closely linked to a 'developed' economy, that of the emerging Carolingian empire, with a documented two-way contact particularly in the sphere of religion. As in the previous period, fortified political centres, which by now can be shown to be of royal status, controlled access to this foreign trade and redistributed the imports to their destinations. These centres show signs of craft specialisation, large-scale production, concentration of wealth in the form of gold and silver, control over substantial human and natural resources, and conspicuous consumption of luxury goods. Trade may have been articulated through a number of neutral island-sites such as Scilly, Dalkey Island, and possibly Caldey Island, but there are few signs of separate trading-emporia like the later Saxon *wics*. It would seems that all the ingredients for the development of a full-scale market-economy were in place at an early date, but that there was no further development.

In contemporary Anglo-Saxon England there is also contact with neighbouring areas of France, but distributions of items, such as pottery flasks, show this is mainly concentrated on Kent.[35] There is some distributional evidence for ports of trade under royal control, at sites such as Sarre and Dover, but as yet no archaeological evidence.[36] Coinage was beginning to be circulated and minted, but only as high-value gold coins unsuitable for market transactions. It is not until the end of the seventh century or early eighth century that economic development entered a new phase with the establishment of trading-centres at Hamwic, Ipswich, and London, the widespread use of silver coinage, and the regulation of trade by royal law-codes.[37]

From the later seventh century the two areas rapidly diverge in economic terms with Anglo-Saxon England developing a market-economy, while in the 'Celtic' areas the trading-functions of the royal sites, and much of the visible wealth, may have been transferred to monastic centres which were themselves badly disrupted by the Viking raids from the late eighth century onwards.[38]

There are many factors which may have contributed to these different paths of economic development: differences in quality of land; differences

---

34 Summarised recently by Huggett, 'Imported grave goods'.
35 Evison, *A Corpus.*
36 Hawkes, 'Anglo-Saxon Kent', p. 76.
37 Seventh-century evidence is sparse or lacking at all the known sites, see Brisbane, 'Hamwic'; Vince, 'The economic basis'; Wade, 'Ipswich'.
38 Doherty, 'Exchange'.

of scale in population and, therefore, in surplus production; or different social attitudes to the accumulation of capital. These may all have had some part in this pattern, although there is evidence to argue against this being significant,[39] but it seems possible that the major cause was a simple geographical one, related to the rise of the southern English *wics*. These were situated within a day's sailing of northern France, a far quicker and safer journey than the hazardous route around Land's End, through the Irish Sea and into the dangerous waters of western Scotland. It can be suggested therefore that the failure of western 'Celtic' areas to develop a full market-economy was due to their peripheral situation in relation to the economic 'core' of contemporary Europe, the Carolingian empire, and not to a lack of human, or natural resources. Nor should it be forgotten that despite this low level of economic development, eighth-century Ireland was perhaps the leading artistic and intellectual centre in north-west Europe.

[39] Campbell, *Imported*, p. 223.

VI

POST-ROMAN IMPORTS IN BRITAIN AND IRELAND: A MARITIME PERSPECTIVE *

A. Bowman

Imported Mediterranean fine wares and amphorae were first recognised in Britain and Ireland in the 1930s. In 1956 Radford discussed the imported pottery found in excavations at Tintagel, Cornwall.[1] In 1959 Thomas produced a revised distribution-map of known finds around the British Isles,[2] and this has since been updated.[3] The pottery has been classified systematically throughout Britain as shown in Figure 1.

On the basis of the provenance of the imported ceramics it is clear that the goods were transported by sea, or waterway, for at least a part of their journey, and it is also likely that, from time to time, vessels carrying such cargoes destined for Britain were wrecked on route. Parker has commented on the importance of wrecked cargoes, which offer a yardstick by which to judge the significance of trade-goods found in remains of rubbish or occupation on land.[4] He suggests that broad-based categories of information such as date, type of cargo, and location are enough to generalise about ancient cargoes. Using this hypothesis, the significance of the fifth- to seventh-century ceramic imports in Britain should not be discussed without first looking at contemporary wreck-cargoes in the area in which the material was produced and transported. Fulford has pointed out to me that wreck-evidence is not representative of the pattern of Mediterranean trade, which can be constructed from other sources. This should not, however, mean that we simply disregard this source of evidence. On the contrary, these data provide a crucial control of our interpretation of terrestrial assemblages and textual sources.

There are seventy-four recorded shipwrecks in the Mediterranean dating from the end of the fourth century to the end of the seventh century.[5] Little

---

* Paper written in 1992.
1 Radford, 'Imported Pottery'.
2 Thomas, 'Imported Pottery'.
3 Thomas, 'A Provisional List'.
4 Parker, 'Stratification and Contamination'.
5 Parker, personal communication, appendix and figure 2.

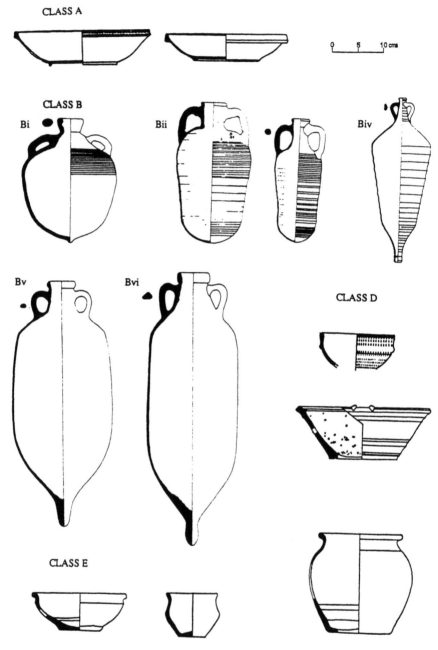

Figure 1. Imported pottery types.

98

is known about many of these. The two ships found at Punta Secca in Italy, for example, had apparently been abandoned and contained no cargo.[6] Few of the wrecks have been completely, or well, excavated. Exceptions include the two wrecks at Yassi Ada, Turkey, of which one is early seventh-century, the other the late fourth-century.[7] A comprehensive study of Mediterranean wrecks, their cargoes, and significance for trade, is currently being carried out by Parker. This chapter is limited to those wrecks for which there is readily accessible information.

Known cargoes are principally of amphorae, with the exception of the wreck at Saint Gervais B, which was carrying wheat, and the 'church wreck' at Marzameni B, Sicily, so-called because it contained almost a complete set of elements for a Byzantine church.[8] There are also three examples of wrecks carrying metal ingots, and three with a cargo principally of roof-tiles. The wrecked vessel found at Taranto had been carrying grinding-stones. The wrecks at Pantano Longarini and Vendicari in Sicily, and Yassi Ada A and B in Turkey, all included amphorae equivalent to the British type Bi. Yassi Ada B also had examples of British Bii. I have been unable to identify any wrecks carrying Biv, Bv or Bvi amphorae, but this may be largely because the material has not been classified by fabric or form. Pottery-types similar to class A (African Red Slipware [ARSW] and Phocaean Red Slipware [PRSW]) have been found at Yassi Ada A and B.

The distribution of wrecks from 400–700 in the Mediterranean shown in Figure 2 seems to reflect the distribution of contemporary amphora types on land.[9] They occur in the Black Sea, and around the Greek islands and Turkey. There are also significant concentrations around Sicily and off the south coast of France, but surprisingly few off north Africa. This is prob-ably, in part, a reflection of the distribution of archaeologists and divers, and Bv amphorae have been found widely in north Africa on land.

It should be noted, when interpreting the distributions of imported ceramics in Britain and Ireland, that the numbers of actual vessels repre-sented at any one site, to date, is very small – typically one or two vessels. Even at Tintagel where extensive excavation over fifty years has probably produced sherds representing somewhere in the region of one hundred to two hundred vessels (the exact figure following the recent excavations is not available), this number falls far short of a typical Mediterranean cargo of Byzantine amphorae. Wreck A at Yassi Ada, for example, produced eight hundred to nine hundred amphorae. This evidence has been used in the past

---

6 Parker, 'Method and Madness'.
7 Bass and Van Doorninck, 'A Fourth Century Shipwreck'; *Yassi Ada*.
8 Käpitan, 'The Church Wreck'.
9 Fulford, 'Pottery'.

to argue a minimalist view of the number of voyages necessary to explain the amount of pottery found.[10] This need not be the case.

Fulford has demonstrated that even a few sherds of pottery can be an index of a large-scale trade.[11] For example, there is only scattered ceramic evidence for the movement of goods across the North Sea in the middle ages, but there is a historical case for a thriving trade in wool, cloth and foodstuffs, as Wooding shows in this volume.

Peacock has distinguished between pottery and amphorae as evidence of trade.[12] He sees pottery as an index of the frequency with which different routes were plied, but amphorae as a direct witness of trade in certain items. McGrail has argued that fine, ancient Greek pottery, transported for economic and practical reasons, would have travelled only as a space-filler and not as a cargo, or ballast, in its own right.[13] Such a practice was evidently in operation in the cargo of the first-century wreck at Madrague de Giens. This may also be the case for the class A pottery, but Thomas suggests that classes D and E may have been traded in their own right.[14]

On the other hand, one might expect a larger quantity of amphorae to be represented, since these, or rather their contents, were the object of trade, though not necessarily the primary one. In fact, larger quantities of amphorae than pottery are found as imports in fifth- to seventh-century Britain and Ireland. Of the minimum number of vessels recorded by Thomas in 1981, 41.5% were of class B, 37% class E, 16% class A, and 5.5% class D. The low percentage of classes A and D wares suggests that these may have been travelling only as space-fillers. Class E is slightly anomalous and should be treated separately, since it may not be contemporaneous with the other wares. Of course, amphorae might be reused several times and this would reduce the amount likely to become incorporated into the archaeological record. It is necessary, therefore, to think more carefully about the depositional context of ceramics on archaeological sites, when discussing their use as indicators of trade.

The quantity of post-Roman imported wares recovered from archaeological sites has increased considerably, and as the recent excavations at Whithorn show, more sites will doubtless yield this material in future. It is difficult, therefore, at this stage to know the significance of the quantity of material recovered and the intensity of trade it reflects. Fulford pointed out that no terrestrial assemblage, Iberian or Frankish, or in the western Mediterranean generally, has ratios of eastern Mediterranean amphorae, or Phocaean Red Slipware and African Red Slipware, to match those found in

---

[10] Thomas, '*Gallicae Nautae*'.
[11] Fulford, 'Pottery'.
[12] Peacock, *Pottery in the Roman World*.
[13] McGrail, 'The Shipment'.
[14] See above, note 3.

western Britain.[15] This difference, however, is perhaps because there was no other local ceramic tradition to compete with the imports. In my opinion, it would be more useful to compare estimated numbers of vessels present, rather than comparing the percentage of different types within the whole assemblage.

The frequency of trade might be limited by the sailing season in operation in the ancient Mediterranean. The *Codex Theodosius* (13.9.3) written in *ca* A.D. 380, and addressed to the shippers of Africa, allowed trade only between 13 April and 15 October.[16] From November to April navigation was suspended. Moreover, the speed and nature of a journey would limit the number of voyages carried out in each year. Casson calculated that a speed of two to six knots per hour could be realised (depending on the favourability of the wind and weather) based on written records of the length of journeys.[17] For example, it was possible to complete the journey between Ostia and Africa, a distance of 270 nautical miles, in two days. Nevertheless, the evidence seems to indicate that a return journey from, for example, Turkey to south-west Britain would take at least half of the sailing season to complete.

Parker shows that there is a general trend towards smaller ships in the Late Roman to post-Roman period.[18] By the fourth century, in both the west and east Mediterranean, ships were being built with a greater reliance on iron-bolt and nail-fastenings rather than the laborious mortise and tenon jointing (for example, La Luque B and Yassi Ada A). He sees this evolution as a result of a decline in the volume, and probably the profitability, of trade, although it may simply indicate change in the organisation of trade to conduct more and shorter journeys.

All of this would suggest that a regular, direct trade between the eastern Mediterranean and Britain is unlikely. Either goods changed hands when journeys were occasionally made for social or diplomatic reasons, or different routes and mechanisms of trade were in operation.

The distribution of wreck-sites and of pottery- and amphorae-types in the Mediterranean gives some indication of the routes by which the material may have travelled. There is a single wreck-site in the Straits of Gibraltar, but this is so badly preserved it is of little use in determining where it was travelling to or from, or what it was carrying. There is more substantial evidence for the use of the route overland from the south of France, with a cluster of nine wrecks in the vicinity of Marseilles. Fulford also suggested that African amphorae were transported across France to Bordeaux whence

---

[15] Fulford, 'Byzantium and Britain'; personal communication.
[16] Casson, *Ships and Seamanship*.
[17] *Ibid.*
[18] Parker, 'Classical Antiquity'.

they were shipped to Britain, and this might explain the introduction to Britain of D and E wares.[19]

It is, therefore, unlikely that Mediterranean pottery found in Britain and Ireland is a result of trade-voyages direct from the eastern Mediterranean. All of the pottery may easily have derived solely from contact with France, the pottery here being obtained from the south of France, where there was contact with, for example, north Africa, Italy or eastern Spain. Individual voyages would, therefore, be shorter and trade might continue throughout the year. Such a trade-mechanism might explain why ships were generally smaller and more lightly built in the late and post-Roman period.

Such a system of transhipment was in operation throughout the Roman empire and was used for military supplies and administrative communications, as well as for commercial traffic.[20]

Rutilius's *De Reditio Suo* gives an account of a coasting voyage in this period. Such evidence is also backed up by archaeological artefact distributions and finds of river craft and harbour-sites. This hypothesis is substantiated by the lack of western Iberian ceramics in terrestrial assemblages in Britain, which on the Continent are commonly found in association with African Red Slipware and Phocaean Red Slipware. If vessels were travelling by the Straits of Gibraltar and up the western seaboard of the Iberian peninsula one would expect these wares to be found on board.[21]

It remains to be seen whether the appearance in Britain of ceramics from the eastern Mediterranean is the result of a 'directional trade' between producers and consumers, or whether the material was transferred independently between centres and eventually ended up in Britain.[22] There is certainly evidence in the Mediterranean of directional trade of, for example, Calabrian wine, which is supported by amphora finds on wrecks at Dramont F and Pian de Spille, Tarquina.[23]

Trade within the Mediterranean was clearly complex and this can be demonstrated by the evidence of two wrecks. The Saint Gervais B wreck was carrying a cargo of wheat, probably from Italy, Africa or Spain, and pitch from south-west Gaul. The pottery was east Mediterranean and the graffiti on the amphorae was Greek. Parker has suggested that this indicates that the cargo may well have been 'directed' but that Syrians were probably doing the carrying, and that they had evidently travelled a long distance. On the other hand, at the Byzantine wreck at Yassi Ada, Bass suggested that the vessel with its merchant-captain on board, plied its trade wherever it could. Trade here was opportunist rather than 'directed'. Millett has also

[19] Fulford, 'Pottery'.
[20] Milne, 'Maritime Traffic'.
[21] Millett, personal communication.
[22] Arthur, 'Some Observations'.
[23] *Ibid.*

noted that Mediterranean sea-captains were frequently of Greek, or east Mediterranean, origin and that this may help to explain why, even in cities like Naples, Greek remained the principal language throughout the Roman period.[24]

For the Late Roman period Fulford identified two main trade-routes between Britain and the Continent: the first between the Rhine and Thames estuaries and the second between Brittany and the Hampshire/Dorset coast.[25] The distribution in Britain of the Biv, Bv and Bvi amphorae around the Thames, as well as further afield, may indicate that the Rhine-route was still in operation but the sheer quantity of material from Cornwall suggests that there was also direct contact with one or more centres there. Such a centre might logically be on the south coast of Cornwall, but the volume of fifth- to sixth-century pottery from Tintagel, on the north coast, is outstanding, and the site, now interpreted as probably royal and secular rather than monastic, may have acted as a port from which material was redistributed. This mechanism can explain only the A, B, and D, wares since, as yet, no E-ware has been found at Tintagel. Interestingly, this ware has the widest distribution, especially in Ireland and Scotland, and it may be that this trade was under Irish (in part, at least, monastic) monopoly, as suggested by Irish textual sources.[26] It should, however, be noted that E-ware which dates to the second half of the sixth century, or later, probably post-dates the other wares and may relate to a change in the trading-networks.

It should not be assumed that the east Mediterranean pottery found in Britain got there as a result of commercial trade with the producers, or that it was the producers who were directing and/or carrying the goods. The material may have reached Britain as the outcome of a series of independent transactions.

Various routes for trading can be, and have been, identified using archaeological evidence found on land and underwater, and textual evidence. The significant of maritime archaeology lies in its ability to identify the mechanism by which goods were transported. It is often possible to identify who was directing, or carrying, the goods which eventually turn up in terrestrial assemblages. By distinguishing how these assemblages differ from the cargoes of which they were once a part it may, then, be possible to suggest how, where, and why, exchange was carried out.

---

[24] Millett, personal communication.
[25] Fulford, 'Pottery'.
[26] Breen, 'Some Documentary Evidence'.

Acknowledgments
I would like to thank Colin Martin, Toby Parker, Michael Fulford, Helena Hamerow, Martin Millett and Jeremy Taylor for commenting on an earlier draft of this paper. Toby Parker provided information on Mediterranean shipwrecks. Moraig Brown kindly drew Figure 2.

Appendix

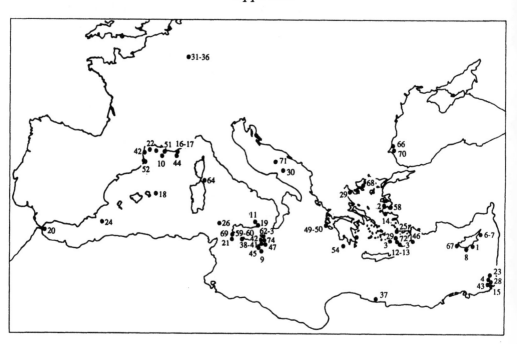

Figure 2. Mediterranean wrecks A.D. 400–700.

Mediterranean wrecks ca A.D. 400–700

This information is supplied by A. J. Parker unless otherwise stated. Size of ship is given as length, beam, and tonnage, where known.

Map Number	Name	Cargo, Date and Context
26	Isis	Amphorae (Spatheia, Roman unclassified and late Roman cylindrical types)
64	Sud-Lavezzi A	Maximum 450 amphorae (Almagro 50, Roman unclassified, Almagro 51A, Almagro 51C)
52	Port-Vendres A	Amphorae (Almagro 50 and 51C). Hull 18–20 x 8 Metres with an estimated capacity of 70–75 tons
70	Varna	Amphorae (Roman, unclassified)
73	Yassi Ada B	Amphorae (Roman, unclassified). Hull reconstructed 20 metres long
17	Dramont F	Amphorae (Late Roman cylindrical, Almagro 51A, Roman unclassified, and a single Calabrian amphora). The vessel has an estimated length of 10–12 x 4.5 metres. Excavated cargo only 3 tons.[27]
67	Plemmirio A	Copper and bronze goods. The condition and date of the wreck is unknown
31	Mainz B	No information available
32	Mainz C	No information available
33	Mainz D	No information available
34	Mainz E	No information available
35	Mainz F	No information available
36	Mainz G	No information available
23	Hof Ha Carmel B	Amphorae (Byzantine, unclassified)
21	Graham Bank B	Amphorae (Late Roman cylindrical)
42	Mateille A	Amphorae (Late Roman cylindrical, Almagro 51A and 51C), iron bars, copper and bronze goods, works of art
51	Port-Miou	Amphorae (Late Roman cylindrical), *terra sigillata*, lamps

[27] Arthur, 'Some Observations'.

16	Dramont E	Amphorae (Late Roman cylindrical, Spatheia), *terra sigillata*. The vessel was estimated at 15–18 x 5–6 metres
43	Newé Yam B	Amphorae (type unknown)
59	Rocca di San Nicola B	No information available
60	Rocca di San Nicola C	No information available
66	Tcerny Nos	Amphorae (Spatheia)
69	Triscina C	Amphorae (Spatheia, Late Roman cylindrical)
4	Caesarea B	Amphorae (Roman, unclassified)
30	Lostovo	Amphorae (Roman, unclassified)
11	Cefalu	Amphorae (Byzantine, globular; Byzantine, baluster shape). Timbers were preserved over an area 35 x 6 metres
55	Povile	Amphorae (Byzantine globular, Late Roman cylindrical)
24	Hormiga, Las	Amphorae (Late Roman cylindrical)
74	Vendicari	Amphorae (Spatheia, Byzantine globular, Byzantine unclassified)[28]
14	Delphinion	Amphorae (Byzantine, unclassified)
29	Kalithéa	Amphorae (Byzantine, unclassified)
49	Pomorje A	Roof-tiles
71	Vis E	Amphorae (Byzantine unclassified)
48	Plitharia	Amphorae (type unknown)
68	Iassos A	No information available
19	Filicudi Porto	Amphorae (Late Roman cylindrical)
38	Marzameni B	Marble architectural elements for a Byzantine church, tiles and bricks, pithos water reservoir[29]
12	Datça A	Amphorae (Byzantine globular)
3	Bozburun	Amphorae (Byzantine unclassified)
54	Porto Longo	Amphorae (Byzantine unclassified)
5	Cape Andreas A	Roof-tiles
9	Capo Passero	Roof-tiles scattered over an area 20 x 36 metres

[28] Parker, 'Stratification'.
[29] Käpitan, 'The Church Wreck'.

18	Favaritix	Metal ingots, works of art
65	Taranto A	Grinding-stones
20	Gibralter C	No information available
10	Carro A	Amphorae (type unknown)
53	Porto Cheli	Amphorae (Byzantine globular)
56	Prasso	Amphorae (Byzantine globular)
46	Pefkos	Amphorae (Byzantine globular, Byzantine unclassified)
7	Cape Andreas B	Amphorae (Byzantine unclassified)
7	Cape Andreas E	Amphorae (Baluster shape), other cargo
40	Marzameni K	Amphorae (Byzantine unclassified)
62	Siracusa B	Amphorae (Byzantine unclassified)
63	Siracusa C	Amphorae (Byzantine unclassified)
44	Palu, La	No information available
28	Israel	Pottery (unclassified)
39	Marzameni J	No information available
37	Marsa Lucch	No information available
1	Arwad B	Amphorae (Byzantine unclassified)
27	Iskandil Burnu A	Amphorae (Byzantine unclassified), coarseware. Vessel estimated at 20 x 5 metres
67	Thalassinies Spilies	Amphorae (Byzantine globular)
2	Ayios Stephanos	At least 1000 amphorae (Byzantine baluster shape, Byzantine unclassified) scattered over an area 24 x 12 metres
61	Saint Gervais B	Amphorae (Byzantine unclassified), grain (*Triticum speltum*), pitch and east Mediterranean painted pottery
45	Pantano Longarini	Several sherds of late Roman pottery under frames of hull. Estimated length 30 metres, capacity of 200–300 tons, built from Italian cyprus[30]

[30] Throckmorton and Throckmorton, 'The Roman Wreck'; Throckmorton and Käpitan, 'An Ancient Shipwreck'.

72	Yassi Ada A	850–900 amphorae (Byzantine globular, Byzantine baluster shape). Vessel reconstructed at 20.5 x 5.25 metres with a tonnage of 50–58 tons[31]
22	Grazel B	Copper and bronze goods
8	Cape Kiti A	Amphorae (Byzantine unclassified)
15	Dor	Amphorae (Byzantine unclassified)
6	Cape Andreas C	Amphorae (Byzantine unclassified)
57	Punta Secca A	Hull only. Byzantine date[32]
58	Punta Secca B	Hull only. Byzantine date[33]
13	Datça B	Amphorae (Byzantine globular, Byzantine baluster shape)

[31] Bass and Van Doorninck, *Yassi Ada*.
[32] Parker, 'Method and Madness'.
[33] *Ibid.*

VII

SEASONED WITH SALT:
INSULAR-GALLIC CONTACTS IN
THE EARLY MEMORIAL STONES AND CROSS SLABS

Jeremy Knight

It might be thought a measure of the native perversity of the Welsh, the Irish, and the southern Scots, that three hundred years of either close proximity to the Roman Empire, or actual incorporation within its frontier regions, seems to have had little effect on their tribal society. Within a century, at most, after the end of Roman rule, some among them were putting up tombstones with inscriptions in a home-made Irish alphabet, or in Latin: they were also importing amphorae of oil, wine, or other goods, and feasting from pottery from Gaul or the Mediterranean. Within the Roman period the impact, of what a more Imperial generation called 'romanisation', seems to have been slight. Although there have been claims of a sustained commercial traffic, most of the Roman coins and small objects found in Ireland are probably recent losses. They include, for example, Alexandrian pieces which never circulated in the West in ancient times, and other coins which may be recent imports from Britain, or from Rome itself. There is also a striking absence of Roman coarse pottery.[1]

However, once this static, or background noise, of uncertain chance-finds is removed, we get a much clearer signal from material with reliable archaeological associations in hoards or burials, reflecting, for example, the repercussions of events like Roman military activity in north Britain under Agricola and Antoninus Pius. For the very Late Roman period there are the hoards of silver *siliquae* and hacksilver from Ballinrees (Co. Derry) and Balline (Co. Limerick), the former including fragments of a silver-gilt military belt-set of exceptional quality.[2] There are also the coins, including gold *solidi*, offered to whatever deity was supposed to reside in the chambered tomb at New Grange.[3] At Dalkey island, near Dublin, Late Roman North African amphorae, recently recognised by Ewan Campbell, may

---

1 Bateson, 'Roman material' and 'Further finds'. Compare Casey, 'Roman coinage' for Scotland.
2 Mattingley and Pearce, 'The Coleraine hoard'.
3 Dolley 'Roman coins'. Bateson, 'Roman material', pp. 46–7.

represent an early phase of a coastal trading-emporium.[4] The influx of silver, gold, and other valuable goods, such as slaves, could have acted as a catalyst on Irish society, particularly on its élite, and, reinforced by the Irish settlement in Dyfed, initiated a process of change which included the beginnings of literacy.

Wales and southern Scotland had been controlled in the first and early second centuries by a network of Roman auxiliary forts, but they were now a thing of the very distant past. Where post-Roman Latin or ogom inscriptions occur on such sites, they are of great interest as evidence of early mediaeval re-occupation of Roman forts, but have little to do with the Roman past. The seventh-century memorial of Catacus, son of Tegernacus, from the fort of Pen-y-Gaer, Breconshire[5] is now at Llanvihangel Cwmdu church, but when Colt Hoare drew it in 1803, it was lying in a field outside the fort.[6] There had been no Roman garrison at Pen-y-Gaer since the time of Hadrian. A similar discontinuity is evident in the epigraphic record. The Roman tombstones from sites such as London, Caerleon or Bath are heavily weighted towards the first and second centuries, and to the army, the civil service, and resident foreigners. Of the Late Roman type, reading *Memoriae* or *Dis Manibus et Memoriae*, so common in Gaul, there are only three or four in Britain, compared with, for example, at least 170 from Lugdunensis Prima alone.[7] Only, perhaps, on Hadrian's Wall and its hinterland were there Late Roman monumental masons who might have been able to pass on their craft to post-Roman times. It would seem that the Class 1 inscriptions of western Britain were a fresh post-Roman introduction.

The earliest phase of the insular memorial-stone sequence is presumably that of the Irish ogom stones, which must pre-date the ready accessibility of Latin literacy from British Christian slaves like Patrick. There are plenty of examples of the invention of alphabets by members of native, learned classes in areas on the fringes of nineteenth-century European literacy, like West Africa, or among the North American Indians.[8] It has often been suggested that ogom might be based on a system of wooden tally-sticks or the like, perhaps like the yew-wood staffs with short Runic texts known from Frisia.[9] Perhaps one day, an Irish wetland site may produce the ogom equivalent of the writing-tablets from Springmount Bog (Co. Antrim),[10] or (in another medium) the fragment of mudstone from Traprain Law with part of a Latin alphabet scratched on it (R.I.B. 2131). My main concern is not

---

4 Edwards, *The Archaeology*, pp. 69–71; Campbell, this volume.
5 Nash-Williams, *The Early Christian Monuments*, no. 54.
6 Thompson, *The Journeys*, p. 238.
7 Audin and Burnand, 'Alla ricerca', 'Chronologie des épitaphes'.
8 Kroeber, *Anthropology*, pp. 344–57.
9 Elliot, *Runes*, plates IV–VIII.
10 Armstrong and Macalister, 'Wooden book'.

with the origin of ogam, but with the Latin memorial-stone sequence. However, it might be easier to understand the continental borrowings like the *Hic Iacet* formula if they are seen not simply as Gallic imports, but as something grafted on to an existing tradition.

Nash-Williams showed that the *Hic Iacet* formula goes back to a Gallic prototype of the second quarter of the fifth century, which can be dated, at least in the Rhône Valley where many of the memorial-stones bear consular dates,[11] but there is now no need to follow Nash-Williams in deriving the insular series from Lyonnais, for *Hic Iacet* inscriptions occur far more widely in Gaul, including areas like the Bordelais, Aquitaine, and the Vendée, where direct contact with Britain is geographically more likely. The idea of a link between the insular churches and that of Lyon had its roots in Victorian church-history, where it did away with the need to derive the British churches from Rome.[12] Apart from three problematical, possibly third-century, inscriptions, the main Christian epigraphic sequence from Gaul begins with a lost stone of A.D. 334 from Lyon (I.C.G. 62, C.I.L. XIII, 2351). There are about ten to a dozen fourth-century Christian stones from Gaul. They are well represented in Aquitaine, but there is nothing like them in Britain. The series ends in 405, on the eve of the great invasions of 406–407.

Our insular *Hic Iacet* series derives from the succeeding and separate phase, probably of north Italian inspiration, where a two-figure, or two-word formula, like *Hic Iacet* or *Hic Requiescit*, stands at the head of the text as an initial formula. Five from Lyon have consular dates from A.D. 422–449; elsewhere in Gaul consular dates are rare at this time. Another inscription from Lyon, of A.D. 454, introduces the next phase, of broadly A.D. 450–480, using 'four-figure' formulae like *Hic Requiescit In Pace*. If the Insular series does not derive directly from the Lyonnais, these stones can no longer be used to date the former directly, other than as a general *terminus post quem*, and as we have seen, the *Hic Iacet* formula itself may not mark the beginning of the insular series. The *filius* inscriptions of Dyfed and Dumnonia are heavily influenced by the ogom series and are, indeed, often bilingual. As Bu'lock pointed out, there is a distributional contrast between these and the *Hic Iacet* stones, which are the dominant tradition in Gwynedd.[14] Both, however, are centred on the unromanised west and north, again emphasising the discontinuity with any surviving Romano-British tradition. The romanised south-east, where there is evidence of organised

---

11 Nash-Williams, *The Early Christian Monuments*, p. 55.
12 Knight, 'The Early Christian', *In Tempore*, pp. 58–9.
13 *Corpus Inscriptionum Latinarum*, XIII, 2353–7; 11, 207; *Ibid.*, 2359.
14 Bu'lock, 'Early Christian memorial formulae'.

Christianity at Caerleon and Caerwent,[15] has only a late and secondary 'Compound' series, for example, *Tegernacus Filius Marti Hic Iacit*.[16]

The British stones showing the closest links with the Gallic series are a small group whose best and most characteristic examples, combining the *filius* and *Hic Iacet* formulae, are the memorial of Cunaide from Hayle in Cornwall, the memorial of Rosteece from Llanerfyl in Montgomeryshire, and the Latinus stone from Whithorn in Galloway.[17] These have comparatively long Latin texts cut in horizontal lines, usually on a prepared face. They retain features like the age of the deceased, a final *In Pace*, the use of stops, and the use of an initial formula at the head of the text, in place of the normal insular custom of putting the name first (*Hic In Tumulo Iacit Rosteece*, rather than, for example, *Carausius Hic Iacit*). This closeness to the Gallic prototypes, together with their spread along the Atlantic coasts of Britain from Cornwall to Galloway, suggests that they may be a primary series among the Gallic-derived British latin memorial-stones. However, they use not 'two-figure' formulae, like *Hic Iacit*, but the slightly later 'four-figure' type – *Hic in Tumulo Iacit* (Rosteece and Cunaide) or *Hic in Pace Requievit* (Cunaide). If the group is indeed primary, it implies a *terminus post quem* of 450–480 for the Gallic-derived insular series.

In looking at the Gallic background of the British memorial-stones, we are looking at only one half of the equation. Equally important is their context at the insular end. Although it has been argued in the past by MacNeill, and others, that the ogom script was pagan in origin,[18] and it is sometimes pointed out that the Dyfed *filius* series need not be specifically Christian, the Gallic series is unquestionably Christian, and there can be little reasonable doubt that its adoption in Britain was through the medium of the Christian Church. Ann Hamlin has suggested that, in Ireland, many ecclesiastical sites associated with ogom stones could belong to a very early horizon of diocesan church-sites, which were overtaken in importance by the development of the monastic-dominated Church from the sixth century onwards.[19] Like the ogom stones, the British series occur in a wide variety of contexts, from high isolated moorlands where it is most unlikely that there had ever been an associated church, to important church-sites like Llandeilo Fawr, or Towyn. Hamlin's suggestion, though, finds support in the contexts of some of our earliest British-Latin stones. Bede was specific

15 Gildas, *De Excidio*, 10; Boon, 'A Christian monogram'.
16 Nash-Williams, *The Early Christian Monuments*, no. 270; Knight, 'Glamorgan', pp. 336–8.
17 Macalister, *Corpus Inscriptionum Insularum Celticarum*, nos. 479, 520; Nash-Williams, *The Early Christian Monuments*, no. 294.
18 For references see Hamlin, 'Early Irish stone carving', pp. 283–5.
19 Hamlin, 'Early Irish stone carving', p. 285.

about Whithorn (with the Latinus stone) – Nyniau was a British bishop.[20] Llanerfyl, in Powys, with the Rosteece stone, fits well with Hamlin's description of the equivalent Irish churches – important early ecclesiastical sites, but of great historical obscurity. It still retains the remarkable wooden reliquary and shrine of its patron, St Erfyl, which may imply a corporate body of clergy in mediaeval times, to serve and foster her cult.[21]

The use of Latin memorial-inscriptions based on Gaulish models was, then, introduced to western Britain in the later fifth century through a church organised along the same lines as in contemporary Gaul, with rural minsters (to borrow anachronistically, the convenient Anglo-Saxon term) of secular clergy, with each 'minster' serving a rural diocese ('minster parish'). Church councils divide clergy into three categories – those on the roll of clergy of a city, those in the *ecclesiae diocesanae*, or rural minster, and those who live on a villa or estate (for example, *Council of Clermont 535*, c. 15; (*Council of Agde*, 506, c. 21),[22] and Gregory of Tours lists the rural churches founded in the *vici* of Touraine by successive bishops from Martin onwards.[23] Gildas himself, seemingly a member of the secular clergy, perhaps a deacon,[24] again suggests a similar pattern. He attacks the British clergy of his day, many of whom, like their Gallic counterparts, were married, neatly inverting the rulings of a series of Gallic church councils in order to do so. (*De Excidio*, 66, compare *Council of Angers* (A.D. 453) c. 4 – priests to avoid familiarity with strange women and be looked after by an aunt, mother, or sister; Munier (1963. I. 137–8); *Ist Council of Orleans* (511), c. 29; *Council of Clermont* (535) c. 16 etc).[25] At the same time, the monastic element in the British Church was still slight, for, evidently, as in Gaul, the great monastic expansion of the later sixth and seventh centuries was still to come.

There is no great problem about contacts between Britain and Gaul in this period. Quite apart from the slightly earlier visits of Germanus of Auxerre, we have the transmission of texts like the *Vita Martini*, or the early sixth-century *Passio Albani* from the Auxerre region,[26] both perhaps used by Gildas. We even have a snapshot of textual transmission in action with the British-born Bishop Faustus of Riez sending a complimentary copy of his latest book from Provence to friends in Britain, or Brittany, even if the whole story, as told by Sidonius Apollinaris, sounds suspiciously like a pastiche of the story of Joseph and his Brethren.[27] We also have a

---

[20] Bede, *Historia Ecclesiastica* III, 4.
[21] *Archaeologia Cambrensis*, 1915, pp. 438–42.
[22] Munier, *Concilia* I, 202–3; II, 109.
[23] Gregory of Tours, *Historiae Francorum*, X, 31; Stancliffe, 'From town to country'.
[24] Chadwick, 'Gildas'.
[25] Munier, *Concilia* I, 137–8, II, 12, 109–10; Knight, 'Glamorgan', pp. 339–40.
[26] Levison, 'St Alban'.
[27] Sidonius Apollinaris, *Letters* IX, 10 (ed. Anderson, pp. 530–47).

fourth-century sarcophagus from Arles re-used in the early or mid-fifth century for a young Briton, Tolosanus, *Britannus Natione*, using a version of the *Hic Iacit* formula.[28] In the following century, Gildas tells of British clerics going to Gaul and obtaining ordination as bishops by simony. Apart from the simony, this was not wholly irregular – after all, St Augustine of Canterbury was ordained bishop in Gaul. The simony is borne out, so far as Gaul is concerned, by a papal letter of 595 to Childebert II, complaining of laymen who, horrible to relate, have been made bishop through the pestiferous sin of simony.[29] We have already noted how Gildas can refer obliquely to married clergy in a way which suggests that his readers would have been familiar with a lost British equivalent of the surviving Gallic conciliar rulings. Overall, there is reasonable evidence of regular contact between Gaul and Atlantic Britain in the fifth and early sixth centuries, particularly in ecclesiastical circles.

One Welsh inscription has sometimes been taken to imply contacts, direct or indirect, much further afield. The sixth-century stone from Penmachno in Gwynedd with an apparent consular dating to 'the time of Justinus the Consul' has been the subject of much comment and speculation since it was found, built into the garden-wall of the Eagles Hotel in Penmachno, by a member of the staff of the Welsh Royal Commission in 1915. Its publication was John Rhys's last, indeed posthumous, contribution to early Welsh epigraphy.[30] There are, in fact, two inscriptions on the stone, one vertical, one horizontal. The vertical text reads FILI AVITORI, the second line of a text originally reading something like 'so and so Hic Iacit/Fili Avitori'. It is quite separate from the horizontal text, but it does show, as Rhys realised, that the stone has, at some stage, split vertically and that what we now have is only its left-hand half. This is borne out by close examination of the stone, for the left-hand face is an ancient and much weathered natural bedding plane, whereas the right-hand face is freshly broken, and the stone surface is still fresh and unweathered, with a crystalline texture.

The horizontal inscription is the consular date. Whereas the vertical text is a straightforward memorial inscription, this is very odd in several ways. It was cut almost immediately above the original ground level, as traces of differential weathering on the butt show, and instead of being a normal funerary inscription, is merely a dating clause. It reads as follows:

IN TE(M)PO[RE]
IVSTI[NI] CON[SVLI(S)]

The expansions are Rhys's, who identified the subject of the inscription as

[28] Benoit, *Sarcophages*, pp. 67–8, no. 98.

[29] *Registrum*, v, 60, quoted Wallace-Hadrill, *The Frankish Church*, pp. 115–16.

[30] Rhys, 'An inscription'. See also Knight, 'Penmachno revisited: the consular inscription and its context.'

Flavius Justinus, eastern consul in 540. He was also the penultimate consul, for, after his successor Basilius in the following year, Justinian, in effect, abolished the consulship by failing to appoint any successors.

As Cameron and Schauer have emphasised,[31] the system of consular dating was by this time archaic, inefficient, and impractical. After the division of the Empire, the practice had grown up of the western and eastern Augusti each appointing one of the pair of consuls, but no western consul had been proclaimed since 534, and Justinus was sole consul. Due, in part, to the huge cost of the games which the consul was expected to fund, and to various political and diplomatic upsets, there had been many gaps in the *fasti* in the previous decades. This, together with the shortcomings in the official machinery for publicly proclaiming the new consuls of the year, had led to a system of post-consular dating – so many years after the consulship of X. This system, using as a base the consulships of Justinus in 540 and of Basilius in 541, continued in some areas of the west, particularly Burgundy and the Rhône valley, where it persisted until the late seventh century, perhaps as a symbol of the area's continuing romanitas, even though it had been annexed to the Frankish kingdom. In practice, the system was usually combined with the fifteen-year cycle of indictions, and in 537 Justinian ruled that legal documents should also be dated by regnal years. This was a practice which, in the case of inscriptions, became increasingly common in the barbarian kingdoms of the west.

It is not clear whether the Penmachno inscription can be, as some have assumed, dated precisely to 541, or whether it belongs to the post-consular series, for there could be room for a numeral at the missing end of the second line. Unless it can be shown that the formula used is specific to a consular, not a post-consular dating, the reference to Justinus can only be regarded as a *terminus post quem*. The eccentric positioning of the inscription, low down on one face, just above the original ground-level, can readily be explained if, as on contemporary Gallic inscriptions, the dating formula formed the end of a longer inscription (there would be room for about ten lines) on the now missing right-hand face of the stone. The stone-cutter evidently ran out of space and finished his text 'round the corner'. There is a parallel for this in the Capel Bronwen stone from Anglesey,[32] and what would we make of this if we had only the face with the end of the inscription – *Auro et Lapidibus* – 'gold and gems'

We can readily explain the Penmachno inscription on the basis of a British cleric who had visited Lyon, which lay on the main route to Rome, and had, there, learned of the dating formula. However, the text is odd. It is hard to parallel *In Tempore*, either as a consular date (one would expect something like *Iustini V(ir) C(larissimus) Consulis*, or as a post-consular

---

[31] Cameron and Schauer, 'The last consul', p. 137.
[32] Nash-Williams, *The Early Christian Monuments*, no. 33.

dating when one would expect the abbreviation *P(ost) C(onsulatum)*. Thus, a typical Lyon inscription of the year after Justinus's consulship reads:

IN HOC TVMVLO REQ
VIISCET BONE MENOR
IAE NECTERIA QUI VIXIT
ANNOS XXV OBIIT IN
PACE PRIDE KAL MAIA
S P. C. IVSTINI[33]

(30th April 541). Parallel indictional datings are very common by this date, although far from universal, and the absence of one at Penmachno is not significant.

Rhys's interpretation of the text has been challenged by Mr Gwyn Thomas, who suggests the alternative reading:

INTEP [IDI]
IVSTI [SSI(MI)]
CON [IUX]

(The grave of) a most loving and righteous husband.[34] This has the merit of being fairly easy to parallel, in phrasing and sentiment, on several Welsh memorial-stones, as at Capel Bronwen on Anglesey (E.C.N.W. s33) – (. . . *Iva Sanctiussima Mulier*), or on some of longer laudatory texts like Capel Bronwen or the memorial of Paulinus from Cynwyl Gaeo.[35] The new reading presents problems, not least in the final O of line 1 (*Intepo*), and for the moment the matter must be left open.

The Gallic memorial inscriptions end in the mid-seventh century. The latest dated inscription from Lyon is of 656 with a regnal dating of Clovis II, the latest from Vienne of 625+. The public display of Latin inscriptions was characteristic of the ancient world, and assumed that there were people who could read them (though little Latin would be needed for the average Welsh memorial-stone). Their end may reflect the way in which literacy had become a largely clerical preserve. Similarly, the insular inscriptions, carrying the names and lineages of an élite, were replaced by anonymous (and, alas, largely undatable) cross-slabs of Nash-Williams Class-II. Study of this series presents a number of difficulties. Nash-Williams's partly notional date of the seventh to ninth century for the Welsh series was the middle section of a tripartite 'chest of drawers' classification which made possible the ordering and classification of a body of very disparate material. But it would be illogical to think that the spread to Wales of sculptured crosses would mean the end of the cross-slab series, which fulfilled quite different functions.

---

[33] *Corpus Inscriptionum Latinarum*, XIII, 2380; Diehl, *Inscriptiones Latinae Christianae Veteres*, 3563 A.
[34] *Archaeologia Cambrensis*, 1970, 170.
[35] Nash-Williams, *The Early Christian Monuments*, no. 139.

Figure 1. Cross slabs representing the Crucifixion. For references for individual stones, see text.

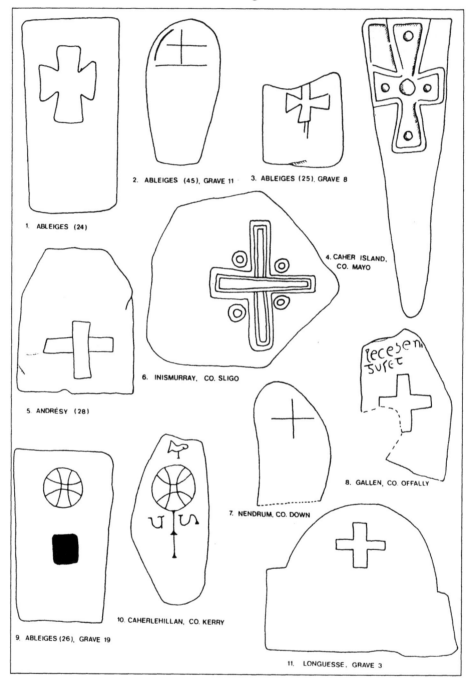

Figure 2. Cross slabs from the Vexin française (after Sirat, 1966, 1970) and from Ireland.

118

The Lives of monastic saints like Samson of Dol, Columba, and Columbanus make very clear the role of the sign of the cross in monastic life.[36] Apart from its ritual and curative role it was cut on food bowls and on tool handles, and was made over food before eating. As part of this literature is continental in origin, we might expect that the travels of a Samson or a Columbanus might be reflected in Gallic parallels for our Insular cross-slab series. Cross-slab H from Reask, Co. Kerry, has a pair of doves or birds flanking the cross, as on Gallic and other memorial-stones.[37] The general range of cross-forms used in the primary series of Insular stones can be matched readily enough on, for example, the Burgundian memorial-stones, which have similar birds, but the distribution of these forms is far too wide for them to be cited as parallels between one area and another. Presumably some more portable medium, like an ivory or book illumination, served as a model. Slightly more distinctive than the cross-types are the Chi-Rho monograms which occur on both Latin memorial-stones and early cross-slabs,[38] and the 'crucifixion representation' slabs, where the central cross is flanked by two smaller ones, as, for example, Inishmurry, Co. Sligo;[39] Llantrisant, Glamorgan[40] Nantes[41] and Mandourel (Aude).[42] A slab from Ardwall Island, Kirkcumbright, probably a portable altar[43] has a snake twined around the central cross, as on a sarcophagus from Pouillé (Vienne) in Poitou.[44] Here, the central cross is shown as a tree, making clear the reference to the belief that Christ's cross was fashioned from the tree which had grown in the garden of Eden.

These suggest continuing routine interchange of ideas and artistic motifs, but much remains to be done on the distribution, typology, and contexts, of the Insular cross-slab series. There is a great range of comparable material in Gaul, in a variety of media, and rather more examples of crosses cut or incised on stone, like the Insular series, than is generally realised. The most striking examples are the hundred or more cross-slabs from a group of late Merovingian cemeteries in the French Vexin north-west of Paris, some

---

[36] Fawtier, *La Vie de S. Sampson*; Taylor, *The Life*; Anderson and Anderson, *Adomnan's Life*; Jonas, *Vita Columbani* (ed. B. Krusch, *Monumenta Germaniae Historica, Scriptores rerum Merovingicarum*, 4, I (1905).
[37] Fanning, 'Excavations', pp. 145–7 and Fig. 31; compare, e.g. Thomas, *Christianity*, p. 165, Fig 21.
[38] Hamlin, 'A chi-rho'.
[39] Wakeman, W. F., *Survey of Antiquarian Remains on the Island of Inismurray*, Journal of the Royal Society of Antiquaries of Ireland, Special Volume (London and Edinburgh, 1893), Figs. 32, 72, 79, 84.
[40] Nash-Williams, *The Early Christian Monuments*, no. 219.
[41] Costa, *Art Mérovingien*, no. 222.
[42] Salin, *Civilisation Mérovingienne*, 2, p. 88, Fig. 44.
[43] Thomas, 'Ardwall Isle', p. 162, Fig. 34.
[44] Salin, *La Civilisation Mérovingienne*, 2, p. 151, Fig. 84.

found *in situ* over the early eighth-century graves.[45] Many are strikingly similar to Irish examples, although they are usually on shaped headstones. As often, it is difficult to say in which direction the flow of connection is running (direct eastern contact has been suggested), but we are, by now, in the Francia of Columbanus. The sorts of contacts implicit in the Hiberno-Frankish Church of the seventh century may be reflected, for example, in the Merovingian *trientes* from near Trim (Co. Neath) and Port Laoise (Co. Laois),[46] or the way in which the tiny amounts of Mediterranean and Gaulish pottery which reached Ireland in the fifth and sixth centuries are followed by the radically greater amounts of insular E-ware from some thirty Irish sites. The situation in other areas, not least Wales, remains obscure, but by the seventh century the patterns of contact between Francia, Ireland, and the developing Anglo-Saxon world, were already in place.

---

[45] Sirat, 'Les Steles Mérovingiennes', 'Inventaire complementaire'.
[46] Dolley, *The Hiberno-Norse Coins*, pp. 13–14; Rigold, 'The Sutton Hoo coins', pp. 669–70.

VIII

POUNDBURY, DORSET: SETTLEMENT AND ECONOMY IN LATE AND POST-ROMAN DORCHESTER

Christopher Sparey-Green

Eight years have passed since the appearance of *Poundbury Excavations Volume I*, covering the settlement sequence outside Poundbury Camp hill-fort, a sequence that extended from the Neolithic to the early post-Roman periods. This paper provides an opportunity to review the post-Roman aspects of the site and further discuss the latest major period of activity on the site in relation to the evidence which it provides for the economy and external contacts of fifth- and sixth-century Britain.[1]

The Poundbury settlement lay on the eastern side of a spur in the South Dorset downs, overlooking the Frome valley to the north and facing the defences of the Roman town of Dorchester on the neighbouring hill to the south-east (Figure 1). The summit of the spur was occupied by Poundbury Camp, a hill-fort of Iron Age origin but later use, while the hillside was occupied by a sequence of prehistoric and Roman activity culminating in a major Late Roman cemetery.

Any description of the Poundbury post-Roman settlement must relate it to the remains of this cemetery, an adjacent settlement and the possible re-use of the hill-fort earthworks. Volume I of the excavation report attempted to place these elements within the sequence of settlements and cemeteries, while Volume II, covering the cemeteries in greater detail, includes a reappraisal of the relationship of the latest burials to the post-Roman settlement.[2]

---

[1] The sequence of settlements from the Neolithic to the early post-Roman period is covered in Green, 'Excavations at Poundbury 1964–1980, Volume I' which, in this text, I will refer to as Poundbury Volume I followed by page number and microfiche reference. The method of referring to buildings by a prefix (R = Roman, PR = post-Roman) and number will be adhered to here, although some building numbers have been assigned new phasing by a subscript 'a' and 'b'. This chapter will cover much of the data included in sections six, seven and twelve of that report but will attempt a reinterpretation of the early post-Roman sequence. Also included are reference to some new discoveries and old finds not reported in Volume I.

[2] Volume II, covering the sequence of Roman cemeteries, is published as: Farwell, D. E. and Molleson, T. I., *Poundbury Volume II: The Cemeteries (Dorset Natural History and Archaeological Society* monograph, 1993). The writer is grateful for the opportunity to

Here, I shall concentrate on the evidence for the economy, building types and settlement-pattern of the early post-Roman period at Poundbury, setting it in the context of a revised phasing for that occupation and a reinterpretation of the relationship between it and the latest Roman activity, both domestic and funerary.[3] This site can then be placed within the local settlement-pattern during the time of change from the end of the Roman economy to the subsistence farming and craft-activity of the succeeding period. Finally, Poundbury is discussed in the wider context of post-Roman settlement types.

The early post-Roman settlement may represent simply a continuation of the latest Roman occupation which was apparently confined to the east of the excavated area (sites F and G) and extended into the base of the combe beyond the limits of excavation.[4] This settlement partly co-existed with, and partly adjoined, the urban cemetery on its eastern and townward side and may have served some function in relation to it besides continuing the previous farming activity. The extent to which the settlement continued to the end of what can be defined as the Roman period is uncertain, just as the latest phase of burial can only be dated approximately on typological grounds, in the absence of radiocarbon dating for the skeletal remains.

The Late Roman settlement and cemetery

The main activity on the site during the fourth and early fifth centuries was undoubtedly funerary, the scale of burial suggesting the cemetery's use by a large and chiefly, urban, population. This aspect of the site lies beyond my scope at present, but reference will be made to the latest use of the site as a burial-place and particularly to the survival thereafter of features, such as the mausolea and the cemetery boundaries. The latter appear to have influenced and even to have been incorporated within the pattern of post-Roman settlement where this was established upon the downhill area of the burial ground (cemetery sectors 3A–C in the excavator's terminology).

At the time of the establishment of the main cemetery (cemetery 3) in the late third or early fourth century major changes had taken place, buildings R13–15 on site C being abandoned at approximately the time that

---

see and comment on drafts of the latter. For the cemetery, see also Sparey-Green 'The Rite of Plaster Burial'.

3 *Poundbury Volume I*, pp. 71–90. The post-Roman buildings will not be described here except where additional details or a new interpretation is introduced.

4 *Poundbury Volume I*, pp. 52–69. Observation in 1964 on the site 30 metres to the east of buildings R12–14 suggests the presence of at least one building, now sealed beneath the present warehouse.

a coin hoard of Carausian date was deposited in their vicinity.[5] Burial in cemetery 3B, the eastern sector of the main cemetery, had started at approximately the same period and then extended over the three ruined buildings during the fourth century. However, settlement could have continued in the vicinity; building R12 lay just beyond the south edge of the burial-ground and at least one further building was observed in building work beyond its eastern limits.

To the north, on sites D, F, and G, beyond the north-eastern edge of cemetery 3, occupation certainly continued. Buildings R16 and 17 were not encroached upon by late burials and R16 at least appears to have been respected by post-Roman features; its interior contained debris from its dereliction at some date in the fourth century or later. On site G, in the north-eastern corner of the excavated area, traces of a metalled surface, adjoined by occupation of the late fourth century, may represent a road leading from R16 and R17 to the west or north gate of the town.[6]

The economic basis and date of this latest Roman settlement are not certain but some finds both indicate activity into the late fourth century and betray long distance trade links. This evidence comprises, firstly, finds of a distinctive form of the local Black Burnished ware (BB1) which appears to date to the late fourth and early fifth centuries and, secondly, sherds of imported Mediterranean amphorae.[7]

Occupation debris within R16 could be dated no later than the mid-fourth century but one feature produced a sherd of Africana amphora and the destruction levels contained large freshly broken sherds of another of east Mediterranean type. A sherd of Biv amphora was included in the top silting of a nearby pit.[8]

---

5 *Poundbury Volume I*, p. 69. The coin-hoard was discovered in 1986 close to building R14 and is currently being studied by Kathy King of the Ashmolean Museum. I am grateful to Mr Honeybun for details of its discovery and to Kathy King for preliminary details of the approximately 10,000 coins of the late third century comprising the hoard.

6 *Poundbury Volume I*, pp. 61–63. R16 and R17 could have co-existed with the post-Roman settlement and enclosure system; the foundations at least of R16 were not robbed out until the medieval period. Furthermore, although building rubble in a pit adjacent to R16 was sealed by fourth-century burials this debris could have derived from renovation of the building rather than its final demolition. For the north gate of Dorchester see RCHM, *Dorset*, p. 551. The presence of an early gate is suggested by seventeenth-century references in Hutchins, *The History*, p. 343.

7 In *Poundbury Volume I*, this late form of Dorset Black Burnished ware (BB1) is represented by fig. 88, vessels 36, 41 and 50, p. 127. The more bulbous shape of some vessels coincides with interior marks compatible with the use of a wheel, a technique otherwise not present in the earlier products of this industry. The ware has been recognised at Dorchester, Bath and Exeter: see Esmonde-Cleary, *The Ending*, p. 157. Late groups published from other sites in Dorset and Somerset appear to include examples; the most important series, from Dorchester Baths, awaits publication, Andrews in Batchelor forthcoming.

8 *Poundbury Volume I*, pp. 117, 140 Mf 3 C1–C4.

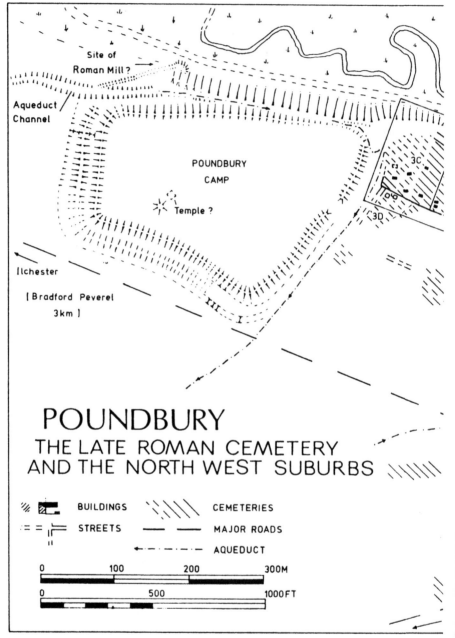

Figure 1. Poundbury. The site in relation to the Late Roman topography: the town, the cemeteries and the hill-fort.

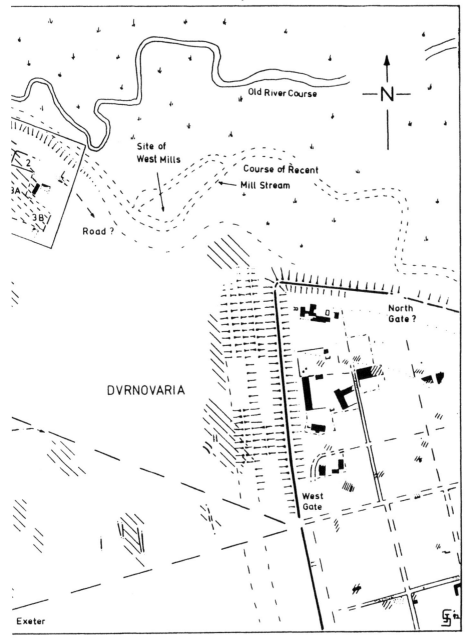

The adjacent structure R17 produced late BB1 ware and some unusual red colour coated ware, one sherd having impressed decoration.[9] The latter, although similar to the expanded-arm cross-designs on later North African Red Slip Ware, appears to be simply an aberrant form of Oxfordshire Ware. Coins associated with the structure comprised late-third-century issues but also others of fourth century flan, defaced by burning which had also discoloured some of the colour coated ware. A crude paving in this building may also have been identified 15 metres to the south where it was associated with traces of a timber structure and large quantities of late-fourth-century pottery. This adjoined a gully which roughly aligned with similar features to the south cutting the burials of cemetery 3B. The latter and perhaps the ruins of R12 and R14, appeared to form an early post-Roman boundary enclosing the eastern side of the phase 1 post-Roman settlement.[10]

Late BB1 ware was also recovered in the vicinity of the eastern cemetery-boundary on site C, and the metalled area on Site G.[11] Late Roman occupation deposits overlying and extending beyond the cemetery edge in the area of C191, produced a mixed third- to fourth-century assemblage which included late BB1 ware. A few sherds of Biv, Coptic and Africana amphorae were also recovered from this area but only as abraded sherds in the uppermost layers.[12]

The late BB1 ware provided some evidence for the economy, bowls and large storage vessels with multiple perforations producing evidence for cheese or butter-making; in one case this material was associated with a sickle blade. This would indicate the continuation of the sheep farming of the late third and early fourth centuries.[13] In addition the amphora suggested the importation of at least oil and honey as well as, presumably, wine, although not on any large scale.[14] As always with amphorae, these may only constitute one specialised item, wine and grape-juice products from Gaul and the Rhineland having been imported on a larger scale in wooden barrels, forming a trade invisible to archaeology except where wood survives in waterlogged conditions. The lead-burden of population within the cemetery suggests a heavy exposure to the metal within the urban environment; in a hard-water district one of the few conceivable food sources for such

[9] *Ibid.*, p. 120; Young, *The Roman Pottery*, pp. 131–2 Stamp 6 and 17.
[10] The interpretation of the Late and post-Roman features on site C and G have here been considerably revised. *Poundbury Volume I*, pp. 57, 62–63 figs 40, 41 and 51.
[11] *Ibid.*, p. 63.
[12] *Ibid.*, p. 59. These sherds were mostly derived from the uppermost Late Roman levels downhill of the buildings R12–14 and the vicinity of R16.
[13] *Ibid.*, pp. 119, 143.
[14] *Ibid.*, pp. 132, 143 Mf 4 G9.

contamination is grape-juice products or some other food processed in lead vessels, but this must remain purely conjectural at this stage.[15]

Late Roman activity in the vicinity of Poundbury could have included, besides a settlement on the valley margins stretching east towards the north-west corner of the town, some activity within and adjacent to the hill-fort. The aqueduct was still carrying water in the fourth century and earthworks below the north-western corner of the hill-fort suggest a side channel fed a watermill at the base of the hillside. Hand-querns were present on the excavated site but only as scattered fragments, too infrequent to suggest their wide use. Pottery and a coin hoard of the mid-fourth century come from the hill-fort and parch marks of a square structure within it might even mark the site of a Romano-Celtic temple.[16]

The Post-Roman Settlements

The transition between the Late Roman and the earliest post-Roman settlements is not immediately apparent in view of the usual problems of dating the development of a site continuing into a period of poverty in the surviving material culture. However, contexts included in the Roman phases, as defined here, were characterised by quantities of unabraded and freshly-broken Roman pottery and an association with mortared stone structures. The post-Roman features were notable for their lack of pottery, other than residual Roman sherds and their association with structures of timber and drystone construction. The economic implications of this will be discussed below.

A revised phasing of the post-Roman settlement is proposed here, consisting of three stages, numbered 1 to 3, themselves only a simplification of an even more complex development. Some revision and sub-division of the building complexes is also made but the individual buildings will not be described in detail.[17] The relationship of the first phase of settlement to the cemetery will also be outlined. Here it should be noted that it is assumed that features such as the cemetery boundaries and the mausolea survived to influence or be incorporated in the post-Roman scheme. The boundary-ditches are interpreted as having been accompanied by banks, in view of the presence of strips of ground free of burials along their inner edge, the

---

15 Molleson, 'The Human Remains', pp. 185–6; Molleson, Eldridge and Gale, 'Identification'.

16 *Poundbury Volume I*, p. 69. Watermills were often positioned to take advantage of a head of water from an aqueduct at a higher level: Singer *et al.*, *History*, p. 602.

17 *Poundbury Volume I*, p. 71. The phasing of the post-Roman features was often hindered by the similarity of fills in intersecting features, but in complexes such as PR1 up to four phases of building and pit-cutting can certainly be recognised.

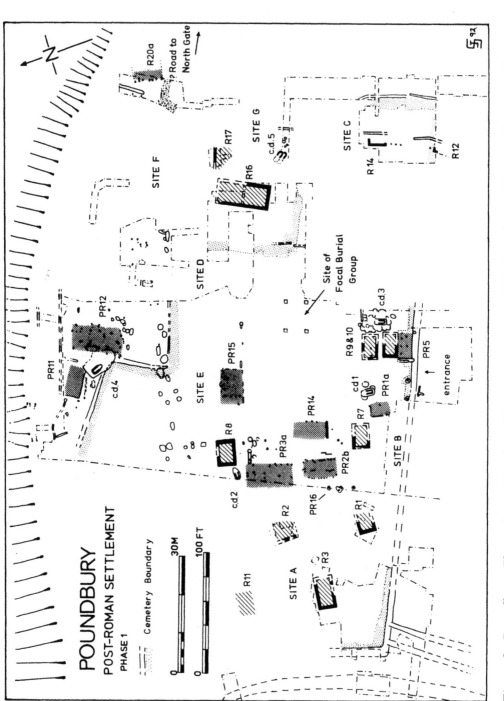

Figure 2 Poundbury. The main surviving Late Roman structures, and the first phase of the post-Roman settlement.

banks at least surviving into the early post-Roman period even though the ditches themselves had silted up in the late fourth century. Some at least of the mausolea, R7–R10 in particular, survived to be incorporated within at least the earlier phases of the settlement layout, R8 also producing evidence that it had been used in association with the adjacent corn-drying oven. Some of the mausolea burials appear to have been robbed at an unknown date but this may have been as late as the medieval period when the wall foundations were being removed.

More problematical is the relation of the settlement to the latest of the ordinary burials. Without radiocarbon dates for the skeletal remains the only evidence for the latest phase of burial is the scatter of 119 shallow un-coffined or stone cist burials, a type of burial which has elsewhere in south-west Britain been dated to the late fourth or fifth century or even later.[18] Some overlapped with the currency of the standard nailed wooden coffins but the majority were stratigraphically the latest. In relation to the settlement 110 of the uncoffined/cist burials coincided with open ground although nine were overlain by buildings, notably a group of three beneath PR2. These uncoffined and cist burials were distributed through the centre of the cemetery, clustering around mausolea R8 but extending into the central area to the south-east. Further groups can be recognised on the north-west edge of cemetery 3, near building R16 and on the very northern edge of the cemetery close to buildings PR11 and 12. The latter group were notable for their proximity to a coffined inhumation with an iron fitting at the head end of the lid in the form a star, or anthropoid, monogram. This burial appeared to lie adjacent to an open area approached by a pathway through the cemetery.

In addition, amongst the standard, coffined burials was a group of approximately ten south of mausoleum R8 that lay on an aberrant and more stricly oriented alignment, part of this group being overlain by the founda-tion-trenches of a substantial timber building PR4. Although apparently similar in the character of their fill and stratigraphical relationship to other post-Roman structures the possibility remains that these features were originally the foundations of some unusual form of Late Roman mausoleum or post-Roman memorial.[19]

Whether or not there was any general respect for, or knowledge of, the earlier burials the incidence of serious disturbance to human remains by post-Roman features was extremely low and of perhaps ten cases through the whole cemetery three were of the robbing of stone coffins from

[18] *Ibid.*, pp. 90–1, 150. For a local example of such a cemetery at Ulwell, dated to the late seventh or eighth century, see Cox, 'A Seventh-Century'.

[19] *Poundbury Volume I*, p. 77, fig. 56. The plan suggests the trenches may have replaced earlier post-settings represented by pits B178, 184, 2014, 2075. Note the adjacent B2054 which was not a posthole but a stone marker set in the upper fill of a late grave.

mausolea. The dead were effectively left in peace during the succeeding phases of post-Roman activity.

Phase 1 – The earliest post-Roman settlement

To the north of the latest Roman settlement a further series of structures can be suggested as belonging to the earliest phase of the post-Roman period and overlapping with the latest phase of burial. On the northern edge of sites E,F and G, adjoining the steep scarp to the flood-plain of the Frome, was a series of timber buildings which, although poorly dated, seem by analogy with the main area of the settlement to belong to the post-Roman period (Figure 2).

On site G the Late Roman metalled surface was not at first cut by any enclosure ditch, suggesting continued links with the town. Structure R20a, on the north side of the metalling, was perhaps the western side of a rectangular earth-fast post building extending beyond the excavation limits. The proximity of corn-drying oven 5, the Late Roman paving and the still extant buildings R16 and R17 may be significant in view of the association of other corn-driers with large rectangular buildings uphill. Immediately downhill and to the south a boundary, noted above, employed ruined structures and an intermittent gully to form a perimeter east of R16, R17 and corn drier 5.

Further uphill, PR11 and 12 lay in close proximity to corn drier 4 and its threshing floor, all four features seemingly constrained on the south by the line of the main cemetery's north boundary. The structural remains consisted of, in the case of PR11, a shallow terrace associated with slight earth-fast features and, in PR12, of an irregular rectangular posthole pattern, neither structure associated with rubble scatters or Roman occupation debris. Although irregular the latter's plan suggested a timber building of, perhaps, four bays and thirteen metres long by five or nine metres wide with a central door or porch on the east. An irregular enclosure was appended to the north-west end of PR11 while another linear boundary to the north may have defined both this and phase 2 of the settlement on the north. The position of the buildings, drier and floor is of some significance. They straddled the corner of an earlier Roman enclosure and the line of a trackway skirting the cemetery, perhaps serving to link the combe settlement with the hill-fort. These structures effectively blocked this route, two gullies to their north marking the realigned track. On the south this complex was constrained by the dog-leg northern boundary of the burial area, their respect of this boundary suggesting the cemetery was still in use at the time, the boundary acting as a shield to drier and floor.[20]

Included here in phase 1, but representing a discrete and perhaps slightly

[20] For PR11–12 and Drier 4, *Ibid.*, pp. 82 and 87.

later development, are the structures established within the cemetery between Mausolea R7, 8, 9 and 10. The construction of buildings, PR1a, 2b,
3a, PR5, PR15 and possibly PR14 marks a major change in the use of the
cemetery, the buildings overlying the burial rows of the formal cemetery.
Not all these buildings were necessarily contemporary but the general
scheme appears to have incorporated the mausolea in a three-sided layout,
open to the eastern and downhill side and covering an area 50 metres
north–south and 30 metres east–west.

The majority of these structures consisted of patterns of postholes and,
in the case of PR1a, post-in-trench construction. In general terms these
rather slight and irregular earth-fast post construction buildings may have
been similar to PR11 and 12.

Corn Driers 1–5 appear to belong with this early phase, drier 1 adjoining
building 1a but sealed beneath its later replacement 1b, Drier 3 adjoining
PR5 but buried beneath a later pit complex and a boundary. Drier 2 is
noteworthy since it lay outside both a possible doorway at the north end of
PR3a and the west door of mausoleum R8. While PR3a in construction and
size is similar to building 12, associated with drier 4, the interior of R8
produced charred cereal remains from a crop of post-Roman type, confirm-
ing that that building was standing and still in use.

On the north a row of pits (the weathered remains of large post holes?)
separated this complex from PR11 and PR12. On the south, the earliest
phase of PR5 filled the space between the mausoleum and the south
cemetery boundary; immediately west two large post holes on this boundary
may mark a gateway to the whole complex giving access across the partly
silted south cemetery boundary ditch northwards into the central open
space.

The western and eastern limits are less clear but uphill the postholes of
structure PR16 could have been part of a western post row rather than the
east side of a building. Downhill a shallow boundary feature defined the
cemetery's eastern limit and separated it from the zone of the latest Roman
activity.

The relationship of this post-Roman structural complex to the latest
phase of the cemetery has already been described in general terms but one
further feature of this postulated plan is that the central group of special
burials north of R9 and R10, perhaps originally marked by a columnated
structure, would have lain at the centre of the postulated open area.

Phases 2 and 3 – Later phases of post-Roman settlement
The extent to which specific elements of the above layout continued cannot
be known but it is assumed that some at least of its component buildings
were incorporated into the new plan of phases 2 and 3 (Figure 3).[21]

---

[21] *Ibid.*, pp. 91–92.

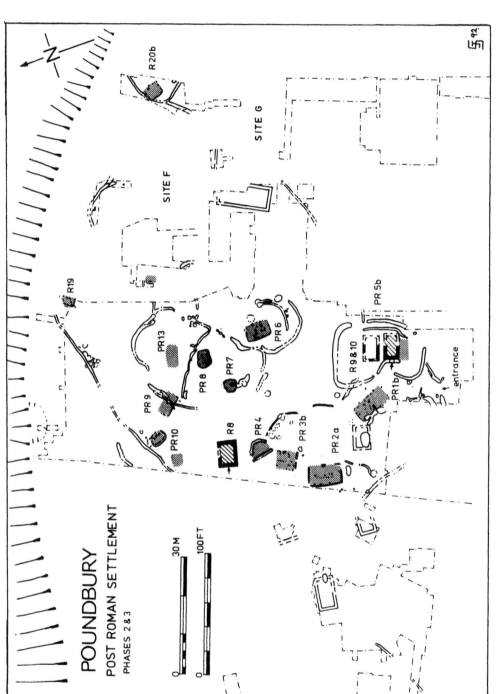

Figure 3 Poundbury. The later phases of the post-Roman settlement.

Phase 2 is distinguished, however, by the appearance of the small terraced or sunken floored buildings of post and wattle construction, each surrounded by irregular ditched enclosures (PR6–10 and PR13). Also included here would be the terraced posthole structure PR1b which, like these huts, has an alignment which diverges from that of the cemetery and is more strictly oriented to the compass points. The ditched enclosure around mausolea R9 and R10 also belongs to this period. On site G the terraced hut R20b and possibly also F1037 and Rl9 may represent other huts of this type.

Phase 3 would, then, comprise surviving elements of the two previous plans with the addition of PR4. PR2a and PR3b, both of which were sealed by burnt rubble from their final destruction, could also belong to this latest phase. The outer boundary-system, set on a more strictly east–west and north–south alignment, would belong with this phase, the late date of this enclosure-system indicated by the way it cut across structures PR11 and 12, corn drier 4 and also passed between PR10 and its northern enclosure ditch. The inclusion of PR4 in this latest phase is based on its alignment and the similarity of its foundations to other slighter structures of this period; as already noted it may be a survival from a late stage of the cemetery. Evidence for burning and fallen drystone rubble, noted in PR2b and PR3b and in the ditch system around PR5, may mark some substantial destruction at the end of this phase. Rare examples of crouched burials may also have been interred at this stage. The topsoil produced a scatter of material from Late Saxon to recent times but this appears to have been no more than debris from agricultural use, a phase confirmed by environmental evidence.

In summary, the settlement sequence is here seen to commence with a group of at least two buildings, representing an uphill extension from the latest and ill-defined activity in the fourth-century settlement. These structures respected the cemetery and were, perhaps, contemporary with its latest use. Thereafter, settlement expanded south to incorporate the most significant mausolea in a rectilinear layout, following the cemetery's alignment and focused on its centre. A new system of boundaries on the same alignment surrounded it. In phase 2 perhaps eight huts in enclosures were added within the central zone and to the north-east, their alignment following a new orientation. This layout was then enclosed in phase 3 by a new more strictly-oriented boundary system aligned with the apsidal structure. The latter may have been either a survival from the cemetery or indeed a newly created post-Roman structure. The end of the settlement's life is marked by evidence for destruction followed by agricultural use.[22]

---

[22] *Ibid.*, pp. 92, 153. For environmental data for the later use of the site, p. 93.

The character of the buildings

The individual buildings have already been described in detail but some
account and further discussion is called for here in view of the relevance of
constructional methods to the cultural milieu in which the settlement grew
up. In general the buildings are of non-standard plan, not adhering to regular
plans or constructional methods and employing a variety of materials. Their
elucidation is further hampered by the erosion consequent on the later
agricultural activity which has denuded their eastern, downhill, sides.[23]

The structural traces appear to fall into two broad categories, firstly,
rectangular patterns of postholes often on terraces sealed by rubble scatters
and, secondly, smaller terraces, or scoops, bearing patterns of stake and
postholes not associated with rubble scatters. In the former category one of
the best preserved buildings was PR2, the pattern of postholes suggesting
two structural phases, each with two major roof supports on the axes of
their irregular rectangular outlines, each measuring approximately 8.5 by
4.5 metres. The earlier phase PR2a had irregularly-placed uprights around
the perimeter while its replacement PR2b was bounded by gullies on three
if not four sides and rare uprights along two sides. From the profile and fill
of these gullies they appear not to have held timbers but to have acted as
drip gullies. Associated with this later outline was a dense scatter of
limestone and flint which bore traces of burning, as also did the packing of
many postholes. The interior surface beneath had been terraced, the chalk
bearing the marks of heavy wear, frequent stake-hole structures and other
internal features. Two sub-rectangular slots may mark the sill of a door in
the east wall. The outside walls were not otherwise apparant but may have
been of drystone in their lower courses, hence the overlying burnt rubble.

Buildings of similar size and plan to PR2b may be represented by PR3a,
11, 12 and 14; PR2a may be paralleled by PR1b, 3b and 9, possibly also by
the fragmentary PR14, PR15 and R20a. Buildings PR3a and 12 appear of
similar size with irregular and widely-spaced patterns of posts partly
defined by drip gullies, forming a sub-rectangular outline of up to 13 by 5
metres. In the case of PR3a, 12, 14 and 15 the surviving post sockets,
possibly of more than one period, would hardly have supported a building
of any dimension and thus may have formed only one element in a structure
which relied as much on sleeper walls of drystone and cob for its support.
Paired posts at the north end of PR3a and on the east side of PR 14 suggest
doorways in walls otherwise not extant; PR2a and 12 provided evidence for
doorways on the eastern, downhill, side.

Structures PR1a, 4 and 5 are more enigmatic, each south of and in close

[23] *Ibid.*, pp. 75–77. The description and interpretation of the timber structures here differs
in detail. In particular the sequence of structures 2a and 2b is reversed in view of the
evidence of the final rubble spread associated with the perimeter of PR2a sealing the west
side of 2b.

proximity to a mausoleum. The first was a timber-slot and post building adjoining R7, disturbed by later pit groups and building PR1b and possibly extending outside the excavated area. PR4, a very substantial foundation trench of apsidal form, has already been noted as a most puzzling structure which overlay and apparantly aligned with a group of strictly-oriented burials beside R8. The trench's rubble fill may have preserved indications of major timber uprights, the stone including part of a capital hollowed out and reused as a basin.[24]

The remaining structures PR6–8 and 10 all fall into the second major category defined above, namely terraces or scoops containing traces of small huts. No two buildings were the same but PR8 was closest to the classic sunken-floored building in plan and contained fragments of clay loom weights and a bone comb. The terraces of PR6 and PR10 were both occupied by wattle and post huts approximately 3 by 4 metres, traces of other wattle structures surviving also on the chalk surface immediately west of PR10 and within enclosure PR13. Lower down the hillside F1036, R19 and R20b may all be examples of similar huts.

Even allowing for frequent reconstructions or overlapping re-builds the post-Roman structures are somewhat irregular in plan and construction, showing none of the sophisticated earth-fast timber construction evident at, for instance, Cowdery's Down or Chalton.[25] As already noted, a four-bay plan might be discerned in building PR12 from the posts on the perimeter but there are also two lines of slighter posts within the interior. PR2a and PR2b were both furnished with substantial supports for a central ridge but the outer walls differed, the later phase incorporating drystone construction. Slots or trenches formed a feature of structures PR1a–5, 9 and 11 but only in PR 1a, 4 and perhaps 14 could an interpretation as foundation trenchs be sustained. The quantity of rubble suggested drystone construction and was also incorporated in buildings PR1b and PR3b, while some ditches surrounding PR5 were apparently filled with collapsed walls. Lumps of cob from at least one pit suggest that this material was also in use. The groups of irregular pits near some structures could be interpreted as the quarries for this material, as in the case of the similar features on local pre-Roman Iron Age settlements.

The economy of the settlement
This revised settlement sequence is proposed here as a background to a further discussion of the evidence for the economy and outside contacts of this settlement. Without repeating detailed descriptions already published the evidence will be summarised and updated with the addition of further reference to relevant comparable sites. The major feature of the site's

[24] *Ibid.*, p. 108, fig 76, object 28.
[25] James, Marshall and Millett, 'An Early Medieval'.

economy is the contrast between the material poverty of the remains and the relative sophistication of some aspects of the farming and industrial technology.[26]

The material poverty is illustrated by the lack of identifiable fifth- and sixth-century finds in observation of building work. Prehistoric, Roman and later finds from the topsoil allowed the period of occupation on the hillside to be estimated but the extensive post-Roman settlement was only recognised once open-area excavation commenced and the buildings, pit complexes and ditches were revealed, cutting the outlines of the Late Roman burials. The contents of these features comprised chiefly limestone rubble, flint and animal bones, accompanied by the occasional residual sherd of Roman pottery or coin. The rare iron knives, bone objects or whetstones were the only recognisably contemporary artefacts; there were only two featureless sherds of handmade pottery which appeared to be associated with this occupation.[27]

The lack of the distinctive imported pottery of the early post-Roman period is significant in view of the presence of the North African and East Mediterranean amphora sherds in the latest Roman levels lower down the hillside. The lack of such pottery inhibited close dating of the site and, other than the relative dating provided by the preceding Late Roman cemetery and the medieval pottery in the topsoil, reliance had to be placed on radiocarbon dating of charcoal and charred cereal remains. The latter did, however, provide clear evidence for a date within the early post-Roman period even if there were insufficent determinations to allow dating of each phase.[28] Roman coins occurred relatively frequently but the pattern of coin loss showed no preponderence of issues from the late fourth century; the coin was presumably rubbish survival from the cemetery period and not an active currency.

In general terms the agricultural economy was of a varied, subsistence nature contrasting with the Late Roman period when the emphasis had appeared to be on pastoralism and dairying, with little evidence for processing or storage of cereals. Turning first to the osteological evidence, in the Late Roman period sheep/goat and cattle were equally important with pig also of some significance. For the former species at least there was evidence for their rearing on site, while the high proportion of mature

[26] The small finds from the post-Roman settlement were discussed by Ann Ellison in *Poundbury Volume I*, p. 140, the evidence for the economy, by the writer on p. 143. The combs and bone pins are typical of the culturally anonymous objects found on early post-Roman sites but can be paralleled best in the 'Celtic' west rather than the 'Anglo-Saxon' east.

[27] *Ibid.*, p. 128. This has serious implications for the identification of comparable sites. Dorset and adjoining areas seem to be virtually aceramic from the demise of the Black Burnished ware industry through to the tenth or eleventh century.

[28] *Ibid.*, p. 132 Mf 4 G1–G2.

animals and pottery evidence for processing of milk products further suggested that both species may have served primarily as milk producers. A specialised husbandry can be suggested, providing both choice meat (veal and lamb from the milking animals' young?) and milk products for the local market, the suburban farm capitalising on the valley pasture, the downland and perhaps even grass cover in the cemetery itself.[29]

In the post-Roman period the proportion of sheep/goat increased, the other two main domesticates declining significantly. The proportion of mature animals declined slightly and some sheep at least were slaughtered as lamb. Pig was less common but the proportion of adults was much greater, presumably to maximise their body weight. At the same time there was an increase in the albeit relatively small number of red deer taken. Meat was being consumed on-site, the animals in each case being slaughtered at the optimum time but the maintenance of some adult cattle for milk and traction and of sheep/goat for milk is likely. The butchery technique of chopping across the bone, which appeared in the Late Roman period, increased in frequency and was used now on the lamb and mutton joints.

Comparing the agricultural economy of the Roman and post-Roman periods is more difficult in view of the relative lack of evidence for arable cultivation in the former period, but the absence of corn-drying ovens, and of obvious storage facilities, supports the earlier settlement's interpretation as a pastoral farm. By contrast the post-Roman settlement was notable for the series of five large ovens containing quantities of ash and charred cereal, undoubtedly features connected with the processing of crops rather than normal cooking activity. The scale of this activity need not have been large if the use of these ovens had been sequential but, interestingly, at least three of the driers were datable to the first phase and the others were not demonstrably late in the sequence. If cereal drying was a feature of only the earliest phase this has important implications for the economy thereafter and, in view of the reliance on cereal remains for the radiocarbon dating of the post-Roman settlement, it could even allow the end of the settlement to be somewhat later than previously suggested.[30]

Comparison of the cereals from occupation levels and domestic ovens in the Roman settlement with this large quantity of material from the post-Roman corn driers and from late activity in mausoleum R8 suggests major changes in cereal cultivation. In the Late Roman settlement the cereals in use were mainly wheat and barley with only a small component of oats, perhaps as a contaminant. In contrast, the samples from the fifth-century post-Roman ovens showed high levels of oats as well as the presence of new varieties of wheat and barley. While one drier produced high numbers of barley grains the others contained mainly mixes of wheat and oats, the

---

[29] *Ibid.*, pp. 129–132.
[30] *Ibid.*, pp. 87–9.

un-sprouted state of the grain showing that these were drying rather than malting kilns. Oats, in particular, need parching in their processing.[31]

The introduction of free-threshing wheat and of six-row barley marks a major technical advance, the few comparable samples from Late Roman contexts locally suggesting that this is truly an innovation of the fifth century. However, bread-wheat does occur in Late Roman contexts, such as an oven at Colliton Park, Dorchester and a malting oven at Catsgore, Somerset.[32]

The sample from a late level in Mausoleum R8 is particularly interesting in that the new bread wheat and large quantities of barley are present but very little oats, this material coming from a context during the currency of the late Black Burnished Ware and of glassware, prior to the destruction of the building. This is particularly significant as a bridge between Late and post-Roman activity.

The weeds from the Poundbury samples give some clue as to the agricultural methods at this date, some species suggesting that part of the crops was derived from a clayey soil, which in this context could be the clay with flints on the downland beyond Poundbury Camp. Other weeds would be compatible with Winter-sown crops, presumably the wheat and oats, while the barley and peas would belong to a spring sowing.

Other than the cereals, potential food plants represented include peas and beans and the presence of flax may also be significant. In contrast to the evidence for cereal processing, querns were rare, as in the Late Roman period the few fragments may have been residual. In view of the number of features excavated, and the number of corn-drying ovens identified, the lack of querns must be a significant absence, suggesting that other methods than on-site milling of cereals were in use and that, from the Late Roman period, firstly the aqueduct and then, perhaps, the river itself were powering watermills close-by. As already noted, an earthwork below the north-west corner of the hill-fort was conceivably the site of a Late Roman horizontal mill serving the suburban settlement (Figure 1).[33] For later periods a more accessible location in the valley floor at West Mills would have been suitable for a vertical mill driven by the river; a mill at the latter spot is likely to be one of the twelve listed in Domesday for Dorchester.

At Poundbury, little evidence for craft or industrial activity was recovered but small-scale smithing and weaving had been carried on in at least two buildings. Smithing slag was recovered, most notably from a heavily trampled and burnt area in the northern part of PR2a. However, the most

31 *Ibid.*, pp. 134–7.
32 For the mausoleum deposit Van der Veen, 'Charred Grain'. *Poundbury Volume I*, pp. 85, 136 .
33 *Ibid.*, p. 51. The aqueduct on the east of the hill-fort was silting up in the fourth- to fifth centuries; was this partly the result of the water's diversion upstream to the mill-stream?

significant feature of the iron technology was the quality of the steel in use at this period. Although small and unprepossessing the knives that were one of the few recurrent finds in this period proved, from x-ray and metallurgical examination, to be technically far superior to the standard edge-tool of the Roman period.[34] These post-Roman tools were sometimes pattern-welded and often skilfully made with a softer flexible back welded to a blade with a much greater hardness than was usually attained in the previous period. There is no way of knowing if these had been made on site or imported but superficially similar knives have come from the earliest Anglo-Saxon burials in the Dorchester area.[35] However, one is reported as coming from beneath a damaged Late Roman mosaic in Colliton Park; such edge-tools deserve technological study to identify the origin and early development of this significant development.

Whetstones appear to have been simply roughly shaped slabs of stones available in the region and were typologically undistinguished. Tools such as the chisel and saw blade show that woodworking was, unsurprisingly, carried out.[36]

Evidence for weaving on-site was more common, several fragments of combs and spindle whorls were recovered from buildings. PR8, a sunken floored building of phase 2/3, produced a possible antler weaving tool and weights similar to the fittings of upright looms found in Anglo-Saxon buildings of this type.[37] In addition rubbing or polishing stones may have been connected with the finishing of leather-work or linen; as already noted, flax was identified amongst the charred seeds. Rectangular pits such as one on the site of PR12 could have served for retting or tanning.

In such a summary of evidence for the necessary domestic or craft activities the lack of evidence for vessels or containers is constantly surprising. For a site to be aceramic at a date within one or two generations of the currency of the latest Black Burnished ware is surprising; equally surprising is the lack of evidence for the use of metal vessels, even allowing for their recycling. The apparant coincidence in the final occupation of Mausoleum R8 of late BB1 ware and cereal remains of post-Roman type is tantalising. Could such pottery have continued in careful use into the fifth century, to be discarded in such a way as to only rarely survive in the archaeological record? However, obviously old, reused and worn vessels cannot be identified amongst the stratified post-Roman deposits.

---

[34] *Poundbury Volume I*, p. 98, fig 70. For the report on the iron technology: p. 143, Mf 2 C10–12.

[35] For the Trumpet-Major finds see Green, 'Early Anglo-Saxon'. Personal observation during work on the Bradford Peverel site reported in Keen, 'Dorset Archaeology'; the latest burials are reported by Hawthorne and Pinder, 'Bradford Peverel'.

[36] See above, note 34.

[37] *Poundbury Volume I*, p. 109, fig. 79; p. 112, fig. 81. The use of combs in weaving is still debated.

Organically-tempered pottery continuing a sub-Roman tradition is known from Somerset but all that is represented here at Poundbury are one or possibly two sherds comparable to the earliest Anglo-Saxon wares.[38]

Imported fine pottery and amphorae, such an important indicator of early post-Roman activity and of the trading links and status of contemporary sites in south-west Britain, were absent. The sherds already noted from the eastern edge of the site may have been either rubbish survival from Late Roman activity or just possibly sherds disposed of away from the core of the post-Roman site. But in that case it seems strange that no such sherds occurred in the many post-Roman features. Poundbury in the fifth- to sixth century was apparently not on the trade route or gift-exchange system which included Tintagel, South Cadbury, Cadbury Congresbury (and also perhaps, Ilchester) but which did not extend to Exeter or Dorchester.[39]

A single small bronze vessel is known from the site but this is a small liquid container or lamp of fourth-century type and was associated with a miniature axe-head. This was probably from a funerary context, possibly recalling the larger and more ornate post-Roman hanging-bowls, rather than a domestic utensil of the post-Roman period.[40]

Fragments of two stone containers were recovered, the most interesting a very burnt and abraded fragment of a basin or stoop carved from a Hamstone column capital. This was incorporated in the rubble fill of PR4's foundation trench and thus could be earlier but the use of such basins as

[38] The distribution of pottery types and sherd-size in the latest Roman levels and the post-Roman features deserves study. The lack of pottery in the majority of post-Roman features could simply reflect their location on the site of the main cemetery, away from the contemporary Roman settlement and its associated domestic debris. In the latter area the early post-Roman features may be masked superficially by the presence of much residual material in their fills. This would apply, for instance, to the latest use of buildings R16 and 17.

[39] Arnold, *Roman Britain*, pp. 98, 116. For a commentary on the lack of post-Roman imports at Exeter see Holbrook and Bidwell, 'Roman Finds', pp. 13–14. As Thomas, 'Gallici', suggests for his phase 2 of imports, Gallic wine could have been imported in barrels. But why not also in phase 1, since, whether east Mediterranean amphorae and special table-ware or E-ware, why should not the bulk of the cargo on the final leg of the journey still have been of Gallic origin? A trade in wine from the Bordeaux region is attested epigraphically in the early third century. The containers in use then appear to have been barrels, attested both by actual survivals and, in central Gaul and the Rhineland, by sculptural evidence: see Salway, *Roman Britain*, pp. 580, 653–4. That much of the transport of wine from that date was in such organic containers, and thus an 'invisible' trade item under normal aerobic conditions, is not surprising in view of the greater efficency, strength and relatively light weight of barrels in comparison with amphorae. The contents also tasted better; who wants to drink retsina every day? Furthermore, the writer suggests that the harnessing of the native Celtic craft of cooperage to the developing wine industry of Gaul and the Rhineland may explain the latter's relative success and the Imperial rescripts attempting to limit the trade.

[40] For a similar bronze bowl of mid-fourth-century date see Johns and Carson, 'The Water Newton'; for a recent study of hanging-bowls see Brenan, *Hanging Bowls*.

fixed containers for water in a ritual context could still be of significance for that building or the preceding mausoleum.[41] In the absence of domestic pottery one has to conceive of a range of organic containers and carefully conserved metal vessels for everyday use.

Some estimate of the nutritional standards enjoyed by the occupants can be obtained from the range of meat and cereal foods available. All the main food animals are present including domestic fowl and deer but evidence for milking animals is not as clear as in the Roman period. The cereals included a more nutritious wheat species and oats while the presence of beans, peas and other edible plants may be significant. The absence of pottery precludes identification of food remains, especially any traces of milk products.

The contemporary diet, at its most basic, is perhaps recorded in the descriptions in penitentials. The combination of dried *paxmati* bread (or fresh bread on Sundays), some dish with fat or butter, garden vegetables, eggs, British cheese, milk and whey would be a reasonably balanced diet, especially if, as implied later in the text, the full diet included meat and beer. Archaeology can corroborate only the basic raw materials of such a diet.[42]

The picture of the site's economy is, then, of a remarkable asceticism when compared with the material prosperity of the the Romano-British settlement and the sophistication of the cemetery which had only recently before occupied the site. Yet amongst the material that did survive there is evidence for continuity of Late Roman technology and innovation in the types of cereals in use and in the quality of iron edge-tools available.

The absolute basics of everyday life were available, perhaps at a similar level to that of the poorest rural communities in the Roman period, but with the addition of these small but significant advances. No perceptible developments occurred during the period of post-Roman settlement although the stratigraphical evidence for an early date for the driers could suggest some change over time in the cereal-processing methods.

---

41 *Poundbury Volume I*, p. 106, fig. 76.
42 Winterbottom, pp. 84–86 and 146–7. It is, perhaps, significant that the Greek word *paxmati* is used rather than the Latin *biscuitum*; is this a reflection of a Byzantine origin for at least this aspect of early monastic regulation in western Britain? However, the text makes no mention of wine or other Mediterranean imports, which reinforces the suggestion that evidence for such foodstuffs need not be a feature of the finds from a monastic site, although, presumably, wine would still be used for eucharistic purposes.
43 *Poundbury Volume I*, pp. 69, 87–9, 153.

The Poundbury settlement in the local context

The lack of comparable settlement remains from the Dorchester area limits any discussion of the site within its local context but some consideration must be given to its relationship with the adjacent Poundbury Camp, to the latest Roman or sub-Roman activity within Dorchester's defences and to evidence for other contemporary sites in the vicinity of the town.

Evidence of Late Roman activity within the hill-fort has already been noted. The excavated post-Roman settlement adjoined the earthworks of Poundbury Camp, corn drier 6 lying immediately outside the eastern rampart, amidst the outer defences levelled in the construction of the aqueduct several centuries earlier.[43] However, the south and western defences had remained in a better state of preservation, the ditches much less silted than at present and the ramparts not scarped by agriculture and recent defensive work. The present south and south-western entrances may not have been in existence. Re-interpretation of sections of the inner rampart on the west and south of the east gate also suggests that it had possibly received a heightening faced with drystone work at this period.[44] Access to the hill-fort from the external settlement would have been easily effected via the original east gate or the gap created for the aqueduct at the north-east corner, the defences north of the east gate being effectively replaced by the southern boundary of the settlement. The latter, although admittedly slight, did produce evidence for substantial drystone work near the settlement's south entrance, a construction method that echoes that of the inner rampart.

The post-Roman re-use of the hill-fort must remain only a suggestion in the absence of substantial investigation of the defences and the enclosed area. If there was major use of the hill-fort then the hillside settlement would, in terms of area, be only an adjunct, in a more sheltered location, to a much more extensive hilltop enclosure. Indeed, whether the hill-fort served as military strongpoint and lookout, a refuge for population or merely a defended cattle corral, its considerable area, comparable to that of South Cadbury, Somerset, is an indicator of the site's importance.[45]

Within Dorchester evidence has only rarely been glimpsed for the town's decline into a sub-Roman phase and for the development of a truly post-Roman or Anglo-Saxon culture. But the coin list for the town, late

---

[44] *Ibid.*, pp. 32–36, 39. Neil Sharples' review of *Poundbury Volume I* in *Proceedings of the Prehistoric Society* vol. 54 (1988), overlooks references to the evidence for redating the Iron Age defences. For the late drystone walling in the western defences see Richardson, 'Excavations', pp. 433–4, plates LXIX, LXVIII and LXXIII, 1.

[45] Alcock, *By South Cadbury*, fig. 33, pp. 182–193.

fourth-century hoards 'and the presence of late BB1 ware on several sites provide evidence for continuity to the end of the Roman period.[46]

Frequent reference has been made to Colliton Park, the nearest sector of the walled area and also the most extensively excavated. Lying on the fringe of the early urban core, it was enclosed by the defences established in the second century and thereafter flourished, producing evidence for activity continuing to the end of the Roman period and possibly into the time of Poundbury's post- or sub-Roman phase. Building 5 at the Library site and the town house (Building I) in the Colliton Park excavations underwent substantial alteration in the second half of the fourth century but thereafter received the addition of crude hearths, roughly paved areas and drystone structures in or above the latest Roman levels. Late BB1 ware and a coin series to the early fifth century were recovered from both sites.[47] Unfortunately the post-Roman structures, the excavator's 'slum or squatter activity', did not produce clear building plans or distinctive post-Roman finds but the hearths and rough paving are similar to the latest activity in the vicinity of R17 and PR20 at Poundbury. A sunken-floored timber building, Room 19 of the town house, appears, interestingly, to fall within the Roman period and to be sealed by a Late Roman path.[48]

Some individual finds can be highlighted, even if their dating is insecure at present. Building VII revealed a smithing hearth of fourth century or later date which yielded both farrier's tools and half-finished projectile heads.[49] Building VI, another fourth-century town house, yielded a delicate set of scales from a hole in one mosaic floor, the only hole apparant in the published photograph appearing to be a posthole of stepped profile. This object is of some significance in view of its potential use for weighing coin; its occurrence in such a late context is intriguing. More refined examples, with suspension shears and balance indicators, occur in Anglo-Saxon graves of the sixth- to seventh century but the present example appears to be of an earlier, less developed, form illustrated, for example, in scenes on Pompeian wall paintings of gold coin production by winged cherubs.[50] Recent excavations in the vicinity of Building V, a large basilican type barn,

---

46 RCHM, *Dorset*, p. 538.
47 Aitken, 'Excavations', p. 99, vessels 6 and 30, fig. 17; Draper, 'Some Further discussion', p. 158; Drew and Collingwood-Selby, 'The Excavations', pp. 12 and 13.
48 The Colliton Park excavations of 1937–8 deserve to be better known as one of the earliest, large-scale, planned rescue excavations of a Roman town. The excellent records and many of the finds do survive and are to receive publication in the near future. Undoubtedly this will help to clarify the nature of the post-Roman activity recorded in the original work in this area. See Dark, *Discovery*, pp. 95–7 and 114.
49 Drew and Collingwood-Selby, 'The Excavations', pp. 11–12; RCHM, *Dorset*, p. 558, Mon 183.
50 Drew and Collingwood-Selby, 'The Excavations', pp. 9–10; RCHM, *Dorset*, p. 560, Mon 186; Scull, 'Scales'.

have revealed an oven similar to the Poundbury post-Roman corn driers and containing charred cereal grains, most notably bread wheat of the type introduced in the fifth century.[51]

To the east, in Glyde Path road, another building appears to have been furnished with tessellated floors in the late fourth century and has also produced a knife of early post-Roman type, reportedly from beneath the pavement but conceivably from one of the many disturbances cutting it.[52] Casual finds from nearer the town's core, in the Somerleigh Court area, are noteworthy since they include the early fifth-century hoard of coin and Christian spoons and a pair of delicate compasses with stamped Chi-Rho symbols.[53] Two spiral-headed bronze pins of early post-Roman type, one from this area the other from South Street, may be the only early post-Roman objects yet identified in the town.[54] The Baths site in the south-eastern sector of the walled area has proved the type site for a well-stratified and dated deposit of the distinctive late BB1 pottery, the ruined building also producing inhumation burials with radiocarbon dates in the early fifth century.[55] Recent work on a building nearby has also recovered posthole structures of Late or sub-Roman date within a building, perhaps adapting it rather than replacing it.[56]

These few indications of very Late Roman and early post-Roman activity in the town form only part of the evidence but the finds from Colliton Park in particular serve to illustrate that the tenuous structures and rare artefacts of this period at Poundbury may yet be identified within the town. Eventually the latter may be recognisable as a distinct extramural zone complementary to a reduced sub-Roman urban core.

South-east of the walled area Fordington Hill is notable for an extensive Roman cemetery zone with pre-Roman origins, a much more extensive and varied equivalant of the earlier cemeteries at Poundbury, differing in character to the standardised rite of the main Poundbury graveyard.[57] The present village is seen as having originated in the Anglo-Saxon period and

---

[51] Smith, 'Excavations'; Van der Veen, 'Charred Grain'; RCHM *Dorset*, p. 560, Mon 189.

[52] Draper and Chaplin, *Dorchester*, pp. 103–110.

[53] Moule describes these compasses as found during the construction of Somerleigh Court and gardens in 1862 or 1875: Moule, *Dorchester*, pp. 34, 74. For a similar pair of compasses (also stamped?) from Cirencester see Buckman and Newmarch, 'Illustrations'. The Dorchester example has been interpreted as indicative of a scriptorium in the town: Henig, 'A Probable Chi-Rho'. The spoons with Christian symbols from the Somerleigh hoard are illustrated in RCHM, *Dorset*, p. 562, Mon 190.

[54] Green, 'Notes'; The Somerleigh find is identical but unpublished. Although parallels in the Bronze Age were quoted for the latter these small delicate pins from post-Roman contexts are more comparable to those at, for instance, Hartlepool: Daniels, 'The Anglo-Saxon'.

[55] Batchelor, forthcoming; the pottery report by Gill Andrews will appear in the same report.

[56] Adams, 'Excavations'; Frere, *Roman Britain*, pp. 284–7.

[57] RCHM, *Dorset*, pp. 573–5, Mon 216.

to have focused on a church which conceivably is a mid-Saxon foundation. The remains of a rectangular masonry building recorded beneath the nave during extensive rebuilding in 1900 may be such an early church rather than a pre-existing Roman building; the fine early Roman funerary inscription found at the time was in a re-used context and probably derived from a grave monument of Classical type. Earlier burials on a north–south alignment underlie this building.[58]

The next spur in the chalk downs beyond Fordington has, however, produced remains of a complex of settlements, funerary and religious monuments which culminates in a phase datable to the early or mid-Saxon period. West of the Mount Pleasant hilltop and bisected by the present Alington Avenue a complex of early post-Roman date can be identified, adjacent to a Late Roman farmstead. To the north of the road, probably the line of a route to Purbeck, a cemetery of sixth or seventh-century date can be recognised while to the south a contemporary settlement has now been excavated. The latter comprised large rectangular timber buildings set around one or two open areas, the larger buildings of approximately 15 by 7 metres having single post-lines for the walls with opposed doorways in the long sides. There were also two possible grain-drying ovens and other slight structures and post lines from enclosures.[59] One structure at St Georges Road, 400 metres to the north-east, closer to the flood plain, appears to be of the same general character but 3.5 by 9 metres long and apparently open on one side. There are also two isolated burials of Anglo-Saxon type within the earthworks of the Neolithic henge further east along the ridge.[60]

The major cropmark complex at Maiden Castle Road, situated south-west of the town and presumed to mark an extended Roman settlement in its suburbs, has produced three Late Roman timber buildings reminiscent of the small huts at Poundbury. The size of these huts, and their slightly dished floors surrounded by postholes, are reminiscent of PR6–10 at Poundbury.[61]

Maiden Castle, itself, has now been recognised to contain a notable sequence from the Late Roman into the Anglo-Saxon period. The late fourth-century temple was adjoined by some ancillary structure of Roman mortared construction on the north, while to the south a roadway described a dog-leg around the small circular shrine set in the eastern end of the prehistoric long-mound. The road continued westward past a series of oriented graves, to continue into the western sector of the hill-fort. The circular shrine, which produced a curious mixture of fragmentary statuary,

---

[58] Feacey, 'The Sequence'.
[59] Green, 'Early Anglo-Saxon'; Davies, Stacey and Woodward, 'Excavations'.
[60] Schweiso, 'The Anglo-Saxon'; Woodward and Smith, 'Survey', p. 81, fig. 2.
[61] Woodward and Smith, 'Survey', p. 87, fig. 5.

the dregs of the temple's cult objects, has been assigned to the early post-Roman period but it did also produce Late Roman pottery. At least one seventh century Anglo-Saxon inhumation also lay in the east end of the mound.[62]

Finally, to the north west of the town beyond Poundbury, the cemetery at Bradford Peverel should be noted. Here on a hilltop adjacent to the Roman road to Ilchester, a location mirroring Alington Avenue on the other side of the town, lay a cemetery of oriented inhumations of Anglo-Saxon character and dated to the sixth or seventh century. These burials, richer than those at the Trumpet Major in the quality and in the number of male and female gravegoods, are not associated with any known settlement but this should, perhaps, be sought close-by on the ridge to the south-west, above the later Anglo-Saxon village.[63]

Interpretation of these discoveries around Dorchester must remain tentative in advance of final publication but it seems that settlements of the Late Roman and early post-Roman periods may occur on many other sites in the vicinity of the town. Within the town the evidence is poorer for structures but activity of the early fifth century existed and included at least one site where timber structures overlay, or were appended to, Roman buildings. Poundbury is thus not isolated but what is lacking for the town is definition of a continuous sequence through a strictly sub-Roman phase into the Anglo-Saxon period when, in the eighth century, a royal residence existed in Dorchester.[64] Perhaps at an earlier stage a sub-Roman settlement in the town, with an enclave at Poundbury, was encircled by early Anglo-Saxon sites at several points including those described above.

The Poundbury settlement in its wider context

Discussion of the Poundbury settlement in relation to some Roman and early post Roman sites is included in the original report; this should now be complemented with reference to studies of early post-Roman building types.[65] Poundbury can be contrasted with the Alington Avenue site, the only local settlement comparable in the extent of its investigation. At the latter site the earth-fast timber structures are notable for their complexity and size, their layout in a group associated with fenced enclosures, and for their location on the shoulder of a downland ridge. These features place them in the 'early Medieval building tradition' defined by James, Marshall and Millett, and interpreted by them as representing acculturation of Roman

---

[62] Wheeler, 'Maiden Castle', p. 74; Rahtz and Watts, 'The End'.
[63] See above, note 35.
[64] Keen, 'The Towns', p. 208.
[65] *Poundbury Volume 1*, pp. 152–3.

building types. These buildings were possibly occupied by both sub-Roman and Anglo-Saxon, or indeed mixed, communities.[66] The larger Poundbury buildings do not compare either in the regularity of plan or the sophistication of the architecture implicit in the plans of these buildings. The opposed doorways, the double-square plan, the annexes at either end and the appended rectangular enclosures are all lacking but can be recognised at Alington Avenue.

The Poundbury buildings are difficult to parallel but might be compared to the structures erected in the civic centre of Wroxeter in the fifth and sixth centuries.[67] These depended on a combination of timber and drystone to create a variety of structures, many similar in size to the phase 1 structures at Poundbury. The superstructures appear to have been of timber, resting on rubble platforms and reliant on earth-fast timbers for only some features, such as door-ways. The latter were often in the middle of one long side or one end wall. There were also lean-to structures utilising pre-existing Roman buildings. Save for the use of rubble platforms these features are comparable to those of the Poundbury buildings; however, the exceptionally large (high-status?) building at the heart of the Wroxeter complex is lacking.

Orton Hall Farm near Peterborough produced fewer buildings dispersed within the framework of a Late Roman courtyard farm, perhaps re-using some of its structures, such as the aisled buildings, but supplementing them with the introduction of a sunken featured building, six-post structure and a small timber hall with opposed entrances. Here, and at Barton Court Farm, the occupation represents the addition of Anglo-Saxon structure-types to Roman complexes and the introduction of Anglo-Saxon pottery and other goods. What this tells us of the nature of the population is now increasingly debated; whether this signals the replacement of British by Anglo-Saxon peoples, or the intermingling of the two, cannot be decided on building type alone but the relationship might be clearer on cemetery sites.[68]

At present we may not have enough post-Roman building plans to understand the Poundbury examples other than to say these are different from the most widespread 'early medieval' tradition. In particular, the relationship to Late Roman building types, not yet clearly defined, needs examination. At Studland and Colliton Park in Dorset, for instance, a distinct building type with a tripartite room division and a central doorway or porch in one long side can be recognised, a building form that might have influenced structures such as PR2, 3a, 12 and 14 and have even provided an origin for the Wroxeter buildings.

The Poundbury post-Roman settlement has been described in the context of the contemporary settlement pattern of the Dorchester area. As already

---

[66] James, Marshall and Millett, 'An Early'.
[67] White, 'Excavations'.
[68] Macreth, 'Orton Hall'; Esmonde-Cleary, *The Ending*, p. 196.

noted, settlement here in the post-Roman period could be an adjunct to some resettlement of the hill-fort or have been dependent on continuing activity in the town; the cemetery might also have been a particular influence on its location.[69] In relation to the hill-fort there is no evidence as to the form of any re-occupation; perhaps the evidence for its re-defence could relate to the Anglo-Saxon presence at Bradford Peverel on the road to the north-west. In relation to the walled area, the settlement could have continued as a working farm providing surplus to settlements such as that which continued in the Colliton Park area. Poundbury was, however, more than simply a servant's house in the sub-Roman suburbs and was at least a farm of several small households.

The relationship of this settlement to the cemetery raises other possibilites concerning the site's socio-economic context; the cemetery may have been an influence on its location, continuity being marked conversely by a change to domestic use focussed on significant burial monuments. The word 'monastery' was used in *Poundbury volume I* without detailed discussion of the evidence for a monastic interpretation and some consideration should be given here to this possibility which, while not excluding relationships with the town and hill-fort, might explain the particular choice of site. Whether or not one accepts the 'minimalist' view of the cemetery as a whole and the plaster burial rite in particular, seeing the former as simply a well-ordered 'municipal' burial ground without religious significance and the latter as merely a practical method of corpse disposal, the cemetery still has few parallels and the settlement's location is remarkable.[70] For a post-Roman settlement to occupy any Late Roman cemetery is unusual but for it to re-use one with the characteristics of Poundbury is unique in Britain. Here a hillside graveyard was re-occupied when a hill-top fortification, commanding the nearby Roman road, lay close-by. Even if the hill-fort was totally occupied – which is unlikely in view of its area, equal to that of South Cadbury – there was the adjoining downland or, indeed, the combe nearer the town. This re-occupation took place within one or two generations, or even within living memory, of the latest coin-dated graves. These, by no means the latest stratigraphically, fall in the third quarter of the fourth century, and yet the settlement on radiocarbon dating, was in existence by the mid-fifth century. If the case of grave desecration described by Sidonius Apollinaris was not unusual then memory of the position of the latest dug graves should have been current at the time of the settlement's foundation.

---

[69] *Poundbury Volume I*, p. 150.

[70] Philpott, *Burial*, pp. 90–96. Municipal regulation as an explanation for Poundbury type well-ordered cemeteries is hardly appropriate to the situation of late Roman Britain where the *ordo* of Durnovaria may have been pre-occupied with questions of taxation and defence rather than the orderliness of grave-rows. For plaster burials see Green, 'The Significance' and Sparey-Green, 'The Rite'.

Perhaps that is the factor dictating the choice of site; the settlement is here because of the more significant amongst the special burials.[71]

The scatter of shallow uncoffined and cist burials has already been noted as a significant feature both late in their stratigraphical position and in their typology. Such burials would seem out of place in a secular context but might accord more with a monastic site. In particular, a group on the north edge of cemetery zone 3C and south-west of PR11 and 12 is notable, also a group clustered in the central area east and north of PR4 and R8. Both groups could have been interred at any point during the settlement's life and could be likened to the disposition, for instance, of the burials at such a site as Church Island.[72]

As to the buildings, those of phase 1 and the corn-driers signify a working farm but the formal layout in relation to cemetery features, incorporating decorated mausolea and reserving the central burial focus within an open area, seems to serve no 'practical' farming purpose. In phases 2 and 3 the buildings are of a very different nature and set within newly created self-contained enclosures on a different axis.

The general pattern is unusual and the individual units can hardly each have served even a nuclear family and were particularly poor in finds. At Hartlepool a series of small buildings, of an admittedly different pattern but self-contained and lacking any familial hall, were seen as an important feature of the historically-attested monastic site.[73] At Poundbury, were these small huts monastic cells, the with re-used mausolea, PR2 and structure PR4 serving as conventual buildings? The latter in particular has no obvious domestic use.

In size and simplicity of plan the mausolea are comparable to the earliest extant churches in this region and could have served just that function. Both R8 and R9, significantly those with painted interiors, had exterior pavings as if for western doorways, while the latter also received structural additions and enclosure at a 'late' date.[74]

The boundaries around the site were of the slightest construction and hardly seem defensive. In phase 1 they continue the alignment of the

---

71 Sidonius Apollinaris, *Letters* Bk III, xii quoted in Reece, 'Burial'. The radiocarbon dating of the representative series of burials covering the span of the cemetery's use, preferably including groups with stratigraphical relationships, is essential to resolve the issues pertinent to both cemetery and settlement. At present the argument depends on comparing data from two disparate dating methods.

72 O'Kelly, 'Monastic Sites'. A rare example of a fully excavated early monastery where burials are set in scattered clusters across the site, sometimes overlapped by later structures, at other points set in open spaces. However, this is a rather distant example and in a specialised island setting where use of space was circumscribed.

73 Daniels, 'The Anglo-Saxon', p. 205. The buildings here were compared to Whitby and interpreted as small examples of the 'early medieval' tradition as defined by James, Marshall and Millett as befitted a seventh-century Anglo-Saxon foundation.

74 *Poundbury Volume I*, pp. 85, 90, 151.

cemetery, but they extended its bounds to the east and north to include building groups and grain-driers on its periphery. The re-orientation of buildings in phase 2 and of the enclosure in phase 3 is illustrated by the change in bearing of the structures. In phase 1 the enclosures followed an alignment of 105 degrees, similar to the cemetery, the buildings' short sides being aligned between 103 and 117 degrees (but with one on 32 degrees). In phase 2 the buildings had shifted to 67–110 degrees, with one on 41, while the phase 3 enclosure had its axis on 70 degrees. This major re-orientation serves no obvious purpose, reflecting neither man-made nor natural topography and requires some other explanation. Possibly the realignment of buildings and enclosure in the later stages was a conscious move to a more strictly oriented layout, dictated by religious views, as, for instance, in the early minster at Exeter.[75]

The material culture is remarkably ascetic but the site produced no distinctive finds specific to liturgical nature. The finds are those of a farming settlement but the presence of animal bones and the evidence for meat-eating is not an impediment to a monastic interpretation, nor is the absence of imported fine pottery or amphorae.[76] Arguably however, Roman Dorchester has produced better evidence for the equipment which might be expected at a religious establishment.[77]

The early settlement phase of the fifth century might be seen by some as too early for a monastic site but, as noted above, phase 2 and 3 fall considerably later. Perhaps the major re-organisation in layout marks the point when a religious community supplanted a more secular settlement focused on a cemetery of special status and memory.[78] Whatever its development it was cut short by the final destruction before the currency of objects such as the strap-end of the ninth- to tenth-century date retrieved

---

[75] The phase 1 enclosure measured 95 metres by 95 metres or more, the phase 3 enclosure 70 metres by 110 metres. Large near-rectangular enclosures have been identified at some sixth-century monastic sites: Thomas, *The Early*, p. 32. Major alterations in the orientation of Roman to post-Roman ecclesiastical sites occurred at, for instance, York and Exeter. At the latter site a sub-Roman cemetery on the alignment of the city grid (135 degrees) was succeeded by a Middle Saxon Cemetery on a mean alignment of 93 degrees, in turn replaced by the Late Saxon Minster on 70 degrees: Henderson and Bidwell, 'The Saxon'.

[76] See above, note 42. The quantity of amphorae sherds at Tintagel is now taken as evidence of its high-status, secular character, not of its monastic origins. For the development of this interpretation, see Dark, 'The Plan', pp. 16–17; Thomas, 'Tintagel', p. 430; Thomas, *Tintagel. Arthur*, pp. 93–5; Dark, *Discovery*, pp. 80–6.

[77] See above, note 53.

[78] Thomas, *Christianity*, p. 348 suggests an origin in south-west Britain in the late fifth century. Again, Gildas implies monasticism was well established in his day. See Dark, *Civitas*, pp. 56–7, 60 and 66–8.

from the topsoil. Unsurprisingly, perhaps no tradition carries any record of the site into the early history of Dorchester.[79]

To raise issues such as the identification of monastic sites is to stray into areas beyond simple matters of external contacts and economy, although, of course, the introduction of monastic communities is a particularly significant example of a non-trading link with the Mediterranean world. But whatever the status of the Poundbury settlement, and it must be admitted its monastic credentials are pretty unimpressive, it is a site that seems to chronicle the level of the subsistence economy and the poor nature of the material evidence which should be anticipated on contemporary settlements. In the Dorset countryside there could be many 'Poundburys' which, in the absence of the distinctive tracer-finds of imported, or native handmade, pottery, lie unrecognised; this one was only found by accident. But then it did have, as proposed above, a close relationship to an important Late Roman site and other such sequences are recognisable in Dorchester and beyond.[80]

This site's material poverty, when compared with the rich town-houses and villas of the Roman period, which must have been decaying in the surrounding contemporary landscape, can easily obscure the innovations manifest in the technology of the ironwork, the new cereal types and the, admittedly tenuous, evidence for watermills in the vicinity. It would be interesting to know whence these innovations derive and when exactly they appear. Are these the technological developments of the Late Roman economy, short of manpower but developing systems of food supply and factory production of weapons and clothing for official purposes, or are they the product of the inventive barbarian mind recorded in the *De Rebus Bellicis*?[81] At Dorchester the change appears to take place in the early fifth century, from the lack of evidence for these innovations in Late Roman contexts but from their presence in the Poundbury post-Roman levels. The late style of BB1 ware, perhaps specific to the late fourth and early fifth centuries, could be a useful key to defining archaeological sequences and refining these changes and innovations, at least locally. The introduction of watermills, including horizontal shaft mills, certainly falls well within the

---

79 For the later history of the site see *Poundbury Volume I*, p. 153. The site deserves attention in the context of neighbouring early Christian sites such as Charminster, a foundation of presumed Anglo-Saxon origin two kilometres to the north-west on the opposite side of the valley. The one-time existence of lost monastic sites is, perhaps, supported by evidence for 'Celtic' dedications at sites such as Halstock and Sherborne. It is only chance survival of early place-names that gives any clue as to their origins: Pearce, *The Early Church*, pp. 75, 99.

80 See above, note 79. The large villa close to Halstock has produced traces of extensive timber structures overlying the Roman buildings. Note on the interim plans in Lucas, 'Halstock', the many postholes around and inside buildings in the north and south wings.

81 Singer *et al.*, *History*, p. 605; Greene, 'Perspectives'.

Roman period and its origin was in the Classical world but the source of changes in cereal types is less certain. Is this a product of thriving Romano-British agricultural skill?[82] The developments in iron-making and edge-tool manufacture could be a very late development of the extensive Roman iron production centres and weapon-making, but seem equally likely to originate in central European technology. Is this the mechanical inventiveness of the barbarian peoples at work? If so, it had reached Dorchester in the mid-fifth century, well before the arrival of Anglo-Saxon settlers.[83]

Much more could be done, both in relation to Poundbury and elsewhere, to study these changes; scientific study of finds and environmental evidence from this period may yet further clarify external contacts and the economy trade and define the extent of acculturation both in demographic and technological terms.[84] This is clearly an instance where the most prosaic of finds and the least dramatic of settlement types could illuminate the early post-Roman period in Britain.

[82] Salway, *Roman Britain*, pp. 618–20.
[83] Biek, 'The Ethnic Factor'.
[84] Esmonde-Cleary, *The Ending*, p. 201, where this question has been addressed in terms of settlement-type but technological and economic factors could equally be valid means of discrimination.

BIBLIOGRAPHY

Adams, N. J., 'Excavations at Charles Street (Wessex Court), Dorchester', *Proceedings of the Dorset Natural History and Archaeological Society* 112 (1990), 115–17

Addison, K., Edge, M. J., and Watkins, R. (eds), *North Wales Field Guide* (Coventry, 1990)

Aitken, G. and N., 'Excavations on the Library Site, Colliton Park, Dorchester 1961–3', *Proceedings of the Dorset Natural History and Archaeological Society* 104 (1982), 93–126

Alcock, L., *Dinas Powys, an Iron Age, Dark Age and early medieval settlement in Glamorgan* (Cardiff, 1963)

———, *Economy, Society and Warfare among the Britons and Saxons* (Cardiff, 1987)

Allan, J., 'Some post-medieval documentary evidence for the trade in ceramics', in *Ceramics and Trade*, edited by Peter Davey and Richard Hodges (Sheffield, 1983), pp. 37–45

Andersen, S. T., 'Identification of wild grass and cereal pollen', *Danmarks Geologiske Undersøgelse Årborg* (1978), 69–92

Anderson, A. O., and M. O. (eds and transl.), *Adomnan's Life of St Columba* (Edinburgh, 1961)

Andrews, M. V., Beck, R. B., Gilbertson, D. D., and Switsur, V. R., 'Palaeobotanical investigations at An t-Aoradh (Oronsay), the Strand and Loch Cholla (Colonsay)', in *Excavations on Oronsay*, by P. Mellars (Edinburgh 1987), pp. 57–71

Armstrong, E. C. R., and Macalister, R. A. S., 'Wooden book with leaves indented and waxed found near Springmount Bog, Co. Antrim', *Journal of the Royal Society of Antiquaries of Ireland* 50 (1920), 160–6

Arnold, C. J., *Roman Britain to Saxon England* (London, 1984)

Aston, M., Austin, D., and Dyer, C. (eds), *The Rural Settlements of Medieval England* (Oxford, 1989)

Atherden, M. A., 'Late Quaternary vegetational history of the North York Moors. III. Fen Bogs', *Journal of Biogeography* 3 (1976), 115–124

Audin, A. and Burnand, Y., 'Alla ricerca della trace di Cristianesimo sulle tombe di Lione prima della pace della Chiesa', *Rivista di Archeologia Cristiana* 35 (1959), 51–70

———, 'Chronologie des epitaphs romaines de Lyon', *Revue des Etudes Anciennes* 61 (1959), 320–52

————, 'Chronologie des epitaphs romaines de Vienne', *Revue des Etudes Anciennes* 63 (1961), 291–311

Baillie, M., 'Do Irish Bog Oaks Date the Shang Dynasty?', *Current Archaeology* 117 (1989), 310–13

Baillie, M. G. L., 'Suck-in and smear: two related chronological problems for the 1990s', *Journal of Theoretical Archaeology* 2 (1991), 12–16

————, 'Dendrochronology raises questions about the nature of the AD 536 dust-veil event', *The Holocene* 4 (1994), 212–17

Baillie, M. G. L., and Munro, M. A. R., 'Irish tree rings, Santorini and volcanic dust veils', *Nature* 332 (1988), 344–6

Balaam, N. D., Levitan, B., and Straker, V. (eds), *Studies in palaeoeconomy and environment in South West England* (Oxford, 1987)

Barber, K. E., *Peat stratigraphy and climatic change* (Rotterdam, 1981)

Bartley, D. D., and Chambers, C., 'A pollen diagram, radiocarbon ages and evidence of agriculture on Extwistle Moor, Lancashire', *New Phytologist* 121 (1992), 311–20

Bartley, D. D., Chambers, C., and Hart-Jones, B., 'The vegetational history of parts of south and east Durham', *New Phytologist* 77 (1976), 437–68

Bartley, D. D., Jones, I. P., and Smith, R. T., 'Studies in the Flandrian vegetational history of the Craven District of Yorkshire: the lowlands', *Journal of Ecology* 78 (1990), 611–32

Bartley, D. D., and Morgan, A. V., 'The palynological record of the King's Pool, Stafford, England', *New Phytologist* 116 (1990), 177–94

Bass, G. F., and van Doornick, F. H., *Yassi Ada, a seventh-century Byzantine shipwreck* (Texas, 1982)

Bass, G. (ed.), *A History of Seafaring based on Underwater Archaeology* (London, 1972)

Batchelor, D., *Excavations at the Roman Baths, Woolaston Field, Dorchester*, forthcoming

Bateson, J. D., 'Roman material from Ireland, a reconsideration', *Proceedings of the Royal Irish Academy* 73C (1973), 21–98

————, 'Further finds of Roman material from Ireland', *Proceedings of the Royal Irish Academy* 76C (1976), 171–80

Beales, P. W., 'The Late Devensian and Flandrian vegetational history of Crose Mere, Shropshire', *New Phytologist* 85 (1980), 133–61

Beckett, S. C., and Hibbert, F. A., 'Vegetational change and the influence of prehistoric man in the Somerset Levels', *New Phytologist* 83 (1979), 577–600

Bell, M., 'Environmental archaeology as an index of continuity and change in the medieval landscape', in *The Rural Settlements of Medieval England*, edited by M. Aston *et al.* (Oxford, 1989), pp. 269–86

Bell, M., and Limbrey, S., *Archaeological Aspects of Woodland Ecology* (Oxford, 1982)

Bennett, K. D., Boreham, S., Sharp, M. J., and Switsur, V. R., 'Holocene history of environment, vegetation and human settlement on Catta Ness, Lunnasting, Shetland', *Journal of Ecology* 80 (1992), 241–73

Bennett, K. D., Fossitt, J. A., Sharp, M. J., and Switsur, V. R., 'Holocene vegetational and environmental history at Loch Lang, South Uist, Western Isles, Scotland', *New Phytologist* 114 (1990), 281–98

Benoit, F., *Sarcophages Paleochretiens d'Arles et de Marseille, Fifth Supplememnt to Gallia* (1954)

Biek L., 'The Ethnic Factor in Archaeotechnology', in *Proceedings of the 22nd Symposium on Archaeometry, Bradford 1982*, edited by A. Aspinall and S. E. Warren (Bradford, 1983), pp. 303–15

Bieler, Ludwig (ed.), *The Irish Penitentials* (Dublin, 1975)

Binchy, D.A., 'Review of Jackson, *Language and History in Early Britain*', *Celtica* 4 (1958), 288–92

————, 'A Text on the Forms of Distraint', *Celtica* 10 (1973), 72–80

———— (ed.), *Corpus Iuris Hibernici* (6 vols, Dublin, 1978)

————, *Críth Gablach* (Dublin, 1940)

Birks, H. J. B., *Quaternary vegetational history of western Scotland* (Cambridge, 1980)

Birks, H. J. B., and West, R. G., *Quaternary Plant Ecology* (Oxford, 1973)

Birks, H. J. B., and Williams, W., 'Late-Quaternary vegetational history of the Inner Hebrides', *Proceedings of the Royal Society of Edinburgh* 83B (1983), 269–92

Blackford, J. J., and Chambers, F. M., 'Proxy records of climate from blanket mires: evidence for a Dark Age (1400 BP) climatic deterioration in the British Isles', *The Holocene* 1 (1991), 63–7

Blagg, T. F., Jones, R., and Keay, S.J. (eds), *Papers in Iberian Archaeology* (Oxford, 1984)

Bohme, H. W., 'Das ende der Romerherrschaft in Britannien und die Angelsachsische Besiedlung Englands im 5 Jahrhundert', *Jahrbuch des Romisch-Germanischen Zentral museum* 33 (1986), 466–574

Boon, G. C., 'A Christian monogram at Caerwent', *Bulletin of the Board of Celtic Studies* 19 (1962), 338–44

Bowman, Sheridan, *Radiocarbon Dating* (London, 1990)

Brenan J., *Hanging Bowls and their Contexts* (Oxford, 1991)

Brisbane, M., 'Hamwic (Saxon Southampton): an 8th-century port and production centre', in *The Rebirth of Towns in the West AD 700–1050*, edited by Richard Hodges and Brian Hobley (London, 1988), pp. 101–8

Brodribb, A. C. C., Hands, A. R., and Walker, D. R., *Excavations at Shakenoak* (5 vols, Oxford, 1968–78)

Brown, A. G., 'The palaeoecology of *Alnus* (alder) and the postglacial history of floodplain vegetation. Pollen percentage and influx data from the West Midlands, United Kingdom', *New Phytologist* 110 (1988), 425–36

Brown, A. P., 'Late-Devensian and Flandrian vegetational history of

Bodmin Moor, Cornwall', *Philosophical Transactions of the Royal Society* B 276 (1977), 251–320

Brown, P., *The World of Late Antiquity* (London, 1971)

Buckman, J., and Newmarch, C. H., 'Illustrations of Remains of Roman Art in Cirencester, the site of Corinium', *Archaeological Journal* 7 (1850), 409–11

Bu'lock, J. D., 'Early Christian memorial formulae', *Archaeologia Cambrensis* 105 (1956), 49–53

Burnham, Barry C., and Wacher, John, *The Small Towns of Roman Britain* (London, 1990)

Buxton, D. (ed.), *Custom is King: Studies in Honour of R. R. Marett* (London, 1936)

Cameron, A., and Schauer, D., 'The last consul: Basilius and his diptych', *Journal of Roman Studies* 72 (1982), 126–45

Campbell, E., 'A Cross-marked Quern from Dunadd and Other Evidence for Relations Between Dunadd and Iona', *Proceedings of the Society of Antiquaries of Scotland* 117 (1987), 105–17

——, 'The Post Roman Pottery', in *Early Medieval Settlements in Wales A.D. 400–1100*, edited by Nancy Edwards and Alan Lane (Cardiff, 1988), pp. 124–36

——, 'A blue glass squat jar from Dinas Powys, South Wales', *Bulletin Board of Celtic Studies* 36 (1989), 239–45

——, 'Imported goods in the early medieval Celtic West: with special reference to Dinas Powys' (unpublished Ph.D. thesis, University of Wales, College of Cardiff, 1991)

——, 'New evidence for glass vessels in western Britain and Ireland in the 6th/7th centuries AD', in *Le Verre de l'Antiquité tardive et du Haut Moyen Age*, edited by D. Foy (Paris, 1995), pp. 35–40

——, 'A review of glass vessels in western Britain and Ireland AD 400–800', in *Glass in Britain, AD 350–800*, edited by J. Price (London, forthcoming)

Casey, P. J., 'The end of garrisons on Hadrian's Wall: an historico-environmental model', in *The Later Roman Empire Today*, edited by D. F. Clark, M. M. Roxan, and J. J. Wilkes (London, 1993), pp. 69–80

Cederlund, C. O. (ed.), *Post-Medieval Boat and Ship Archaeology* (Oxford, 1985)

Chadwick, O., 'Gildas and the monastic order', *Journal of Theological Studies* (1954), 78–80

Chambers, F. M., 'Two radiocarbon-dated pollen diagrams from high-altitude blanket peats in South Wales', *Journal of Ecology* 70 (1982), 445–59

——, 'Three radiocarbon-dated pollen diagrams from upland peats north-west of Merthyr Tydfil, South Wales', *Journal of Ecology* 71 (1983), 475–87

Colgrave, B., and Mynors, R. (eds), *Bede's Ecclesiastical History of the English People* (Oxford, 1969)

Colgrave, B., and Mynors, R. A. B. (eds and transl.), *Historia Ecclesiastica Gentis Anglorum* (Oxford, 1969)

Collins, R., 'Mérida and Toledo: 500–585', in *Visigothic Spain*, edited by E. James (London, 1980), pp. 189–219

Costa, D., *Art Merovingian: Musee Th. Dobree, Nantes. Inventaire des Collections Publiques Francaises 10* (Paris, 1964)

Courty, M. A., Goldberg, P. and Macphail, R., *Soils and Micromorphology in Archaeology* (Cambridge, 1989)

Cox, P. W., 'A Seventh Century Inhumation Cemetery at Shepherds' Farm, Ulwell near Swanage, Dorset', *Proceedings of the Dorset Natural History and Archaeological Society* 110 (1988), 37–47

Crawford, O. G. S, 'Western Seaways', in *Custom is King: Studies in Honour of R. R. Marett*, edited by D. Buxton (London, 1936), pp. 181–200

Cunliffe, B., 'Relations between Britain and Gaul in the First Century A.D.', in *Cross-Channel Trade between Gaul and Britain in the Pre-Roman Iron Age*, edited by S. Macready and F. H. Thompson (London, 1984), pp. 3–23

Daniels, R., 'The Anglo-Saxon Monastery at Church Close, Hartlepool, Cleveland', *Archaeological Journal* 145 (1988), 158–211

Dark, K. R., 'St Patrick's *uillula* and the fifth-century occupation of Romano-British villas', in *St Patrick, A.D. 493–1993*, D. N. Dumville *et al.* (Woodbridge, 1993), pp. 19–24

———, *Civitas to Kingdom* (London, 1994)

———, *Discovery by Design* (Oxford, 1994)

Davey, Peter, and Hodges, Richard (eds), *Ceramics and trade* (Sheffield, 1983)

Davies, G., and Turner, J., 'Pollen diagrams from Northumberland', *New Phytologist* 82 (1979), 783–804

Davies, S. M., Stacey, L. C., and Woodward, P. J., 'Excavations at Alington Avenue, Fordington, Dorchester 1984/85 Interim Report', *Proceedings of the Dorset Natural History and Archaeological Society* 107 (1985), 101–10

Dawes, E. and N., and Baynes, N., *Three Byzantine Saints* (London, 1948)

Day, S. P., 'Post-glacial vegetational history of the Oxford region', *New Phytologist* 119 (1991), 445–70

———, 'Woodland origin and "ancient woodland indicators": a case-study from Sidlings Copse, Oxfordshire, UK', *The Holocene* 3 (1993), 45–53

Detsicas, A. (ed.), *Collectanea Historica: Essays in Memory of Stuart Rigold* (Maidstone, 1981)

Dixon, Philip, 'Life after Wroxeter: the final phases of Roman towns', in

From Roman Town to Norman Castle, edited by Aubry Burl (Birmingham, 1988), pp. 30–9

Doehaerd, R., *The Early Middle Ages in the West: Economy and Society* (transl. by W. G. Deakin, Amsterdam, 1978)

Doherty, C., 'Exchange and Trade in Medieval Ireland', *Proceedings of the Royal Society of Antiquaries of Ireland* 110 (1980), 67–89

———, 'Exchange and trade in early medieval Ireland', *Journal of the Royal Society Antiquaries Ireland* 110 (1980), 67–90

Dolley, M., *The Hiberno-Norse Coins in the British Museum* (London, 1966)

———, 'Roman coins from Ireland and the date of St Patrick', *Proceedings of the Royal Irish Academy* 76C (1976), 181–90

Donaldson, A. M., and Turner, J., 'A pollen diagram from Hallowell Moss, near Durham City, U.K.', *Journal of Biogeography* 4 (1977), 25–33

Draper, J., 'Some further Discussion of the Library Site, Colliton Park, Dorchester', *Proceedings of the Dorset Natural History and Archaeological Society* 105 (1983), 157–9

Drew, C. D., and Collingwood, Selby, K. C., 'The Excavations at Colliton Park, Dorchester 1937–8: First Interim Report', *Proceedings of the Dorset Natural History and Archaeological Society* 59 (1938), 1–14

Driscoll, S., and Nieke, M. (eds), *Power and Politics in Early Medieval Britain and Ireland* (Edinburgh, 1988)

Drury, P. J., and Wickenden, M. P., 'An Early Saxon settlement within the Romano-British Small Town at Heybridge, Essex', *Medieval Archaeology* 26 (1982), 1–14

Dumayne, L., and Barber, K. E., 'The impact of the Romans on the environment of northern England: pollen data from three sites close to Hadrian's Wall', *The Holocene* 4 (1994), 165–73

Dumayne, L., Stoneman, R., Barber, K., and Harkness, D., 'Problems associated with correlating calibrated radiocarbon-dated pollen diagrams with historical events', *The Holocene* 5 (1995), 118–23

Düemmler, E., *Epistolae Karolini Aevi. Monumenta Germaniae Historica: Epistolae*, II (Berlin, 1895)

Dumville, David N. *et al.*, *St Patrick, A.D. 493–1993* (Woodbridge, 1993)

Edwards, H. J. (ed.), *Caesar: Gallic War* (London, 1917)

Edwards, K. J., 'Palynological and temporal inference in the context of prehistory, with special reference to the evidence from lake and peat deposits', *Journal of Archaeological Science* 6 (1979), 255–70

———, 'Using space in cultural palynology: the value of the off-site pollen record', in *Modelling Ecological Change*, edited by David R. Harris and Kenneth D. Thomas (London, 1991), pp. 61–73

Edwards, N., *The Archaeology of Early Medieval Ireland* (London, 1990)

Edwards, N., and Lane, A. (eds), *Early Medieval Settlements in Wales AD 400–1100* (Cardiff, 1988)

158

Elliott, R. W. V., *Runes: An Introduction* (Manchester, 1959)

Ellis Evans, D. (ed.), *Proceedings of the Seventh International Congress of Celtic Studies* (Oxford, 1987)

Esmonde-Cleary, A. S., *The Ending of Roman Britain* (London, 1989)

Evans, D. H., 'Reflections on the study of imported ceramics', in *Studies in medieval and later pottery in Wales*, edited by Blaise Vyner and Stuart Wrathmell (Cardiff, 1987), pp. 199–224

Evans, Jeremy, 'From Roman Britain to the "Celtic West" ', *Oxford Journal of Archaeology* 9 (1990), 91–103

Evison, Vera I., *A corpus of wheel-thrown pottery in Anglo-Saxon graves* (London, 1979)

Evison, V. (ed.), *Medieval Pottery from Excavations: Studies presented to G. C. Dunning* (London, 1974)

Faegri, Knut, and Iversen, J. (revised by Knut Faegri, Peter Emil Kaland and Knut Krzywinski), *Textbook of pollen analysis* (4th edn, Chichester, 1989)

Fanning, T., 'Excavation of and Early Christian cemetery and settlement at Reask, Co. Kerry', *Proceedings of the Royal Irish Academy* 81C (1981), 67–172

Farquhar, R. M., and Vitali, V., 'Lead isotope measurements and their application to Roman lead and bronze artefacts from Carthage', *MASCA Research Papers Science and Archaeology* 6 (1989), 39–45

Fawtier, R., 'La Vie de Saint Samson', *Bibliotheque de l'Ecole des Hautes Etudes* 197 (Paris, 1912)

Feacey, J., 'The Sequence and Evolution of Architectural Styles in the Church of Fordington St George, Dorchester', *Proceedings of the Dorset Natural History and Archaeological Field Club* 30 (1909), 164–70

Fleuriot, L., and Giot, P-R., 'Early Brittany', *Antiquity* 51 (1977), 106–16

Foy, D., 'Le verre de la fin du IVe au VIIIe siècle en France méditer-ranéenne, premier essai de typo-chronologie', in *Le Verre de l'antiquité tardive et du haut moyen âge*, edited by D. Foy (Association Française pour l'Archéologie du Verre/Musée Archéologique du Val D'Oise, Guiry-en-Vexin, 1995), pp. 187–242

Foy, Daniele (ed.), *Le Verre de l'antiquité tardive et du Haut Moyen Age* (Association Française pour l'Archéologie du Verre/Musée Archéolo-gique du Val D'Oise, Guiry-en Vexin, 1995)

Foy, D., and Hochuli-Gysel, A., 'Le verre en Aquitaine du IVe au IXe siècle: un état de la question', in *Le Verre de l'antiquité tardive et du haut moyen âge*, edited by D. Foy (Association Française pour l'Archéologie du Verre/Musée Archéologique du Val D'Oise, Guiry-en-Vexin, 1995), pp. 177–86

Francis, P. D., and Slater, D. S., 'A record of vegetational and land use change from upland peat deposits on Exmoor. Part 2: Hoar Moor',

Proceedings of the Somerset Archaeological and Natural History Society
134 (1990), 1–25

Frere S. S., 'Roman Britain in 1990', *Britannia* 22 (1990), 221–312

Fulford, M., 'Pottery and Britain's foreign trade in the Late Roman period',
in *Pottery and Early Commerce: Characterisation and Trade in Roman
and Later Ceramics*, edited by D. P. S. Peacock (London, 1977), pp.
35–84

———, 'Pottery Production and Trade at the end of Roman Britain: the
case against continuity', in *The End of Roman Britain*, edited by P. J.
Casey (Oxford, 1979), pp. 120–32

———, 'Demonstrating Britannia's economic dependence in the first and
second centuries', in *Military and Civilian in Roman Britain*, edited by
T. F. C. Blagg and A. C. King (Oxford, 1984), pp. 129–42

———, 'Byzantium and Britain: a Mediterranean Perspective on Post-
Roman Mediterranean Imports in Western Britain and Ireland', *Medieval
Archaeology* 33 (1989), 1–6

——— 'The economy of Roman Britain', in *Research on Roman Britain
1960–89*, edited by Malcolm Todd (London, 1989), pp. 175–201

Fulford, M., and Peacock, D. P. S., *Excavations at Carthage: The British
Mission, Volume 1.2: The Pottery from the Avenue du Président Habib
Bourguiba Site* (Sheffield, 1984)

Galinie, H. (ed.), *Recherches sur Tours*, volume 1 (Tours, 1981)

Garnsey, P., Hopkins, K., and Whittaker, C. (eds), *Trade in the Ancient
Economy* (London, 1983)

Garvin, J. N., *The Vitas Patrum Sanctorum Emeretensium* (Washington
D.C., 1946)

Giot, P.-R., and Querre, G., 'Le tesson d'amphore B2 de l'Ile Lavret (Brehat,
Côtes-du-Nord) et le problème des importation', *Revue Archéologique
de l'Ouest* 2 (1985), 95–100

Godley, A. D. (ed.), *Herodotus, Histories* (2 vols, New York and London,
1926)

Godwin, H., 'Pollen-analytical evidence for the cultivation of *Cannabis* in
England', *Review of Palaeobotany and Palynology* 4 (1967), 67–70

Goffart, Walter, *Caput and Colonate: Towards a History of Late Roman
Taxation* (Phoenix, 1974)

———, *Barbarians and Romans, A.D. 418–584: the Techniques of Acco-
modation* (Princeton, 1980)

Graham, A. J., and Lucas, R. N., *Excavations at the Roman Villa at
Halstock, Dorset* (forthcoming)

Grattan, J. P., and Charman, D. J., 'Non-climatic factors and the environmental impact of volcanic volatiles: implications of the Laki fissure
eruption of AD 1783', *The Holocene* 4 (1994), 101–6

Grattan, J. P., and Gilbertson, D. D., 'Acid-loading from Icelandic tephra
falling on acidified ecosystems as a key to understanding archaeological

and environmental stress in northern and western Britain', *Journal of Archaeological Science* 21 (1994), 851–59

Green, C. J. S., 'Notes on Roman sites in Dorchester 1963–65', *Proceedings of the Dorset Natural History and Archaeological Society* 88 (1966), 110–13

——, 'The Significance of Plaster Burials for the Recognition of Christian Cemeteries', in *Burial in the Roman World*, edited by R. Reece (London, 1977)

——, 'Early Anglo-Saxon Burials at the "Trumpet-Major" Public House, Alington Ave, Dorchester', *Proceedings of the Dorset Natural History and Archaeological Society* 106 (1984), 149–52

Greene, Kevin, *The Archaeology of the Roman Economy* (London, 1986)

——, 'Perspectives on Roman Technology', *Oxford Journal of Archaeology* 9.2 (1990), 209–19

Greig, J. R. A., 'The British Isles', in *Progress in Old World Palaeoethnobotany*, edited by Willem Van Zeist, Krystyna Waslikowa and Karl-Ernst Behre (Rotterdam, 1991), pp. 299–334

Hamerow, H., Hollevoet, Y., and Vince, A., 'Migration period settlements and "Anglo-Saxon" pottery from Flanders', *Medieval Archaeology* 38 (1994), 1–18

Hamlin, A., 'A Chi-rho carved stone at Drumaqueran, Co. Antrim', *Ulster Journal of Archaeology* 35 (1972), 22–8

——, 'Early Irish stone carving: content and context', in *The Early Church in Western Britain and Ireland*, edited by Susan M. Pearce (Oxford, 1982), pp. 283–96

Hammer, C. U., 'Traces of volcanic eruptions in the Greenland ice sheet', *Jokull* 34 (1984), 51–6

Hammer, C. U, Clausen, H. B., and Dansgaard, W., 'Greenland ice sheet evidence of post-glacial volcanism and its climatic impact', *Nature* 288 (1980), 230–5

Harris, David R., and Thomas, Kenneth D., *Modelling Ecological Change* (London, 1991)

Hartgrove, S., and Walker, R., 'Excavations in the Lower Ward, Tintagel Castle, 1986', in *Tintagel Papers*, edited by Charles Thomas (Redruth, 1988), pp. 9–30

Hatton, J. M., and Caseldine, C. J., 'Vegetation change and land use history during the first millenium AD at Aller Farm, east Devon as indicated by pollen analysis', *Devon Archaeological Society Proceedings* 49 (1992), 107–14

Hawkes, S. C., 'Anglo-Saxon Kent c. 425–725', in *Archaeology in Kent to AD 1500*, edited by Peter Leach (London 1982), pp. 64–78

Hawthorne, J., and Pinder, C., 'Bradford Peverel Inhumation Cemetery', *Proceedings of the Dorset Natural History and Archaeological Society* 111 (1989), 110–11

Hays, J. W., *Late Roman Pottery* (London, 1972)

———, *A Supplement to Late Roman Pottery* (London, 1980)

Henderson, C. G., and Bidwell, P. T., 'The Saxon Minster at Exeter', in *The Early Church in Western Britain and Ireland*, edited by S. M Pearce (Oxford, 1982), pp. 145–75.

Henig, M., 'A Probable Chi-Rho Stamp on a pair of Compasses', *Proceedings of the Dorset Natural History and Archaeological Society* 105 (1983), 159

Herren, M., 'The Earliest Irish Aquaintance with Isidore of Seville', in *Visigothic Spain*, edited by E. James (London, 1980), pp. 243–50

———, 'Some New Light Upon the life of Virgilus Maro Grammaticus', *Proceedings of the Royal Irish Academy* 79C (1979), 21–71

Hicks, S. P., 'Pollen-analytical evidence for the effect of prehistoric agriculture on the vegetation of north Derbyshire', *New Phytologist* 70 (1971), 647–67

Higham, N., *The Northern Counties to AD 1000* (London, 1986)

Hill, P., *Whithorn III*, and Supplement (Whithorn, 1990)

Hillgarth, J. N., 'Ireland and Spain in the Seventh Century', *Peritia* 3, 1984, pp. 1–16.

———, 'Modes of Evangelisation in Western Europe in the Seventh Century', in *Irland und die Christenheit: Bibelstudien und Mission*, edited by P. Ní Chatháin and E. Richter (Stuttgart, 1987), pp. 311–32

Hochuli-Gysel, A., 'Le verre du IVe-VIe siècles en Aquitaine; un état de la question', in *Le Verre de l'Antiquité tardive au moyen Age*, edited by D. Foy (Paris, 1995)

Hodges, Richard, *Dark Age economics: the origins of towns and trade AD 600–1000* (London, 1982)

———, *The Anglo-Saxon achievement* (London, 1989)

———, 'Some Early Medieval French Wares in the British Isles', in *Pottery and Early Commerce: Characterisation and Trade in Roman and Later Ceramics*, edited by D. P. S. Peacock (London, 1977), pp. 239–62

Hodges, Richard, and Whitehouse, David, *Mohammed, Charlemagne and the Origins of Europe* (Gloucester, 1983)

Holbrook, N., and Bidwell P. T., *Roman Finds from Exeter* (Exeter, 1991)

Hood, A. B. E. (ed. and transl.), *St Patrick: His Writings and Muirchu's Life* (Chichester, 1978)

Howe, M. D., Perrin, J. R., and Mackreth, D. F., *Roman Pottery from the Nene Valley: A Guide* (Peterborough, 1981)

Huckerby, E., Wells, C., and Middleton, R. H., 'Recent palaeoecological and archaeological fieldwork in Over Wyre, Lancashire', in *North West Wetlands Survey Annual Report 1992*, edited by R. H. Middleton (Lancaster, 1992), pp. 9–18

Huggett, J. W., 'Imported grave goods and the early Anglo-Saxon economy', *Medieval Archaeology* 32 (1988), 63–96

Hurst, Derek, 'Major Saxon discoveries at Droitwich: excavations at the Upwich brine pit', *Current Archaeology* 126 (1991), 252–55

Hutchins, J., The History and Antiquities of the County of Dorset (3rd edn, Dorchester, 1870)

Jacobson, G.L., and Bradshaw, R. H. W., 'The selection of sites for palaeo-vegetational studies', *Quaternary Research* 16 (1981), 80–96

Jaffe, Philipp (ed.), *Regestra Pontificum Romanorum* (Berlin, 1885)

James, E., 'Ireland and western Gaul in the Merovingian period', in *Ireland and Early Medieval Europe*, edited by D. Whitelock, *et al.* (Cambridge, 1982), pp. 362–86

——, *The Franks* (Oxford 1988)

—— (ed.), *Visigothic Spain: New Approaches* (Oxford, 1980)

James, S., Marshall, A., and Millett, M., 'An Early Medieval Building Tradition', *Archaeological Journal* 141 (1984), 182–215

Johns, C., and Carson, R., 'The Waternewton Hoard, Durobrivae', *Review of Nene Valley Archaeology* 3 (1975), 10

Jones, Barri and Mattingly, David, *An Atlas of Roman Britain* (Oxford, 1990)

Jones, H. L. (ed.), *Strabo, Geographica* (New York and London, 1949)

Jones, M., and Dimbleby, G., *The Environment of Man: the Iron Age to the Anglo-Saxon Period* (Oxford, 1981)

Jones, V. J., Stevenson, A. C., and Battarbee, R. W., 'Acidification of lakes in Galloway, south west Scotland: a diatom and pollen study of the post-glacial history of the Round Loch of Glenhead', *Journal of Ecology* 77 (1989), 1–23

Keay, S.J., *Late Roman Amphorae in the Western Mediterranean* (Oxford, 1984)

Keen, L. J., 'The Towns of Dorset', in *The Anglo-Saxon Towns of Southern England*, edited by J. Haslam (1984), pp. 203–47

——, 'Dorset Archaeology in 1977', *Proceedings of the Dorset Natural History and Archaeological Society* 99 (1977), 120

Kenney, J. F., *The Sources for the Early History of Ireland: Ecclesiastical* (New York, 1929)

Killeen, J.F., 'Ireland in the Greek and Roman Writers', *Proceedings of the Royal Irish Academy* 76C (1976), 207–15

Knight, J., '*In Tempore Iustini Consulis:* Contacts between the British and Gaulish Churches before St Augustine', in *Collectanea Historica*, edited by A. Detsicas (Maidstone, 1981), pp. 54–62

——, 'Glamorgan A.D. 400–1100 – Archaeology and History', in *Glamorgan County History*, edited by H. N. Savory (Cardiff, 1984), pp. 315–45

——, 'Sources for the early history of Morgannwg', in *Glamorgan County History*, edited by H. N. Savory (Cardiff, 1984), pp. 346–409

——, 'Pottery in Wales: the pre-Norman background', in *Studies in*

Medieval and Later Pottery in Wales, edited by Blaise Vyner and Stuart Wrathmell (Cardiff, 1987), pp. 9–22

————, 'The Early Christian Latin inscriptions of Britain and Gaul: chronology and context', in *The Early Church in Wales and the West*, edited by N. Edwards and A. Lane (Oxford, 1992), pp. 45–50

————, 'Penmachno revisited: the consular inscription and its context', *Cambrian Mevieval Celtic Studies* 29 (Summer, 1995), 1–10

Kroeber, A. L., *Anthropology* (New York, 1948)

Krusch, B. (ed.), 'Jonas: *Vita Columbani*', in *Passiones Vitaeque Sanctorum aevi Merovingici*. *Monumenta Germaniae Historica: Scriptores rerum Merovingicarum*, edited by B. Krusch and W. Levison (Hanover, 1902–10), vol. IV, pp. 64–108

————, *Liber Historiae Francorum*. *Monumenta Germaniae Historica: Scriptores rerum Merovingicarum II* (Hannover, 1888)

Krusch, B., and Levison, W. (eds), *Passiones Vitaeque Sanctorum aevi Merovingici*. *Monumenta Germaniae Historica: Scriptores rerum Merovingicarum*, volumes IV–VI (Hanover, 1902–10)

Lamb, H. H., 'Climate from 1000 BC to 1000 AD', in *The Environment of Man: the Iron Age to the Anglo-Saxon Period*, edited by M. Jones and G. Dimbleby (Oxford, 1981), pp. 53–66

Leech, R., 'The Roman Interlude in the South-West: The dynamics of economic and social change in Romano-British South Somerset and North Dorset', in *The Romano-British Countryside: Studies in Rural Settlement and Economy*, edited by David Miles (2 vols, Oxford, 1982), pp. 209–67

Levison, W. (ed.), 'Vita Filiberti', in *Passiones Vitaeque Sanctorum aevi Merovingici*. *Monumenta Germaniae Historica: Scriptores rerum Merovingicarum*, volumes IV–VI (Hanover, 1902–10), vol. V, pp. 568–604

————, 'Eddius: *Vita Wilfridi*', in *Passiones Vitaeque Sanctorum aevi Merovingici*. *Monumenta Germaniae Historica: Scriptores rerum Merovingicarum*, volumes IV–VI (Hanover, 1902–10), vol. VI, pp. 163–263

————, 'St Alban and St Albans', *Antiquity* 16 (1941), 337–59

Lewis, A. R., 'Le Commerce et la navigation sur les côtes atlantiques de la Gaule du Ve et VIII siècle', *Le moyen âge* 59 (1953), 271–2

Lewit, T., *Agricultural production in the Roman Economy AD 200–400* (Oxford, 1991)

Lindsay, W. M., *Isidori Hispalensis Episcopi, Etymologiarum Siue Originum* (Oxford, 1911)

Lucas, R. N., 'Halstock Roman Villa 1985 Excavation', *Proceedings of the Dorset Natural History and Archaeological Society* 107 (1985), 163–4

MacNiocaill, G., and Mac Airt, S. (eds), *Annals of Ulster* (Dublin, 1983)

Macready, S., and Thompson, F. H. (eds), *Cross-Channel Trade between Gaul and Britain in the Pre-Roman Iron Age* (London, 1984)

Macreth D. F., 'Orton Hall Farm, Peterborough, A Roman and Saxon Settlement', in *Studies in the Romano-British Villa*, edited by M. Todd (London, 1978), pp. 209–38

Mallory, J. P., 'Silver in the Ulster Cycle of Tales', in *Proceedings of the Seventh International Congress of Celtic Studies*, edited by Evans pp. 33–65

Mattingley, H., and Pearce, J. W. E., 'The Coleraine Hoard', *Antiquity* 11 (1937), 39–45

Maynard, D., 'Excavations on a Pipeline near the River Frome Worgret, Dorset', *Proceedings of the Dorset Natural History and Archaeological Society* 110 (1988), 77–98

Meehan, D. (ed.), *Adomnan, De Locis Sanctis* (Scriptores Latini Hiberniae, III) (Dublin, 1958)

Mellars, Paul, *Excavations on Oronsay* (Edinburgh, 1987)

Merryfield, D. L., and Moore, P. D., 'Prehistoric human activity and blanket peat initiation on Exmoor', *Nature* 250 (1974), 439–41

Meyer, K., 'The Oldest Version of Tochmairc Emire', *Revue Celtique* 11 (1890)

———, *Learning in Ireland in the Fifth Century and the Transmission of Letters* (Dublin, 1913)

——— (ed.), *Aislinge Meic Conglinne* (London, 1892)

——— (ed.), *Tecosca Cormaic* (Dublin, 1909)

Mighall, T., and Chambers, F. M., 'The environmental impact of iron-working at Bryn y Castell hillfort, Merioneth', *Archaeology in Wales* 29 (1989), 17–21

———, 'Holocene vegetation history and human impact at Bryn y Castell, Snowdonia, north Wales', *New Phytologist* 130 (1995), 299–321

Miles, J., 'Vegetation and soil change in the uplands', in *Ecological Change in the Uplands*, edited by M. B. Usher and D. B. A. Thompson (Oxford, 1988), pp. 57–70

Miller, M., 'Hiberni Reversuri', *Proceeding of the Society of Antiquaries of Scotland* 110 (1978–80), 305–27

Molleson, T. I., Eldridge, D., and Gale, N., 'Identification of Lead Sources by Stable Isotope Ratios in Bones and Lead from Poundbury Camp, Dorset', *Oxford Journal of Archaeology* 5.2 (1986), 249–53

Moore, P. D., 'Human influence upon vegetational history in north Cardiganshire', *Nature* 217 (1968), 1006–7

———, *European Mires* (London, 1984)

Moore, P. D., Merryfield, D. L., and Price, M. D. R., 'The vegetation and development of blanket mires', in *European Mires*, edited by Peter D. Moore (London, 1984), pp. 203–35

Moore, P. D., Webb, J. A., and Collinson, M. E., *Pollen Analysis* (2nd edn, Oxford, 1991)

Morris, Christopher D. (ed.), *Tintagel Castle Excavations 1993* (Glasgow, 1993)

Morris, E., 'Prehistoric salt distributions. Two case studies from Western Britain', *Bulletin of the Board of Celtic Studies* 32 (1985), 336–79

Moule, H. J., *Dorchester Antiquities* (Dorchester, 1906)

Munier, C. (ed.), *Concilia Galliae Corpus Christianorum* (2 vols, Turnhout, 1963)

Munn, M., 'A Late Roman Kiln Site in the Hermionid, Greece', *American Journal of Archaeology* 89 (1985), 342–3

Myres, J. N. L., 'Lincoln in the fifth century A.D.', *The Archaeological Journal* 103 (1946), 85–8

———, 'The Anglo-Saxon pottery of Lincolnshire', *The Archaeological Journal* 108 (1951), 65–95

Mytum, H., 'High Status Vessels in Early Historic Ireland: A Reference in Bethu Brigte', *Oxford Journal of Archaeology* 5 (1986), 375–8

———, 'Across the Irish Sea: Romano-British and Irish settlement in Wales', *Emania* 13 (1995), 15–22

Nash-Williams, V. E., *The Early Christian Monuments of Wales* (Cardiff, 1950)

Ní Chatháin, P. and Richter, M. (eds), *Irland und die Christenheit: Bibelstudien und Mission* (Stuttgart, 1987)

Nieke, M. R., and Duncan, H. B., 'Dalriada: the Establishment and Maintenance of an Early Historic Kingdom in North Britain', in *Power and Politics in Early Medieval Britain and Ireland*, edited by S. Driscoll and M. Nieke (Edinburgh, 1988), pp. 6–21

Ó Cróinín, D., 'Rath Melsigi, Willibrord and the Earliest Echternach Manuscripts', *Peritia: Journal of the Medieval Academy of Ireland* 3 (1984), 17–42

O'Kelly, M. J., 'Monastic Sites in the West of Ireland', *Scottish Archaeological Forum* 5 (1973), 1–16

O'Mahany, T., and Richey, A. G., *Ancient Laws of Ireland*, vol. 3 (Dublin, 1873)

O'Meara, J. J., 'Giraldus Cambrensis in *Topographia Hibernie*', *Proceedings of the Royal Irish Academy* 52C (1949), 113–78

O'Sullivan, P. E., 'Pollen analysis and radiocarbon dating of a core from Loch Pityoulish, Eastern Highlands of Scotland', *Journal of Biogeography* 3 (1976), 293–302

Olson, Lynette, *Early monasteries in Cornwall* (Woodbridge, 1989)

Parker, A. J., 'Shipwrecks and trade in the Mediterranean', *Archaeological Review from Cambridge* 3 (1984), 99–114

Peacock, D. P. S. (ed.), *Pottery and Early Commerce: Characterisation and Trade in Roman and Later Ceramics* (London, 1977)

Peacock, D. P. S., and Thomas, C., 'Class E Imported Pottery, A Suggested Origin', *Cornish Archaeology* 6 (1967), 35–46

Peacock, D. P. S., and Williams, D., *Amphorae and the Roman Economy* (London, 1986)

Pearce, S. M., *The Kingdom of Dumnonia: Studies in History and Tradition in South Western Britain AD 350–1150* (Padstow, 1978)

Pearce, S. M. (ed.), *The Early Church in Western Britain and Ireland* (Oxford, 1982)

Penhallurick, Roger D., *Tin in Antiquity* (London, 1986)

Pennington, W., 'Vegetation history in the north-west of England: a regional synthesis', in *Studies in the Vegetational History of the British Isles*, edited by D. Walker and R. G. West (Cambridge, 1970), pp. 41–79

Pertz, G. W. (ed.), *Monumenta Germaniae Historica, Diplomatum Imperii 1* (Hanover, 1874)

Pertz, K. (ed.), *Diplomatum Imperii (Monumenta Germaniae Historica: Diplomata, volume 1* (Hannover, 1872)

Philpott, R., *Burial practices in Roman Britain, a Survey of Grave Treatment and Furnishing AD 43–410* (Oxford, 1991)

Plummer, C. (ed.), *Vita Kyarani*, in *Vitae Sanctorum Hiberniae* (Oxford, 1910), pp. 200–16

——— (ed.), *Vitae Sanctorum Hiberniae* (Oxford, 1910)

Preston-Jones, Ann and Rose, Peter, 'Medieval Cornwall', *Cornish Archaeology* 25 (1986), 135–85

Price, M. D. R., and Moore, P. D., 'Pollen dispersion in the hills of Wales: a pollen shed hypothesis', *Pollen et Spores* 26 (1984), 127–36

Prieto, N., 'Algunos datos sobre las importaciones de cerámica "Phocean Red Slip" en la peninsula Iberica', in *Papers in Iberian Archaeology*, edited by T. F. Blagg *et al.* (Oxford, 1984), pp. 540–8

Pucci, G., 'Pottery and Trade in the Roman Period', in *Trade in the Ancient Economy* edited by P. Garnsey *et al.* (London, 1983), pp. 105–17

Quinnell, Henrietta, 'Cornwall during the Iron Age and the Roman period', *Cornish Archaeology* 25 (1986), 111–34

Rahtz, P., 'Pottery in Somerset, A.D. 400–1066', in *Medieval Pottery from Excavations*, edited by V. Evison (London, 1974), pp. 95–126

Rahtz, P., and Watts, L., 'The End of Roman Temples in the West of England', in *The End of Roman Britain*, edited by P. J. Casey (Oxford, 1979), pp. 183–201

Randoin, B., 'Essai de classification chronologique de la céramique de tours du IVe au XIe siècle', in *Recherches sur Tours*, edited by H. Galinie (Tours, 1981), vol. 1, pp. 103–13

Randsborg, Klaus, *The first millenium AD in Europe and the Mediterranean* (Cambridge, 1991)

RCAHMW, *Inventories of the Ancient Monuments in Anglesey* (London, 1937)

RCHM(E), *Dorset Volume II South-East* (London, 1970)

Reece, R., 'Burial in Latin Literature; Two Examples', in *Burial in the Roman World*, edited by R. Reece (London, 1977), pp. 44–5

———, 'Town and Country: the end of Roman Britain', in *World Archaeology* 12.1 (1980), 77–92

——— (ed.), *Burial in the Roman World* (London, 1977)

Reith, E., 'Research on Nautical Archaeology and Traditional Boats in France', in *Post-Medieval Boat and Ship Archaeology*, edited by C. O. Cederlund (Oxford, 1985), pp. 413–20

Rhys, J., 'An inscription at Penmachno', *Archaeologia Cambrensis* (1919), 201–5

Richardson, K. M., 'Excavations at Poundbury, Dorchester, Dorset 1939', *Antiquaries Journal* 20 (1940), 429–48

Rigoir, J., Rigoir, Y., and Meffre, J.-F., 'Les dérivées paléochrétiennes du groupe atlantique', *Gallia* 31 (1973), 364–409

Roberts, B. K., Turner, J., and Ward, P. F., 'Recent forest history and land use in Weardale, Northern England', in *Quaternary Plant Ecology*, edited by H. J. B. Birks and R. G. West (Oxford, 1973), pp. 207–21

Robinson, D. E., and Dickson, J. H., 'Vegetational history and land use: a radiocarbon-dated pollen diagram from Machrie Moor, Arran, Scotland', *New Phytologist* 109 (1988), 223–51

Rowell, T. K., and Turner, J., 'Litho-, humic- and pollen stratigraphy at Quick Moss, Northumberland', *Journal of Ecology* 73 (1985), 11–25

Rynne, C., 'The Introduction of of the Vertical Watermill into Ireland, Some Recent Archaeological Evidence', *Medieval Archaeology* 33 (1989), 21–31

Salin, E., *La Civilisation Merovingienne* (Paris, 1950–59)

Salway, P., *Roman Britain* (Oxford, 1981)

Schweiso, J., 'The Anglo-Saxon Burials', in *Mount Pleasant, Dorset: Excavations 1970–1*, edited by G. J. Wainwright (London, 1979), pp. 181–3

Scott, B. G., 'Some Conflicts and Correspondences of Evidence in the Study of Irish History and Language', in *Studies in Early Ireland*, edited by B. G. Scott (Belfast, 1981), pp. 115–19

——— (ed.), *Studies in Early Ireland* (Belfast, 1981)

Scull, C., 'Scales and Weights in Early Anglo-Saxon England', *Archaeological Journal* 147 (1990), 183–215

Seeck, O. (ed.), *Symmachus, Opera. Monumenta Germaniae Historica, Auctores Antiquissimi, vol. 6* (Berlin, 1883)

Simmons, I. G., and Cundill, P. R., 'Late Quaternary vegetational history of the North York Moors I. Pollen analyses of blanket peats', *Journal of Biogeography* 1 (1974), 159–69

Simmons, I. G., Rand, J. I., and Crabtree, K., 'A further pollen analytical study of the Blacklane peat section on Dartmoor, England', *New Phytologist* 94 (1983), 655–67

——, 'Dozmary Pool, Bodmin Moor, Cornwall: a new radiocarbon dated pollen profile', in *Studies in palaeoeconomy and environment in South West England*, edited by N. D. Balaam *et al.* (Oxford, 1987), pp. 125–33

Sims, R. E., 'The anthropogenic factor in East Anglian vegetational history: an approach using A.P.F. techniques', in *Quaternary Plant Ecology*, edited by H. J. B. Birks and R. G. West (Oxford, 1973), pp. 223–36

Singer, C., Holmyard, F. J., Hall, A. R., and Williams, T. I., *History of Technology*, vol. II (London, 1956)

Sirt, J., 'Les stèles merovingiennes du vexin français', *Bulletin archéologique vexin français* 2 (1966), 73–83

——, 'Les stèles merovingiennes du vexin français – inventaire complémentaire', *Bulletin archéologique vexin français* 6 (1970), 95–103

Smith, A. G., 'The mires of south-western Westmorland; stratigraphy and pollen analysis', *New Phytologist* 58 (1959), 105–27

Smith, A. G., and Green, C. A., 'Topogenous peat development and late-Flandrian vegetation history at a site in upland South Wales', *The Holocene* 5 (1995), 172–83

Smith, K., Coppen, J., Wainwright, G. J., and Beckett, S., 'The Shaugh Moor Project: third report – settlement and environmental investigations', *Proceedings of the Prehistoric Society* 47 (1981), 205–73

Smith, R., 'Excavations at County Hall, Colliton Park, Dorchester', *Proceedings of the Dorset Natural History and Archaeological Society* 110 (1988), 147

Spain, R. J., 'Romano-British Watermills', *Archaeologia Cantiana* 100 (1984)

Sparey-Green, C. J., 'The Rite of Plaster Burial in the Context of the Romano-British Cemetery at Poundbury, Dorset, England', in *Romerzeitliche Graber als Quellen zu Religion, Bevolkerungsstruktur und Sozialgeschichte*, edited by M. Struck (Mainz, 1992)

Stancliffe, C. E., 'From town to country: the Christianisation of the Touraine, 370–600', in *Studies in Church History 16: The Church in Town and Country*, edited by D. Baker (Oxford, 1979), pp. 43–59

Stewart, D. A., Walker, A., and Dickson, J. H., 'Pollen diagrams from Dubh Lochan, near Loch Lomond', *New Phytologist* 98 (1984), 531–49

Stokes, W. (ed.), *Three Irish Glossaries* (London, 1862)

Stuiver, M., and Pearson, G. W., 'High precision bidecadal calibration of the radiocarbon time scale, AD 1950–500 BC and 2500–6000 BC', *Radiocarbon* 35 (1993), 1–23

Tallis, J. H., and Switsur, V. R., 'Studies on southern Pennine peats VI. A radiocarbon-dated pollen diagram from Featherbed Moss, Derbyshire', *Journal of Ecology* 61 (1973), 743–51

Taylor, T., *The Life of St Samson of Dol* (London, 1925)

Thomas, C., 'Imported pottery in dark-age western Britain', *Medieval Archaeology* 3 (1959), 89–111

——, 'An Early Christian cemetery and chapel on Ardwall Isle, Kirkcudbright', *Medieval Archaeology* 11 (1967), 127–88

——, *The Early Christian Archaeology of North Britain* (Oxford, 1971)

——, 'Imported Late-Roman Mediterranean pottery in Ireland and western Britain: chronologies and implications', *Proceedings of the Royal Irish Academy* 76C (1976), 245–55

——, *Christianity in Roman Britain to AD 500* (London, 1981)

——, *A Provisional list of Imported Pottery in Post-Roman Western Britain and Ireland* (Redruth, 1981)

——, 'East and West: Tintagel, Mediterranean imports and the Early Insular Church', in *The Early Church in Western Britain and Ireland*, edited by Susan M. Pearce (Oxford, 1982), pp. 17–34

——, 'The earliest Christian art in Ireland and Britain', in *Ireland and Insular art AD 500–1200*, edited by Michael Ryan (Dublin, 1987), pp. 7–11

——, 'Tintagel Castle', *Antiquity* 62 (1988), 421–34

——, 'The Context of Tintagel: a New Model for the Diffusion of Post-Roman Imports', *Cornish Archaeology* 27 (1988), 7–25

——, '*Gallici Nautae de Galliarum Provinciis* – A Sixth/ Seventh Century Trade with Gaul Reconsidered', *Medieval Archaeology* 34 (1990), 1–26

—— (ed.), *Tintagel Papers* (Redruth, 1988)

Thomas, G., 'Note', *Archaeologia Cambrensis* (1970), 160

Thompson, M. W., *The Journeys of Sir Richard Colt Hoare Through Wales and England 1793–1810* (Gloucester, 1983)

Timby, J. R., 'The Middle Saxon pottery', in *Southampton finds, volume 1; the coins and pottery from Hamwic, Southampton*, edited by P. Andrews (London, 1988), pp. 73–124

Tipping, R., 'Holocene evolution of a lowland Scottish landscape: Kirkpatrick Fleming. Part I, peat- and pollen-stratigraphic evidence for raised moss development and climatic change', *The Holocene* 5 (1995), 69–81

——, 'Holocene evolution of a lowland Scottish landscape: Kirkpatrick Fleming. Part II, regional vegetation and land-use change', *The Holocene* 5 (1995), 83–96

——, 'Holocene landscape change at Carn Dubh, near Pitlochry, Perthshire, Scotland', *Journal of Quaternary Science* 10 (1995), 59–75

Turner, J., 'The anthropogenic factor in vegetational history. I. Tregaron and Whixall Mosses', *New Phytologist* 63 (1964), 73–90

——, 'A contribution to the history of forest clearance', *Proceedings of the Royal Society of London* B161 (1965), 343–53

——, 'Post-neolithic disturbance of British vegetation', in *Studies in the*

Vegetational History of the British Isles, edited by D. Walker and R. G. West (Cambridge, 1970), pp. 97–116

——, 'The environment of north-east England during Roman times as shown by pollen analysis', *Journal of Archaeological Science* 6 (1979), 285–90

——, 'The vegetation', in *The Environment of Man: the Iron Age to the Anglo-Saxon Period*, edited by M. Jones and G. Dimbleby (Oxford, 1981), pp. 67–73

Turner, J., Innes, J. B., and Simmons, I. G., 'Two pollen diagrams from the same site', *New Phytologist* 113 (1989), 409–16

Usher, M. B., and Thompson, D. B. A., *Ecological Change in the Uplands* (Oxford, 1988)

Van der Veen, M., 'Charred Grain Assemblages from Romano-British Corn-Driers in Britain', *Archaeological Journal* 146 (1989), 302–19

Van Doorninck, F., 'Byzantium, Mistress of the Sea', in *A History of Seafaring based on Underwater Archaeology*, edited by G. Bass (London, 1972), pp. 134–56

Van Zeist, Willem., Waslikowa, Krystyna, and Behre, Karl-Ernst, *Progress in Old World Palaeoethnobotany* (Rotterdam, 1991)

Vince, A., 'The economic basis of Anglo-Saxon London', in *The rebirth of the towns in the west AD 700–1050*, edited by Richard Hodges and Brian Hobley (London, 1988), pp. 83–92

Wade, K., 'Ipswich', in *The rebirth of the towns in the west AD 700–1050*, edited by Richard Hodges and Brian Hobley (London, 1988), pp. 93–100

Walker, D., and West, R. G., *Studies in the Vegetational History of the British Isles* (Cambridge, 1970)

Walker, G. S. M., *Sancti Columbani Opera* (Dublin, 1957)

Wallace-Hadrill, J. M., *The Frankish Church* (Oxford, 1983)

Warner, R., 'The Clogher Yellow Layer', *Medieval Ceramics* 3 (1979), 37–40

Watkins, R., 'The postglacial vegetational history of lowland Gwynedd – Llyn Cororion', in *North Wales Field Guide*, edited by K. Addison *et al.* (Coventry, 1990), pp. 131–6

Waton, P. V., 'Man's impact on the chalklands: some new pollen evidence', in *Archaeological Aspects of Woodland Ecology*, edited by M. Bell and S. Limbrey (Oxford, 1982), pp. 75–91

Webster, Graham, 'A Romano-British pottery kiln at Rookery Lane, Lincoln', *Antiquaries Journal* 40 (1960), 214–20

Wheeler, R. E. M., *Maiden Castle, Dorset* (Oxford, 1943)

White, Roger, 'Excavations on the Site of the Baths Basilica', in *From Roman Viroconium to Medieval Wroxeter*, edited by Philip Barker (Worcester, 1990), pp. 3–7

White, Roger H., *Roman and Celtic Objects from Anglo-Saxon Graves* (Oxford, 1988)

Whitelock, D., McKitterick, R., and Dumville, D. (eds), *Ireland and Early Medieval Europe* (Cambridge, 1982)

Whittaker, C. R., 'Late Roman trade and traders', in *Trade in the Ancient Economy*, edited by P. Garnsey, K. Hopkins and C. R. Whittaker (London, 1983), pp. 163–80

Whittington, G. Edwards, K. J., and Cundill, P. R., 'Late-and post-glacial vegetational change at Black Loch, Fife, eastern Scotland – a multiple core approach', *New Phytologist* 118 (1991), 147–66

Whittington, G. and Gordon, A. D., 'The differentiation of the pollen of *Cannabis sativa* L. from that of *Humulus lupulus* L.', *Pollen et Spores* 29 (1987), 111–20

Wickham, C., 'The other transition: from the ancient world to feudalism', *Past and Present* 103 (1984), 3–36

Wild, John Peter, 'Wool production in Roman Britain', in *The Romano-British Countryside: Studies in Rural Settlement and Economy*, edited by David Miles (2 vols, Oxford, 1982), pp. 109–22

Winterbottom, M. (ed.), *Gildas: The Ruin of Britain and other Works* (Chichester, 1978)

Wooding, J.M., 'What Porridge Had the Old Irish?', *Australian Celtic Journal* 1 (1988), 12–17

Woodiwiss, Simon (ed.), *Iron Age and Roman Salt Production and the Medieval Town of Droitwich* (London, 1992)

Woodward, P. J., and Smith R. J. C., 'Survey and Excavation along the Route of the Southern Dorchester By-pass 1986–7, an Interim Note', *Proceedings of the Dorset Natural History and Archaeological Society* 109 (1987), 79–89

Young, C. J., *The Roman Pottery Industry of the Oxford Region* (Oxford, 1977)

Zimmer, H., 'Über direkte Handelsverbindungen Westgalliens mit Irland im Altertum und frühen Mittelalter', *Sitzungsberichte der königlich preussischen Akademie der Wissenschaften* (Berlin, 1909–10).

INDEX

Italicised numbers denote illustrations

Glyde Path, 144
goat, 136, 137
goblets, 73
gold, 65, 73, 89, 95, 110, 115
graffiti, 80, 102
Graham Bank, 105
grain, 107
Grambla, 60
Grammaticus (Virgilius Maro), 69
grape-juice, 126, 127
grass, 24, 38, 39, 41–51
Grazel, 108
Greece, 79, 81, 84, 99, 100
Greenland, 30
Gregory of Tours, 113
grinding stones, 99, 107
Gwynedd, 111
hacksilver, 109
Hadrian, 110
Hadrian's Wall, 36, 39, 40, 110
Hallowell Moss, 33, 35, 45
Hamburg, 69
Hampshire, 103
Hamstone, 140
Hamwic, 95
hand-querns, 127
hanging-bowl, 140
harbours, 102
Hartlepool, 149
Hayle, 112
hazel, 39, 41–51
hearths, 143
heather, 39, 41–51
helmets, 65
Helsington Moss, 29
hemp, 25, 37, 38, 39
henge, 145
Herpes, 76
Heybridge, 58
Hibernia, 69
hides, 72
hoards, 109
Hoar Moor, 33, 35, 46
Hockham Mere, 33, 34, 37, 46
Hof Ha Carmel, 105
honey, 73, 74, 92, 93, 126
hop, 25
horizontal mills, 151

Hormiga (Las), 106
horse trappings, 65
horses, 73
hounds, 77
Humulus Lupulus, 25
hypercoherence, 18, 19, 20, 21
Iassos, 106
Iberia, 81, 85, 86, 88, 100, 102
ice-cores, 30
Ilchester, 140, 146
imports, 83–108, 111
industrial activity, 138
    technology, 136
Industrial Revolution, 3, 4, 5, 14, 18,
    20, 21
ingots, 99, 107
Inismurray, *117*, *118*, 119
ink, 65
inland waterways, 5
inscribed stones, 109–20
inscriptions, 65
investment, 6
Iona, 75
Ipswich, 95
Irchester, 13
Ireland, 29, 68–79, 82, 83, 84, 89, 92,
    94, 96, 97–107, 109, 110, 112, 120
Irish Sea, 92, 96
iron, 73, 105, 129, 136, 141, 151, 152
iron slag, 138
iron-smelting, 10–11, 61
iron-working, 14
Isidore, 69, 72
Isis, 105
Iskandil Burnu, 107
Israel, 107
Italy, 19, 102, 111
ivory, 119
jewellery, 65
John (St), 82
Joseph, 113
Jurassic ridge, 10, 11
Justinian, 17, 81, 86, 115
Justinianic plague, 30
Justinus, 114, 116
Kalithea, 106
Kenchester, 13
Kent, 95

9 780851 156552